Creating the Intercultural Field

Sandra M. Fowler
Daniel C. Yalowitz
Editors

Creating the Intercultural Field

Legacies from the Pioneers

Foreword by Craig Storti

Editors
Sandra M. Fowler ⓘ
Carlsbad, CA, USA

Daniel C. Yalowitz
Greenfield, MA, USA

Foreword by
Craig Storti
Westminster,
MD, USA

ISBN 978-3-032-01369-9   ISBN 978-3-032-01370-5   (eBook)
https://doi.org/10.1007/978-3-032-01370-5

This Palgrave Macmillan imprint is published by the registered company Springer Nature Switzerland AG.
The registered company address is: Gewerbestrasse 11, 6330 Cham, Switzerland

If disposing of this product, please recycle the paper.

We dedicate this book to our grandchildren.
Sandy to Theodore and Alexandra Mumford, already world travelers in
their third decades who, with their Greek heritage, inherit an ancient
culture and in the current era show an eagerness for the life-changing
experiences that this planet has to offer. And to Katelyn, Cade, and Sam
Fowler who share a passion for learning from other cultures and travel to
far off places.
Daniel to his two precious grand-ones, Naomi and Diego, whose parents
represent the coming together of two different cultures, languages, and ways
of being in life ...and to the mysterious ways their energies and synergies will
create new and peaceful ways of being in a radically different world
desperately needing their life skills and perspectives.

And to the grandchildren of all our contributors as well as the community of
people of all ages who hold the potential to carry on the spirit of our work.

Foreword: Ezzrahoui's World

An American Peace Corps volunteer once told me a charming story. He was posted to a small island in Micronesia, not even a mile long, with a village at each end. After a few weeks on the island, he decided one morning to stroll down to the village at the other end to have a look around. When he mentioned his plan to a few friends, they were alarmed. "Oh, you should never go there," they warned. "Those people are *nothing* like us."

And such has been the way of the world for most of human history: what was different caused anxiety, anxiety stoked fear, fear led to dislike, and dislike often morphed into hatred. The Other was synonymous with danger, and we retreated into our tribes to find safety and affirmation. Enlightened individuals emerged from time to time, preaching compassion and tolerance—to give peace a chance—but by and large their message has not prevailed

The problem with the Other is simple: We do not understand Them. Not understanding them, we can never know for sure how they will behave. And that is profoundly troubling. It means we live in a world that is not altogether safe. In the second half of the twentieth century, people such as those in these pages tried again, advancing a new paradigm: Different doesn't have to be unnerving; it just has to be understood. And they set about conceiving and then developing frameworks for getting inside the mindsets of people Not Like Us.

They were modest, as you will see. They did not imagine they would fix an imperfect world or necessarily change millions of minds; they simply created tools for the curious. Nor did they believe that understanding would automatically lead to acceptance. Or even that it always should. They didn't set out, in other words, to do away with judgements, to suggest that if a lot of folks (a culture) do a certain something, then somehow that thing must be OK. They simply hoped that more people would *suspend* judgements *until* they understood. And then they did their level best to create greater understanding, inventing a new field in the process.

In these pages, you will hear from some of these people, what moved them to explore difference and try to reduce the threat of the Other. You'll hear that the Other sometimes comes from very close to home, from those of a different racial, religious, or ethnic background than the majority culture. You'll hear how these people help to found and build organizations to advance the cause. You'll be inspired by their commitment. You may even want to shake their hand.

The co-editors of this collection asked the contributors to describe in fifty words or less an especially meaningful cross-cultural encounter. I like that idea and want to participate, but I'm taking the liberty (as Foreword author) to exceed the 50-word limit.

My story goes like this. As an American Peace Corps volunteer, I taught English as a second language at a high school in Safi, Morocco. Some of my students were from Essaouira, a town some 90 miles distant, and they boarded at my school. Over one Moroccan holiday, a few of the boarders invited me to come along with them to Essaouira, to spend the weekend. I stayed in the home of a student from the Ezzrahoui family where one morning I saw a lady washing the tiles in the courtyard. "Is that your mother?" I asked. "No," he said, "that's one of my father's wives."

I took this in, quite amused, and then much later I thought: My god! Is there any way I could ever understand this boy's world? A home with three mothers (as it turned out), with full siblings and half siblings. How did he regard and get along with the two mothers who were not his? How did they regard him? What did his mother think of the children of the other two wives? How did she get along with those wives? What did my student think of his half siblings? What did they think of this boy not born of their mother? Was there a favorite wife? What was it like to be the first-born son of the favorite? What was this boy's self-image? What did it feel like to be living young Ezzrahoui's life? If not at the time, then certainly now, I realize I will never really understand Ezzrahoui's world.

But that's not because the people in these pages have failed me. On the contrary, it is because of them—and many others like them—that it occurred to me to ask those questions in the first place, to realize my ignorance. And isn't realizing you're ignorant the first step on the path to acquiring knowledge? Only then, after all, will you be prompted to ask questions and find answers. And if you don't always find an answer, then isn't that a kind of knowledge too: realizing that not everything *can* be understood?

So yes, the interculturalists profiled here *have* spent their lives helping people to better understand the Other. If it didn't work for me in this particular instance, it's not their fault; there is still work to be done to figure out those people at the other end of the island. But thanks to the folks in these pages, now in the twilight of their remarkable careers, we are all much closer than we've ever been before.

[Craig Storti, Westminster, MD USA, is a trainer in the intercultural field and the author of nine books on related topics, including *The Art of Crossing Cultures*, *Cross-Cultural Dialogues*, and *Why Travel Matters*.]

Westminster, MD, USA   Craig Storti
February 2025

PREFACE

This book explores the intercultural field with the people who generated and lived it. The individuals whose autobiographies provide the heart of this book contributed to building the foundation and practices that comprise interculturalism.

What is interculturalism, you may ask? You'll find it built into the lives of the implementors of the field who developed it with no template or road map to guide them. Their curiosity, willingness to take risks, skills with networking, and generous sharing of their experiences transformed not only themselves but the intercultural field.

The intention in developing this book was to preserve the narratives of pioneers in the intercultural field because so many have already passed on, making it even more important to capture the stories of those who remain. The surprise is how varied the careers of the intercultural pioneers have been.

Do not read this book with the expectation that the stories are cookie-cutter similar. Rather, enjoy getting to know people who did it their way. The experiences that led them into the intercultural field (which in many cases when they started was not even a field) were as different as the cultures they studied, or lived and worked in. But while their paths diverged, they also converged in projects and professional associations.

What did they learn? A lot about themselves as they came to realize that interculturalism is not just a job but a lifestyle. They lived and breathed intercultural for decades. Do they think interculturalism will save the world? The world needs them, but it is not ready to be saved. When it is, interculturalists of the future will be there to help.

Sandra M. Fowler
Daniel C. Yalowitz

Acknowledgments

First and foremost, we express our gratitude to the contributing authors who provided their stories with enthusiasm, patience, and persistence. We are honored by their participation. We thank Cragi Storti for his willingness to meet with us, his suggestions, and his Foreword. It meant a lot to all of us to reveal, reflect, and examine our devotion to the intercultural field.

At Palgrave Macmillan we are indebted to Beth Farrow, Senior Editor, and Raghupathy Kalyanaraman, Production Editor for Springer Nature, also to Cineha Dhakshinamoorthi and Kali Gayathri, our Project Managers at Straive. Beth was a champion for our book from the time we became acquainted at the American Psychological Association convention during the summer of 2024.

We owe a great debt of gratitude to Ted Mumford who helped with a variety of technical aspects associated with preparing the manuscript, and most of all getting everything to the publisher.

We acknowledge the support provided by Margie Sobil as she made room for one more book. Daniel could not have done this without her.

From the beginning, our goal was to create an informative and enjoyable book for old timers in the intercultural field, newcomers to the field, and introduce the intercultural field to people who had never heard of it. Goals are guideposts—hopefully ours served us well.

Sandra M. Fowler
Daniel C. Yalowitz

CONTENTS

MEET THE CONTRIBUTORS

Nancy J. Adler, PhD S. Bronfman Chair Emerita in Management at McGill University, received her doctorate from UCLA, and as an artist and professor published 10 books and 150 articles. International companies and organizations use her pioneering work on cross-cultural management, global women leaders, and leadership artistry.

Hong Kong, 1979. "We want to take you to lunch." "That's not necessary." "Professor Adler, Socrates' students took Socrates to lunch, it is the least we can do for you." Over lunch I asked, "In Montréal, we say *Bon Appétit*, before eating, what do you say in Hong Kong?" "Oh Professor Adler, if you stop to say anything, everyone else will have finished their lunch!"

Clifford H. Clarke, ABD Designed intercultural innovations in Foreign Student Counseling, 1960s; in teaching intercultural courses, 1970s; in creative consulting for intercultural management and organizational development, 1980s–1990s; in teaching intercultural courses, 2000s; in executive coaching and evaluating educational programs until retirement, 2025.

Culture Shock! Imagine my surprise. Hong Kong, 1962. My first morning shower on the landing outside my host's high-rise home's front door. Hose, bucket, soap, stool... I leaned back to rinse my hair to a chorus of clapping children's hands from each floor's landing above. They were my admiring, yet unexpected audience!

John C. Condon, PhD In the early '70s I wrote the first college textbook on intercultural communication; 50 years later, authored what a reviewer called "the best book on culture and communication"; in between, wrote what's called "the bible for Westerners beginning their work in Japan."

Shortly after Tanzania gained independence from England, I taught a course at a government college on Communication for adult professionals, including regional officials, teachers, labor union organizers, and *freedom fighters* from still-colonized African lands. I asked: "when you think of communication, what do you think of?" The response reminded me of where I was and how much I needed to learn. Classmates agreed: *"Spying."*

Carlos E. Cortés, PhD Cortés was a pioneer in multicultural education and diversity in the media, including serving as Creative/Cultural Advisor for Nickelodeon's "Dora the Explorer" and "Go, Diego, Go!" and Cultural Consultant for the Dreamworks film, *Puss in Boots: The Last Wish.*

In 2013, as an intercultural lecturer on a cruise out of Istanbul, my first lecture on gestures of the world included culturally-diverse offensive gestures, my upraised middle finger as an example. The taped lecture was repeatedly screened into passenger staterooms. Result: nearly two weeks of smiling passengers flashing me the finger or a pornographic gesture from their culture.

Alvino E. Fantini, PhD Emeritus linguist-interculturalist and past SIETAR International President, Alvino stressed language and intercultural interconnections, putting "Communicative" into Intercultural Competence = ICC, supported by research with colleagues in eight countries to define ICC and assess its development in 2200 educational exchange participants.

As the son of immigrant parents, I often found it difficult to adjust when I left the house and to readjust when I returned home, blending cultures and changing languages. Then, during my teens, I fell in love with a new culture during a homestay in Mexico. This was the beginning of my acceptance not only of other cultures but of myself.

Sandra M. Fowler, MS Former president of SIETAR International and SIETAR USA, editor of *The Intercultural Sourcebook: Cross-Cultural Training Methods*, and Director of the U.S. Navy's Overseas Duty Support Program, I also was the Art Co-Director for the *American Psychologist* for 23 years.

Connecting: Beijing, 1982, out for an early morning run, finding Chinese men and one woman running on a track. I joined them, running next to a petite grandmother. Many laps around the track, many glances, smiles, no words, a big hug at the end. I've never forgotten her.

V. Robert Hayles, PhD Best known for guiding public/private, national/international organizations to achieve optimum results using research and evidence-based scientific knowledge, he specializes in customized diagnostics/strategies to enhance effectiveness of organizations whose participants have wide ranges of inherent and acquired characteristics.

I facilitated many meetings of the SIETAR International Governing Council using "Robert's Rules of Order" by Henry Robert (1st edition 1876). Some members from several countries privately expressed appreciation for how Robert ran the meetings but wondered why they had to use *his* rules. Everyone had a good laugh as Robert's rules were explained.

Stephen H. Rhinesmith, PhD After spending 10 years as president and CEO of the American Field service international student exchange program, I was appointed the coordinator of President Reagan's US-Soviet exchange initiative with the diplomatic rank of US ambassador.

Arriving in Germany as a 17-year-old exchange student, I was excited to meet my German father, mother, and three brothers. My new brother, who was my age, introduced himself with a stiff handshake and said, "Christian!" Looking for a nickname, I asked him what he liked to be called. He looked at me puzzled and replied emphatically, "Christian." I quickly learned that not all cultures have shortened names by which they like to be called!

Fanchon J. Silberstein, MA Known for teaching dialogues with art that reveals details of life and perceptions of reality in many cultures. These dialogues build intercultural competence through self-understanding that grows from closely observing multiple value systems and interpretations of experience.

While living in Pakistan, I asked a beautiful friend (with an equally good-looking husband), what it was like to have had an arranged marriage. She replied with a question: "What makes you think you have better judgment than your parents?"

Donna M. Stringer, PhD Co-authored *52 Activities for Exploring Value Differences* the first book focused solely on exercises to explore how cultural values translate to different behaviors across cultures leading to her concentration on helping organizations identify behavioral values for successful engagement of employees and clients.

My first trip to Greece, I was just going to bed when I heard a very loud argument. Looking out the window to be sure a woman was not in danger, I saw a couple having a lovely conversation on their patio. Clearly a more emotive conversational style than the "take turns" conversations my culture had taught me was comfortable.

Sivasailam Thiagarajan (Thiagi), PhD Designer of instructional games and training activities primarily focused on intercultural communication and well known for his game Barnga, a simulation game on cultural clashes, which deals with differences that make a difference.

My well-intentioned colleagues and friends in the USA give me gratuitous feedback: "You have a funny accent." When I go home to Chennai, India, and speak to my friends and colleagues in Tamil, they tell me, "You have a funny accent." Can't win them all!

Michael F. Tucker, PhD Fellow, International Academy of Intercultural Research, known for creating psychometric assessment instruments: Overseas Assignment Inventory; Tucker Assessment Profile; Global Leader Tucker Assessment Profile.

In 1968, I was in Puerto Rico to lead Peace Corps training. The first night I was awakened by a loud thump on the roof, then annoyed all night by chirping of what I thought were birds. What strange bird would be doing that? Next day I learned to my embarrassment the thump was a common bread fruit, and the "birds" were Coquis, a type of tiny tree frog.

Daniel C. Yalowitz, EdD A longtime university faculty and senior administrator known for pioneering work regarding simulations and ethical debriefing in intercultural settings with 4 books and 40+ articles focusing on play, intercultural competence, community-building, leadership, conflict transformation, and social/emotional intelligence.

I'm left-handed—only one in my extended family. On my first trip to India, my wife and I piled into a train car with four generations of people, vegetables, fruit, animals. We had food for the 19-hour trip, but no seats, so we stood for the first several hours. As I ate my food, the car began clearing out—quickly. That's how I learned that eating with my left hand in India was not the right way!

LIST OF FIGURES

CHAPTER 1

Introduction

Sandra M. Fowler and Daniel C. Yalowitz

Interculturalism is a never-ending journey in which readers can partici-pate, not a distant field that they can only view through academic lenses or as distant experiences. The editors and authors of this book—all pioneers in the intercultural field—invite you into our journeys with the audacious wish that hearing our stories will inform your own.

WHY THIS BOOK?

A fundamental reason for this book is that it is rare to have direct, personal access to the people who created a professional and academic field. For example, we can no longer ask Sigmund Freud or Carl Jung or William James to tell us about the early days of psychology and how the field devel-oped. The intercultural field has lost many of its visionaries, but fortu-nately, there are pioneers still among us. Elders in the intercultural field are the people who have been instrumental in its development and

S. M. Fowler (✉)
Carlsbad, CA, USA

D. C. Yalowitz
Greenfield, MA, USA
e-mail: danielcyalowitz@gmail.com

© The Author(s), under exclusive license to Springer Nature Switzerland AG 2025
S. M. Fowler, D. C. Yalowitz (eds.), *Creating the Intercultural Field*,
https://doi.org/10.1007/978-3-032-01370-5_1

1

evolution. In this book they shared their stories of how they found inter-culturalism, and traced the arc of their careers, contributions, and challenges.

A specific impetus for this collection of exciting life stories was the demise of an intercultural visionary. It took months of digging, establishing a timeline, verifying dates for George Renwick, a leader in the intercultural field who was a very private person. But with the help of his brother, Zareen Karani deAraoz, and some of the many people who worked with George over the years, a to chronicle his life and his contributions to the intercultural field was created. It made me (Sandy) think about colleagues in the field who by coincidence were born the same year I was: 1938, in addition to the small group of aging, American interculturalists scattered around the country and further afield. It seemed important that their stories—preferably in their own words—should not be lost.

Serendipitously my longtime friend and colleague Daniel Yalowitz called to inquire if there might be something he could do to become more involved with SIETAR USA (Society for Intercultural Education, Training, and Research). Daniel is a published author, longstanding member in the intercultural field, an excellent writer and editor, and I knew we would work well together based on previous collegial work and projects. I described my idea to Daniel of obtaining autobiographies from 10–12 of the people who had been prominent in the intercultural field for decades. His immediate and enthusiastic yes! led me to believe that this could really be something important and, as they say, the rest is history—that is the histories of the dozen individuals whose stories are the heart of this book.

Daniel and I knew it was a big ask of busy people, but happily they all added to our enthusiasm as we talked with them individually about the project. A few people I called were not old enough to qualify, and we laughed that at our ages we rarely hear that we are too young for something. Authors were selected because of their age, proven ability as writers, having made substantial contributions to the intercultural field, and key intangibles like "plays well with others." The group bonded quickly during our virtual meetings. They all knew me whereas not necessarily each other. We agreed to share early drafts of our stories, and everyone contributed comments and suggestions throughout the process. As editors, Daniel and I believed strongly that we wanted the process and the anticipated book to be as collaborative and connected as possible.

Relationships among our group that previously existed grew stronger, and new relationships were forged in the process. It was a joy-filled ride.

We hope that some of that joy spills over for you as you read the stories from the different authors and learn *with* (not just *from*) them.

Why only American authors? One may ask why all the contributors to this book seem to be from within the United States The answer is simply that the intercultural field has its origins in the United States. John Condon and many others attribute the beginnings of the intercultural field as emerging from Edward T. Hall's work. Our intent from the beginning was to trace the development of the intercultural field in the United Staes. Most of the people who we asked to contribute their stories are indeed living within the United States although there is some cultural, ethnic, and geographic diversity. For instance, Thiagi was born and grew up in India, Cliff Clarke spent much of his childhood and adult life in Japan, Nancy Adler has lived and worked in Canada much of her life. Alvino Fantini's background is Italian, and Carlos Cortes' immigrant grandparents were from Mexico, Austria, and Ukraine. While Europe and Asia have their own intercultural programs, they developed after the birth of the field in the United States. By and large, the earliest pioneers in the intercultural field were in the United States. Hopefully this book will inspire similar works recounting the development of interculturalism in Europe and Asia through the stories of their pioneers in the intercultural field by capturing their stories before their voices are lost.

What is Interculturalism? What is the Intercultural Field?

Standing in a slow line at a Washington, D.C. bank, the lady behind me struck up a conversation. After pleasantries she mentioned that she had recently spent 4 years in London. I asked how it went, and she said it was better after she got over thinking that they speak English so how hard could it be? I smiled when she admitted that their English in the U.K. is different from ours in the U.S., but it took her almost a year to realize it. "How was it coming home?" I asked. She said she must have caught something because it wasn't feeling right at all. I gently explained about culture shock and re-entry shock as her eyes got bigger and bigger. "Oh my gosh", she shouted, "that explains it!" (Sandy Fowler)

The concept of culture shock by no means explains all that intercultur-alism is. Interculturalism is a focus or perspective that the distance between cultures can be bridged with study, knowledge about intercultural com-munication, and intercultural relations. In its beginning the focus was on international intercultural understanding, however more recently attention has also been applied within cultures. Interculturalism is nuanced and complex just as human beings and their interactions are.

The intercultural field refers to the work of professionals who focus on the cultural influences on communication and understanding between people from different cultures. Those differences include such factors as the norms, values, language, perceptions, behavioral patterns, context, and expectations (the list goes on) that affect the ability of people who grew up in different cultures to work and live together. The Intercultural Field is made up of Intercultural Communication, Intercultural Management, Intercultural Relations, Intercultural Research, Intercultural Coaching, Intercultural Education and so forth. In this respect it is no different from many other disciplines. Each interculturalist usually combines several segments of the field, but they all deal with intercultural understanding. It is that focus on the cultural interface that sets us apart regardless of whether we are professors, consultants, or researchers. Our intercultural competence comprises "a set of cognitive, affective, and behavioral skills and characteristics, that support effective and appropriate interaction in a variety of cultural contexts" (Bennett, 2015, p. xxiii).

You will find examples in this book of successful professors involved in the academic/research component of the intercultural field, who have also had successful non-academic professional careers. And as Michael Tucker points out, "many of us outside an academic environment consider ourselves intercultural consultants, performing research and applying research-based methods and techniques to assessment, coaching and training. We do not really define our work as Intercultural Communication. However, there isn't a separate field for us, so I suppose we could be considered an applied branch of Intercultural Communication. We certainly do consider ourselves Interculturalists in our lives and work." (Personal communication, March 15, 2025.) It is not unusual for people joining the field to find themselves making a personal commitment to a lifetime of exploring the depths of cultural diversity and pathways to the harmony that intercultural interactions can create.

Let us introduce the man who fundamentally *founded* the field of intercultural communication: Edward T. (Ned) Hall (1914–2009). He was an American anthropologist and cross-cultural researcher whose long career and visionary work built a professional vocabulary and domain that he sculpted out of his doctoral studies, field work, and global travels.

Hall (1992) described his life "as a story of my gradually increasing awareness of the richness of the grammar and vocabulary of everyday culture, the unwritten rules that provide what order there is to daily life" (p. xv). He called these rules the *unstated rules of everyday life*. He was aware that the cultural rules were largely unconscious just as culture's role in the development of the individual is by and large an unconscious process. Hall valued and built on the work of his anthropological elders, as he crafted his theories but he developed his own perspective, and his approach became known as applied anthropology. He was an early proponent of *theory to practice*, however, he proclaimed that he wasn't interested in theory unless it was rooted in what actually goes on in the world.

John Condon, one of this book's authors recalled Hall's contributions in the early days of the intercultural field: "While *The Silent Language* (1959), Hall's first book, inadvertently launched what became a field of study for academics wanting to expand what we'd been offering and evolved into a profession. There were many people from many backgrounds around the same time who wantd to find something that the available disciplines and professions didn't seem to offer. That's how I remember conversations at the time. Coming together were language teachers and interpreters; missionaries; a rare businessperson; academics in communication, sociology, political science, a collection of people who otherwise might seem to have nothing in common who were itching to find a missing something that brought us all together. Hall's *Silent Language* gave us something with which to scratch that itch. And it seems not surprising that this emerged in the United States—with its history of cultural values and an *attitude* to convert others, and the post-war wealth and power lacking in much of the world devastated by the war, and an idealism that often follows revolutions and wars." (Personal Communication, July 16, 2024.)

Through Hall's work in the U.S. State Department, the Foreign Service Institute, and elsewhere, Hall introduced a number of seminal concepts, including:

- Proxemics. The human use of physical space and how it differs between cultures and relates to territorialism in animals. (Hall, 1959)
- Monochronic Time. Individuals and cultures tend to handle events sequentially, and polychronic time in which individuals attend to multiple events simultaneously. (Hall, 1984)

- High and Low Context. The meaning of words and sentences derives in large part from the context in which they are embedded; the importance of context differs across cultures. (Hall, 1959)

One of Hall's most important contributions was the concept of silent language. Silent language refers, for example, to the ways various cultures perceive time or as he called them, the "voices of time." In addition, silent language refers to non-verbal communication: posture, mannerisms, cadence, emphasis, are all examples of communicating without words.

Building Careers and the Foundation
of the Intercultural Field

The elders whose stories form the heart of this book were the implementors and engaged activists who built the intercultural field not just by doing but by living it. They learned from Hall's contributions as he worked to decode hidden meaning. These early implementors were not averse to risk nor were they afraid to fail. They had no boilerplate, no how-to manuals—they were trying to do things that hadn't been done before. Their curiosity and open-minded attitude enabled them to try things out and make revisions when and where they determined what was most necessary and appropriate. Much of the time they succeeded, but perhaps more important, they learned and changed course when things went wrong. Even more notably they shared their successes and failures—they learned from each other.

What predisposed these early interculturalists to see culture as an entity to be explored and understood, what made them hungry to learn more about themselves and cultural others?

We learn in their stories what it was about intercultural communication that called out to each of these authors. What were their struggles? Challenges? Joys and successes? What opened them to taking certain risks in their lives, moving to other countries to work and explore? Why did they choose to engage with the uncertainty inherent in working in a new field—so new it didn't quite exist? What did this newly minted intercultural field look like as they found like-minded colleagues? What were the highlights of their careers? How has the intercultural profession changed over time? And, how has their work impacted and influenced their life-outlook, values, and vision for the future of our world? You will find their responses to these questions and more in their life stories. They have out-lined the themes that guided their careers in different ways.

Transformational learning theme. Authors were asked to think about the events in their lives that influenced their career trajectories. They reviewed and reflected on their entire lives. Doing this from a perspective developed over decades, one can see patterns and themes that were not necessarily evident while engaged in the business of living. It was an exercise in making meaning as each author reflected on their visions, goals, objectives—the overall mission of their lives. In their stories, you will find that these intercultural elders identified seminal moments and events that transformed their perspectives, brought new meaning to experiences, and changed how the authors chose to show up in the world. These eventful moments catalyzed transformational learning.

Transformational learning events (Donna Stringer refers to hers as a SEE: Significant Emotional Experience) in the sense that the concept is used in writing these autobiographies, is based on a theory that a profound life experience often challenges and even redefines values, assumptions and beliefs, transforms the way a person defines words, and expands their world view. The individual must be open to new meanings that result from reflecting on the transformational experience, such as living in a culture other than the one on their passport or an accumulation of experience in their home culture. The same kind of transformational experience did not happen for all the authors. There are as many ways to enter and contribute to the intercultural field as there are interculturalists.

When intercultural work is part, not all. Some people do intercultural work but are not interculturalists. For example, medical professionals serve patients often from cultures other than that of the doctors, nurses, or technicians. As often happens today, doctors, nurses, and technicians may well be from a variety of cultures, and they too need to learn to work together. Medical treatments differ across cultures as well as patient and doctor expectations and behavior. It serves medical personnel well to receive ongoing intercultural training to work better with their patients but that does not make them interculturalists.

Another example is police personnel who often face situations where issues can escalate quickly due to a lack of understanding of cultural norms. For example, some cultures normally speak loudly and excitedly, while not meaning to exacerbate a situation. However, when police react to some situations according to Anglo cultural norms, escalation and unnecessary force can happen. Similar to medical professionals, their work involves communicating with people from a wide range of cultures, however they would not be considered interculturalists. Intercultural practitioners work with medical professionals, police and many other professions to help them bridge cultural differences and communicate effectively.

An additional area greatly impacted by interculturalism is the field of language education. According to Alvino Fantini, a few decades ago, language courses generally dealt only with vocabulary and grammar, possibly with some added literary works to provide some cultural insights, but this has changed dramatically in the past 50 years or so. Today, appropriate interactional, intercultural performance is commonly dealt with as part of learning to communicate in another tongue. The language education field has benefitted and incorporated a great deal that comes from the intercultural field.

The context within which this book is happening. Edward T. Hall is purported to have said that nothing means anything without context. The 1960's when interculturalism began to blossom was the very opposite of the context of the environment 65 years later when this book is being written. In 1960, with John F. Kennedy forming the U.S. Peace Corps and an upsurge of American corporations expanding abroad it was a time of inspiration and opportunity. The outlook as we write this book is not the same. How this will affect the intercultural field we cannot predict. It is safe to say that interculturalism is well established and it will be important for the world of the future to support our work and use what we know to bring about the peace we all wish for. The stories that recall the beginnings of the field establish the solid foundation upon which the intercultural field rests.

Reflecting on their professional lives authors included events, experiences, and lessons from their personal lives. It is our hope that as a reader of this book, you get to know them and can see for yourself how inclusive and over-arching interculturalism has been for each of these intercultural elders. Interculturalism is not just an academic field or professional domain, but a *way of life: doing, living, being.* Interculturalism is a lifestyle. It is above and beyond an approach to work—it threads itself into and throughout work, career, and personal life. Each author expresses that integration differently, but the impact of an intercultural career is clear in each person's narrative. We welcome you to read on. We invite you to find out for yourself what it means to be an interculturalist. Is that you?

REFERENCES

Bennett, J. (2015). *The Sage Encyclopedia of Intercultural Competence*. Sage Publications, Inc.

Hall, E. T. (1959). *The Silent Language*. Fawcett Books.

Hall, E. T. (1984). *The Dance of Life: The Other Dimension of Time*. Doubleday/ Anchor Books.

Hall, E. T. (1992). *An Anthropology of Everyday Life: An Autobiography*. Doubleday.

CHAPTER 2

Do We Have the Courage and Vision Not to Fail

Nancy J. Adler

We have a responsibility in our time, as others have had in theirs, not to be prisoners of history, but to shape history.
Madeleine Albright[1]

Montreal, Winter 2025. A blizzard howls outside. A white world of blowing snow makes it impossible to travel across the street let alone around the world. Blizzards also ravage our social, political, and cultural worlds, rendering it impossible to know if we, the citizens of the world, will find our way back to civility, humanity, and prosperity before one of the predicted cataclysms makes the question mute. This morning, as I reflect on my life and career, I find myself wondering if anything we have learned is powerful enough to successfully guide our communities, companies, and countries through this seemingly devastating moment in history. We yearn for an interconnected, multicultural, global society that equally celebrates our individuality, our cultures, and our ability to collectively create beauty, stability, and the innovations the world so

N. J. Adler (✉)
McGill Desautels Faculty of Management, Montreal, QC, Canada
e-mail: nancy.adler@mcgill.ca

© The Author(s), under exclusive license to Springer Nature
Switzerland AG 2025
S. M. Fowler, D. C. Yalowitz (eds.), *Creating the
Intercultural Field*,
https://doi.org/10.1007/978-3-032-01370-5_2

11

desperately needs. Which of us has the vision and courage to guide us back to a more optimistic future? To guide us home? What am I, along with my international and cross-cultural colleagues, contributing? Are we obsolete or crucial for the world to flourish? I wish I had the answer. I am not sure I do.

DARING TO CARE: GLOBAL WISDOM
AND THE AUDACITY OF HOPE

I was born an optimistic realist; born into a family encircled with love, to a mother whose courage and ingenuity were crucial to her family's survival. Without recognizing it, I was born to sense danger, not to avoid it. The only questions worth asking are "How do we transform the current global threats into opportunity? How do we transform ugliness into beauty? Transforming potential cross-cultural crises into beauty became my mission and life path, long before I knew what a mission was or understood the path I was on.

Shortly after I moved from my native California to Canada to become an international management professor, I flew back to the West Coast to celebrate American Thanksgiving with my family. As I arrived, Kiara, my not-yet-five-year-old niece met me at the door and began bombarding me with questions, urgently demanding to know who I really was, not just her aunt, but who? In her most serious voice, she began her inquiry:

"Aunt Nancy, what do you do?"
"I teach, Kiara."
"Who do you teach, Aunt Nancy?
"Big people, like your mommy and daddy, and your friends' mommies and daddies."

This perplexed her. Somewhat exasperated with my response, she demanded,

"Do big people still need to learn?"

Pausing only momentarily, she continued her interrogation,

"Aunt Nancy, what do you teach the 'big people'?"

Stumped, I felt I would fail miserably at explaining global leadership and cross-cultural management to an almost five-year-old. I tried.

Kiara's response? Silence. But moments later, she triumphantly proclaimed,

> *"Aunt Nancy, I know what you do. You teach big people from around the world how to play nicely with each other."*

Precisely! That is exactly what we do, or at least it's what we all try to do; we try to get big people from around the world to play nicely with each other. And, I would hazard to say that, against all odds, we urgently need to succeed. What we do, at our best, is exactly what the world most needs.[2]

Courage Beyond the Bubble of Love

Growing up in California, my family's history and stories shaped me into the woman I became. The influences, however, began long before I was born.

When my Austrian mother first met my American father, she no longer wanted to bring children into the world. World War II had destroyed her belief that the world was worthy of children. My father argued that my mother's well-founded anguish at the state-of-the-world did not have to reduce her to cynicism and despair. Luckily, my father convinced my mother that the two of them, Liselotte and Robert, could surround their children in a bubble of love that would protect them from the evils of the world. Four years later, I was born, the second of three children.

Years later, I passed on the wisdom of my parents' story to senior civil-sector leaders from around the world:

> As leaders, your job is to create the global equivalent of my parents' bubble of love; to encircle the world with a sustainable bubble of peace, justice, compassion, and prosperity—a bubble in which humanity is safe to flourish.

My mother, along with every parent who has survived terror anywhere in the world, was forced to ask herself: How do I tell my children about evil and a world gone mad? How do I tell the truth without stealing the essence of my children's hope, optimism, and faith in humanity?

How my mother told me her story defines the very essence of who I became as a human being, an artist, and a cross-cultural professional.

Rather than overwhelm me with horror, fear, and condemnation, she told a story of courage, compassion, responsibility, and love.

The Courage to Live: I Am My Mother's Daughter

Vienna, the city of my mother's birth, symbolizes the height of Western civilization, having given the world great art, architecture, music, philosophy, psychology, and so much more. Both Vienna's heights and nadir have shaped who I became.[3]

The splendor of Viennese culture filled my mother's first 13 years. Then, in 1938, her world, along with that of her neighbors, descended from cultured heaven into unadulterated hell. Following months of violence, two Nazis SS officers arrived at Liselotte's home to interrogate and evict her family. Seeing Liselotte and her brother doing chores, the Nazis trained their guns on her father and ordered him to pay 'the help'—moments later Liselotte and her brother escaped to the street. The Nazis then forced her father into one of Vienna's already overcrowded prisons. This being early in the German occupation, few concentration camps had been built, and none, as yet, had been converted into extermination camps.

Fearing that they would be more easily recognized if they stayed together, Liselotte ran in the opposite direction from her older brother. The petrified teenager hid in the alleys behind Vienna's elegant buildings in a world gone mad with murderous intent aimed at Jews, children as well as adults. On the third day, hungry and scared, she reached the home of the Janns, family friends who, like 97% of all Austrians, were Catholic. Even at risk of the Nazis killing their entire family for hiding a Jewish child, the Janns immediately opened the door and took Liselotte in. If it had not been for their extraordinary courage, my mother would never have escaped, and I, needless to say, would never have been born. The Janns saw my mother as a child who deserved to live; not as a Jew nor as someone different from them. Their humanity transcended cultural difference. Good transcends evil, even as evil eclipses good.

Throughout my life I have asked myself, "*For whom or for what would I open the door?*"

Neighbors grew suspicious and informed the Nazis that they suspected the Janns were hiding a Jewish child. Once again Nazis SS officers arrived at the door, the distinctive clomp of their heavy boots warning the family of their imminent approach. With their lives in jeopardy, the Janns hurriedly hid Liselotte in the laundry bin under the family's beautifully embroidered sheets. The SS officers tore apart the house looking for the fugitive Jewish child. Liselotte, however, evaded their prying eyes and murderous intent. The next night she left, not because the Janns threw her out, but because she refused to further endanger their lives.

I ask myself, "*Would I have had the courage to risk my life to protect someone else?*"

Even if my mother's story had ended there, which it doesn't, it would be impossible not to learn from her that life is sacred, that courage is necessary, and that people of all religions and cultures often act with profound moral integrity. We do not live in a world in which 'our side' has all the good people and the 'other side' manifests the essence of evil. With just this fragment of my mother's story deeply embedded within me, it is not surprising that I chose to focus my professional life on learning how people from every culture, religion, nationality, and race can work together in peace for the benefit of all, rather than resorting to violence to resolve their real and imagined differences.

But let me return to my mother's story.

What now? How do you save your life when you are a hunted teenager alone on the streets of Vienna, with that once elegant culture now attempting to murder you along with all those like you?

Luckily, Liselotte discovered where her mother was hiding. But less than 24-hours later, yet another terrifying 'visit' from the SS threatened their lives. This time she and her cousin hid in plain sight, jumping into the oversized bed and pretending to make passionate love. Laughing and slightly embarrassed, the SS officers backed out of the bedroom.

Liselotte now realized that not even the adults knew what to do. Were her father and brother still alive? They didn't yet know that the family of her brother's Catholic girlfriend was risking their lives to hide him. Stories of courage, stories compassion, stories of horror—all playing out across cultures.

For reasons that remain unimaginable to me from my perspective having grown up in the peaceful, happy world of California, Liselotte took matters in her own hands. Realizing that she did not match the stereotype of a Jew, she hoped that she could pass unmolested as a gentile. Unbeknownst to her mother, Liselotte took the streetcar downtown to meet with a friend's father who, months earlier, had offered to help her family. Liselotte arrived at his address only to discover it was Gestapo headquarters. She entered and asked to see her girlfriend's father. Shocked but remaining true to his word, this very senior Gestapo officer released

Liselotte's father from prison and arranged visas for the immediate family to leave the country. Good transcends evil, even as evil eclipses good.

Days later, with her father back with the family, but having been beaten so brutally that he no longer recognized them, Liselotte's parents agonized over their options. Leave the country immediately and sacrifice the grandparents, who simply could not get exit visas, or stay and risk the entire family being annihilated. An impossible choice. The grandmothers, however, made the decision: "*Leave now! For if not, none of us will survive. For your sake, for the children's sake, and for the sake of their children's children! Leave!*"

Years later I have pondered the meaning of having great grandmothers who loved me, an as-yet-unborn child, so profoundly that they sacrificed their own lives so that I might be born. Great Grandmothers Nina and Laura paid the ultimate price. The Nazis murdered them along with their husbands. They died so that I, the next generation, might be born. Even though I never had the privilege of meeting my great grandmothers, I can hear them speaking to me and can feel their strength:

"*Nancy, you have to speak your truth, for if not, we died in vain.*"

It surprises no one that my ultimate goal whether implicit or explicit, as Kiara has said, is to get big people from around the world to play nicely with each other.

CREAM CHEESE ON PUMPERNICKEL: BRIDGING DIFFERENCES, CREATING SYNERGY

Everyday experiences growing up in California also shaped who I have become as a human being, an artist, and a cross-cultural management scholar, teacher, and consultant. Already during my first week in kindergarten, I encountered the wrath of rejection as my new five-year-old friends judged me not only as different, but weird. My mother had sent me to school with my favorite sandwich: cream cheese on traditional Austrian, dark-brown pumpernickel bread. The other kindergartners laughed in disgust at my sandwich and wouldn't sit next to me. Returning home in tears, I told my mother that I wanted a peanut-butter-and-jelly sandwich on white bread, with the crust cut off, just like the other kids. The next day, I happily arrived at kindergarten with my culturally-appropriate sandwich. The kids no longer ridiculed me for eating a strange sandwich. However, when I returned home I again burst into tears. I hated the taste of the squishy white-bread sandwich. I was much too young for long discussions about identity and the role of culture, or the stigma of being labelled as different and treated as an outsider. My mother, however, transcended the cross-cultural sandwich crisis, not with philosophy, but with pragmatism. For lunch the next day, she prepared two large cream-cheese-on-pumpernickel sandwiches, cutting the second into small squares and telling me to share the small squares with my new friends. Success! As the kindergartners tasted the chocolate-looking squares, their faces erupted in delight: cream cheese on pumpernickel might look strange, but it tasted delicious. Without ever saying as much, my mother had taught me that the challenge is not merely to recognize differences, but rather to bridge them. With those tiny sandwich squares, she had taught me how creativity and generosity can bridge differences. At age five, however, I simply knew that I could have new friends AND continue to enjoy my favorite sandwich. It wasn't either or. Later that understanding grew into my lifelong belief that differences are opportunities; platforms for discovering and creating synergy.

BECOMING EDUCATED: LEARNING BEYOND BORDERS

From kindergarten through high school, I attended public school in California during an era in which the education they offered was top rated. In addition to a wide range of honors classes we enjoyed many opportunities outside our local school. In my senior year, for example, I was one of 60 young people chosen from across the country to participate in a National Science Foundation Summer Science Institute on marine biology and oceanography. With our own boat and daily visits to the beach, it became hard to tell the difference between learning and fun.

Neither of my parents had the opportunity to attend university, yet, my brother, sister, and I all earned graduate degrees. At the final interview for a Regents Scholarship, I felt puzzled when the Committee asked me why I planned to go to university. My answer: "*For the same reason I went to third grade. My family simply assumed that I'd continue my education.*" The Committee's next question did not appear as benign, revealing the era's reluctance to fully open the door to women. After asking me what I would do if I had a lover on the marine-biology research ship, they asked: "*Nancy, what do you think of Nancy Sinatra's new song, These Boots are Made for Walking?*" I sensed a trap. The hit song celebrated empowerment, rebellion, and individuality, particularly for women. Not what I guessed the Committee wanted to hear. So I strategically ducked the question and responded, *"I don't really know that song."* Learning when to fight and when to duck is a skill I was only beginning to learn (and may never have completely mastered).

In 1966, with my prestigious Regents Scholarship in hand, I entered the University of California Los Angeles (UCLA), eager to become a marine biologist. After earning the top grade in UCLA's 400-person Chemistry 1A class, my science career came to an abrupt halt when the computer registration system failed to enroll me in Chemistry 1B. Sadly, I didn't realize that I could have fought the computer's 'decision.' Rather, I believed my only option was to change majors. Following in my Uncle Herb's footsteps, I switched from marine biology to economics. Looking back, I realize how, little-by-little, I learned that there are almost always 'other options', often ones that you need to create and then fight for. Maybe that belief comes from the subtext of my mother's life story. Don't surrender to being a victim! However, in this case, I think it was serendipity. Economics led me to management which led me to global leadership, a much better fit for me than marine biology.

Following both my junior and senior years at UCLA, I spent the summer as a White House Intern, along with other soon-to-be-graduates selected from other top universities. Did we have a great time! Yes! Did I begin to see how culture, politics, and economics influence most consequential decisions? Yes. After graduating, I stayed in Washington D.C. to work for the Coalition to Tax Pollution, my first opportunity to use my new economics degree for something I believed in—environmentally sound economic policy.

From War to Joy: My First Experience Working Abroad

After several years in Washington, I returned to UCLA to earn an MBA in their new Arts Management Program, the first such program in the world. Working in the nation's capital had convinced me that I needed to focus more on what I was for rather than on what I was against. The two, working for versus against (for example, for environmental sustainability versus against pollution), are very similar, simply different paths to the same goal. I later learned from Gunnar Hedlund, my Swedish global strategist friend, that equivalent but different paths to the same goal is called equifinality. Appreciating equifinality has guided me throughout my career in working with people from around the world. In 1972, it reoriented me toward aspiring to bring more beauty into the world rather than continuing to work primarily against what was wrong. I continue to be inspired by how world renowned systems theorist and architect Buckminster Fuller captured the importance of beauty in his own contributions: *"When I am working on a problem, I never think about beauty. I think of only how to solve the problem. But when I have finished, if the solution is not beautiful, I know it is wrong"*.[4]

I feel lucky to have entered professional life just as more opportunities were opening for women. When I joined UCLA's Masters in Business Administration (MBA) program, I was one of only ten women accepted into a class of 400. A small number, but just a few years earlier, no women had been allowed to enrol in any of the country's top MBA programs.

In my first year in the MBA, UCLA selected me to represent them on the Journey for Perspective. Together with two MBA students from each of the five major west-coast universities, I would be going to Europe to meet with senior leaders from government, industry, and the civil sector. It would be my first trip abroad. Needless to say, I was excited as I arrived at the pre-trip briefing hosted by the Journey's sponsor, a major global company. As each of the other nine representatives entered the executive suite, the CEO greeted him with *"Congratulations, Welcome to the Journey for Perspective. We are delighted you'll be joining us."* When I entered. I was greeted with *"Oh my God, look what they've done!"* and immediately taken aside by an executive assistant who pointedly suggested that I could wait outside as no women would be going on the trip. I graciously declined and stayed for the briefing. The next day, the Journey's corporate sponsor emphatically informed UCLA that they needed to replace me with a male representative. My excitement dwindled to dismay. But then something happened that taught me much about organizational and societal change. UCLA not only informed the CEO that I would remain UCLA's representative but also contacted the other four universities to enlist their support. Within days, all five universities notified the company that they fully supported me being the first woman to go on the Journey for Perspective, and that they would collectively disclose the company's discriminatory policy to the press if they failed to treat me with the utmost respect. Given the threat of adverse publicity, the host company immediately welcomed me back onto the Journey. Wow! I had a wonderful first trip to Europe and learned more than I could have imagined about not accepting the status quo, not giving up, and using collective power to negotiate. All lessons that have served me well from that time on. I also learned that just because something has never been done before doesn't mean that now is not the right time for it to happen.

That same year, UCLA arranged for me to work for the Minister of Culture in Israel. My first experience living abroad. My initial weeks in Tel Aviv fit the classic definition of cultural shock. I still remember how astonished I felt, coming from a country where most people speak only one language, English, and are considered brilliant if they speak multiple languages, when I discovered the local fruit vendor happily conversing with my new neighbors in at least six distinct languages.

My real shock, however, came on October 6th, 1973, when the Yom Kippur War broke out. Never in my sunny-Southern-California life had I imagined being in a war. I could neither decode much of what was going on nor assess the imminent threats. As I wrote to my parents on a postcard that they still have: *"I feel like I'm inside an old-fashioned tumble dryer, looking out at the world."* On the first Saturday after the war broke out, the Minister of Culture invited me to join her for Shabbat lunch in Jerusalem's Old City at the home of a prominent Palestinian. The other guests, six Israeli Jews and six Israeli Arabs, all artists, engaged in a vibrant conversation, laughing together, and agreeing on more issues than most would suspect. Far from somber, the lunch was joyous. *Weren't we at war? Weren't we supposed to be enemies?* The following week, with the War still raging, friends from Moscow invited me to their home for Shabbat dinner. My linguist host spoke 17 languages, including English, so we didn't need to navigate the conversation in my rudimentary Hebrew. It was a joyous evening. Mystified, I finally asked: *"How can you be so happy in the middle of a war, especially when we emerged only five minutes ago from the bomb shelter."* Their answer: *"Joy is not what the world gives you, it is what you create for yourself and those you love."* I come from a culture with an extremely high locus-of-control (a term I only learned later), but in that moment, I realized that I had let my own happiness become a puppet of outside circumstances. Whereas I felt despondent because of the War; my friends chose to create a joyful evening in the middle of the same War. What a gift that realization has been for me, as that moment has guided my perspective (and my mood) from that day forward. Based on the same create-your-own-joy philosophy, the Israeli symphony performed throughout the War, even on the many evenings when none of the soldier-violinists were present to play. Years later in Montreal, I listened with profound appreciation as Nobel Peace Prize Laureate Elie Wiesel explained that hope is not an empirical conclusion; it is what leaders bring to a situation. Bring hope. Make beauty. Joyously celebrate life.

Coming Home: Dinner with Andy

In 1974, when I returned from Israel to my home in California, I felt disoriented. I assumed that the War had caused my sense of being disconnected from reality. I was wrong. A few weeks after returning home, I got together with Andy, a good friend who had just come home after two-years working in India with the Peace Corps. Over dinner, Andy described his own intense disorientation. To my surprise, his feelings mirrored my own. It had nothing to do with Israel or the war. Shortly thereafter, the regional Peace Corps director invited me to his home to meet informally with a small group of recently returned Peace Corps volunteers who were among the best performers abroad but, sadly, were among those having the hardest time readjusting once home. The returnees' storytelling continued far onto the night. By 3 a.m., we realized that we all felt profoundly disoriented, no matter which foreign country we had lived in nor the specific challenges we had faced. One woman described being very sick in Africa and losing a lot of weight. Just after she returned home, her family gathered for a sumptuous Thanksgiving dinner. Overwhelmed by the amount of food, both eaten and wasted, she eagerly anticipated sharing her experiences in Africa with the people she loved most. Instead, she remembers only being asked to *"Pass the peas."* Her family seemingly wasn't interested in her time abroad. It took weeks for her to move past feeling unimportant, rejected, and invisible, and to accept that her family was simply involved in their own lives and found it impossible to relate to her time in Africa.

That evening, I knew we had uncovered an important dynamic, the re-entry transition, that neither the literature nor people in organizations seemed to have recognized. Until then, most people assumed that only the initial cross-cultural transition, when a person first moves abroad, was difficult, due to cultural shock, but that the transition back home would be easy because everything would be familiar. It wasn't true. My dinner with Andy and the subsequent evening with the Peace Corps volunteers convinced me to begin asking more seriously, *"What is really going on during re-entry?"*

That evening launched my cross-cultural career and gave me my first major research topic, re-entry, which became my UCLA doctoral dissertation. I received corporate and governmental support for my research, even though I had no research track record at that time. Based on my study, the Canadian International Development Agency (CIDA) and Procter and Gamble hired me to help them design their first re-entry programs. Over the years, more companies, organizations, and government agencies worldwide hired me to help their employees successfully transition not only back into their home country but also back into their home organization. Tellingly, the catalyst for many early re-entry programs was most companies' failure to retain their returning expatriates, the very people who had the most international management expertise and experience.

CROSS-CULTURAL TRANSITIONS: GETTING THERE AND COMING BACK HOME

As I worked more broadly on cross-cultural transitions, I became an expert on getting expatriates there and getting them back home. Alcan, a Montreal-based global company, for example, asked me to produce a film, *A Portable Life*, documenting how much more difficult the role of accompanying spouse was than that of the expatriate employee and children. At that time, in the early 1980s, the accompanying spouse, who was almost always a wife, was rarely allowed to work abroad. That policy changed when companies began sending women managers abroad as professionals. Most companies found it inconceivable that they would require an accompanying husband to remain unemployed while abroad. Once companies changed their policy for male spouses (husbands), it became untenable to continue to restrict female spouses (wives). And so change happens. An unfortunate residual of that era were the companies that continued to believe that women couldn't succeed abroad, when, in fact, it was the role of 'accompanying spouse' that caused most difficulties, not the gender of the person in the role.

Only later, based on conversations with hi-potential and executive women did I learn that expatriation had begun to become a work-life-balance strategy. As one woman succinctly explained, "*There's no way I could hold a senior position in this company and take good care of my family without having accepted an expatriate position—without having a housekeeper, a driver, an excellent caretaker for my children, and a cook. I have no idea what I will do when I return home.*"

As I travelled the world, I learned that many of the challenges faced by North American women were, in other parts of the world, more a consequence of socio-economic status than of gender. As one South American women executive laughingly clarified for me, using a vocabulary that few would use in North America, *"Here, the poor people clean our homes, cook, and take care of the family, not the women in prominent families. Women from prominent families, similar to their brothers, receive the best education and are networked with people who offer them influential senior positions."* Many Asian women executives echoed similar sentiments. Perhaps that explains why more than 100 women have already served in their country's most senior leadership position—as president or prime minister—yet, as of 2025, the United States has yet to elect its first woman President.

CROSS-CULTURAL MANAGEMENT

I joined UCLA's management doctoral program in 1974. One of the professors knew George Renwick, who later became a good friend, even celebrating my 30th birthday by hiking with me into the Grand Canyon by starlight and proceeding to get caught the next morning in a massive snowstorm (but that's a story for another day). The professor told George about this new doctoral student, Nancy Adler, who wanted to learn about people working across cultures. Straightaway George invited me to attend the inaugural conference of the Society of Intercultural Education, Training, and Research (SIETAR) in Washington DC.

On Conferencing as a Way of Knowing

UCLA awarded me a travel grant, rare for a graduate student, with just enough funding for me to take the overnight red-eye flight from Los Angeles to DC. With excitement masking my lack of sleep, I presented myself at the conference registration desk, giving them my name and affiliation, UCLA Graduate School of Management. Nametag in place, I joined the opening reception, only to be met with less than cordial comments: *"Oh, so you help companies profit from employing foreigners"* and *"We're interested in creating cross-cultural relationships, not in forcing foreigners to work for us."*

Even with my fledgeling observation skills, I could decode these not-so-subtle rebukes. I promptly returned to the registration desk and explained that there was a mistake on my nametag. It should read 'UCLA',

not UCLA Graduate School of Management. With my new identity proclaimed on my nametag, I rejoined the conferees and was warmly greeted
with *"Oh, you flew here all the way from California"* and *"Welcome, UCLA
is a great university."* It seems I was using the same strategy my mother
had taught me in kindergarten with my cream-cheese-on-pumpernickel
sandwich-squares.

The next day, I sat in a darkened auditorium watching animated films
portraying various cross-cultural interactions. Without thinking, I said out
load, *"That would make a great executive-decision-making film!"* Instead
of expressing annoyance at me for talking during the film, the person next
to me said *"Absolutely!"* By luck, amongst a sea of cross-cultural communications conferees, I was sitting next to Joe Distefano, a cross-cultural
management professor. Our conversation consumed the rest of the afternoon, spilled over into a Maryland-crabcakes dinner, and didn't begin to
wind down until well after midnight. Joe introduced me to Kluckhohn
and Strodtbeck and explained how their values-orientations could be
applied to organizations, including to management and leadership. That
coincidental meeting led to a lifelong friendship and colleagueship. Joe
seamlessly transitioned from mentor (I was a first-semester doctoral student) to colleague. Over the years, we consulted together for many international companies. From our consulting, emerged theory, the theory was
published, and the insights continue to help companies and students alike.

Beyond Recognizing Differences: Understanding Cross-Cultural Interaction

In 1980, McGill recruited me to join the university as a professor, the first
woman to hold a tenure-track position in Faculty of Management. McGill
is a top-ranked, completely international, English-speaking university.
Located in Montreal, it is in the French-speaking province of Quebec
within the predominantly English-speaking country of Canada. Within
6 months, I launched the first university-based Cross-Cultural Management
course in the world. That course became the basis of *International
Dimensions of Organizational Behavior*, a book that ultimately sold hundreds of thousands of copies in multiple languages.[5]

At McGill, I began focusing on what made people effective when working cross-culturally, rather than continuing to research cross-cultural transitions. I led leadership seminars for Francophone (native French-speaking)
and Anglophone (native English-speaking) managers. Initially, the

managers analyzed cases in teams in which all members spoke the same native language. Anglophone and Francophone teams consistently arrived at equally effective decisions. However, reflecting equifinality, the styles of interacting that they used to arrive at their decisions varied markedly. Months later, we showed videos of the teams to international executives, all of whom regularly conducted business in Quebec but none of whom had participated in the original teams. Suddenly the audio failed. We could see the team members' behavior, but we couldn't hear what they were saying. Nevertheless, the international executives instantly identified which teams were Anglophone and which were Francophone. When asked how they knew, as all participants looked and dressed alike, they listed classic stereotypical behaviors. They noted, for example, that in the Francophone teams, multiple members spoke at the same time whereas generally only one person spoke at a time in the Anglophone teams. Simultaneous versus sequential communication. Francophone team members appeared more expressive, using a wider range of gestures and facial expressions than their Anglophone counterparts. The executives, who had not been looking for cultural differences, expressed surprise at how distinct the differences were among people who are neighbors. More importantly, they knew that in Quebec the differences were rarely interpreted as cultural, but rather assumed to reflect longstanding political animosity between the two cultures. As became evident, misinterpretation of the patterns of interaction was undermining both societal and business dynamics, including by preventing mutually beneficial collaboration.

All of us, me included, left the session with a profound appreciation for the all-too-common potential damage caused by unrecognized and misunderstood cross-cultural dynamics. Would Anglophones and Francophones have a more mutually beneficial relationship if they better understood the underlying patterns of cross-cultural interaction? This is not an idle question as Quebec has become so frustrated with the rest of Canada that it has repeatedly threatened to secede. Societal stability and economic prosperity rest to a much greater extent than most people appreciate on understanding the nuances of cross-cultural interaction. Today, in 2025, one has to wonder to what extent extreme nationalism and anti-immigration sentiment are fueled, in part, by similar cross-cultural misunderstandings and subconscious misinterpretations. If we were all to appreciate our common humanity, be it masked behind superficial or more profound cultural differences, would we again be able to see 'them' as a part of 'us'? With the world now digitally hyper-connected, is there any hope of us acting as if we understood acclaimed documentary film maker Ken Burns' reminder that: "We are US, there is no THEM."[6]

I am eternally grateful that the audio failed that day, and that we were all able to learn something much more important than what I had planned for the evening.

Working with Global Companies

Eastman Kodak was the first company that invited me, along with a strategy, marketing, and finance professor, to help them restructure the company into global-lines-of-business. I was so new to consulting that I hesitated and then suggested that they also hire Joe Distefano. They did. The next two years, directed by the CEO, were challenging and exciting. Together with strategic marketing professor Fariborz Ghadar, we created a framework showing how companies' human resource systems needed to evolve as the company's business strategy and structure progressed from domestic to international, multinational, global, and transnational. The framework advanced scholarship as well as business practice.

For me, consulting, research, and teaching have always been inextricably linked. That said, some of my university colleagues disparaged consulting (viewing it as strictly money-making) and threatened to penalize me when I came up for promotion. I reduced, if not eliminated, the threat by asking my driver to pick me up at home or around the corner from my office where none of my colleagues could see me regularly departing for the airport. Years later, I was promoted ahead of schedule to associate professor, given tenure, promoted to full professor, named the S Bronfman Professor Chair in Management, and ultimately awarded the McGill Medal for Exceptional Academic Achievement, the first person in management to be so honored in McGill's 200-year history. Discrete consulting, loving teaching, and rigorous research and publishing seem to have worked as a career strategy.

PLAYING ON A GLOBAL STAGE: MAKING A DIFFERENCE

The first hint that my work could have a larger impact happened after having delivered a keynote on *Leadership Courage: For Whom or For What Would You Open the Door.* As a part of the talk, I described how my mother had moved beyond historical hatred and now applauded Germany's many initiatives to transcend its own wartime history. To my surprise, a Rwandan diplomat approached me and asked if she could give my speech to Rwanda's President. Kagame then shared my speech about my mother's story with his entire cabinet, in the belief that if people like my mother could move beyond the Holocaust, then Rwanda's Tutsis and Hutus could move beyond the Genocide. Never could I have imagined that the retelling of my mother's story would resonate as a universal story that could help Rwandans move toward peace and prosperity.

Other unexpected opportunities for influence arose. In the 1990s, for example, I was invited to join the Board of the Tel Aviv International School of Management (TISOM). TISOM was patterned after INSEAD (in France), where I had frequently taught executive seminars. INSEAD's founding mission was to foster economic integration in post-WWII Europe, and thus foster peace, prosperity, and stability. TISOM's mission was similar, but for the Middle East. TISOM's Board, faculty, and managerial participants were drawn from countries throughout the Middle East, Arab and Israeli, Muslim, Jew, and Christian alike. Sadly, as we all know, neither TISOM nor other initiatives with similar aspirations, have as yet succeeded. Each courageously launched initiative has aimed at bringing together leaders from multiple countries and cultures for the benefit of all. Each was and is attempting to create global synergy.

I had the opportunity to work with other start-ups, including Uniterra, a 14-country international-development organization founded on a new, non-hierarchical, networked structure. I still remember arriving in Botswana, on my birthday, to co-lead Uniterra's inaugural network-building meeting, only to discover that I would be presenting in the clothes I had flown in—my suitcase having gone astray somewhere between Montreal and Gaborone. The next day, as my Botswana hosts took me to stores to buy replacement clothes, I was repeatedly told, accompanied by laughter, that I wasn't shaped like an African woman.

Another similar project was for Cirque du Soleil's foundation, One Drop, whose mission is to bring potable water to people worldwide. There could not have been a better project for me, as it integrated global leadership and humanitarian purpose with artistic processes. With the support of the Cirque, we drew on multiple art forms to create an innovative South American network that went far beyond the dehydrated language of typical leadership and strategy initiatives.

Most recently, I co-designed and co-led the inaugural Leadership Legacy Retreat for fifteen of Pakistan's most senior leaders. Held in the Himalayas, we wove together a purpose-driven leadership network to address the myriad challenges threatening the country and region. When your neighbors are Afghanistan, China, India, and Iran, neither international peace nor domestic stability can be assumed. No leader acting alone, no matter how brilliant, can successfully address the extremity of the threats facing economically developing countries. Only multisectoral networks have a possibility of making progress.

I awoke just before sunrise on the first morning and hiked further into the mountains, letting the silence and exquisite beauty of the Himalayas inspire me. On day two, several participants joined me. Within a few days, the entire group stood in awe as the early morning sunlight outlining the jagged Himalayan peaks. When faced with the beauty, majesty, and eternity of that moment, no one can think small or short-term. What a gift my professional life has been.

GLOBAL LEADERS: NO LONGER MEN ALONE

Throughout my career, I looked for ways to better understand and support women who work internationally, many of whom were the first in their company to be sent abroad or assume global responsibility. Disappointingly, my first application for a national research grant to study global women leaders was rejected with the curt assessment: *What do women have to do with leadership?*

Research I conducted in the 1980s on women expatriate managers showed that the major challenge for women was having their company or organization send them abroad, not succeeding once sent. The myth that women couldn't succeed, usually misattributed to foreigners' supposed prejudice, created the biggest hurdle. The erroneous belief that women didn't want to go created additional barriers.

In the 1990s, I researched women who were global leaders, many of whom had been rendered invisible by the widely held belief that only men could lead at the most senior levels. I submitted my first global-women-leaders article to *Leadership Quarterly*. To my dismay, the article was rejected. The rejection was not only unfair to me and to the current women leaders, but it was also unfair to all the organizations that could double their talent pool simply by considering both male and female candidates for senior leadership. So, I took the unusual step of calling the editor: "*Hi. Would you have time to discuss my paper. This topic is very important to me.*" The editor cordially responded, "*Sure. As the reviewers stated, your sample size is too small.*" I calmly responded: "*Perhaps the reviewers didn't understand that there was no sampling in my study. I included 100% of the women worldwide who have served as a president or prime minister of their country in the last half century. Perhaps the reviewers confused the entire population of global women leaders, which is in fact small, with a sample. You and I can of course agree that there should be more women presidents and prime ministers; that is, that the population should be bigger. But as a scholar, I can't change the small size of the population; I can only report what are, in fact, paltry numbers.*" The editor paused, then replied, "*You're right. There's no sampling error.*" After several of the editor's additional arguments collapsed, he interrupted me: "*Nancy, would you give me a few days to re-review your article?*" "*Happily. I really appreciate your time.*" Less than a week later, the editor accepted the article for publication with no revisions! Journals almost never publish articles as is.

The stereotype of global leaders being men was so powerful that it had blinded the editor and reviewers to the fact that not only were women holding the most senior leadership positions in countries and companies worldwide, but in both cases—government and business—the numbers were increasing. Luckily, years of teaching cross-cultural negotiating had given me the skills to broaden the editor's perspective. One of the gifts of having entered the field of cross-cultural management just as it was being born, has been the opportunity to expand my own, as well as many others', worldviews.

Drawing on the research on women leaders worldwide, I worked with global companies as they expanded their worldwide talent pool, including on a particularly creative and impactful initiative at Bestfoods. The CEO started by requesting that each region nominate their most senior and highest potential women to attend a Women's Global Leadership Summit that we had designed. With that simple invitation, the CEO ensured that the entire company became aware of the depth of talented women within the organization. As we led the Summit, we discovered how dramatically opportunities and challenges differed for women from various parts of the world. I've always believed that if I don't learn as least as much as my clients and program participants, I have failed. Given how much everyone learned during the Bestfoods' Summit, we certainly did not fail.

LEADERSHIP ARTISTRY: FINDING BEAUTY IN AN UGLY, CHAOTIC WORLD

For years, I lived two parallel lives, one very public as a management pro-fessor and consultant and the other more quietly as an artist.[7] I painted and created monotype prints and ceramics artworks. Best described as two solitudes, I purposely kept my art and management worlds completely separate, not even allowing my artist friends to know that I was an inter-national management professor. I regularly disappeared from McGill into various communities of artists, sometimes as an artist-in-residence at the Banff Centre high in the Rocky Mountains, sometimes as a member of the artistic communities at La Miranda in Italy, Penland in the United States, or Haliburton in Canada's lake district, and once to study with a Kintsugi master in Japan.

When the Emily Carr Institute of Art and Design invited me to come to Vancouver as a guest artist, they agreed that they would not reveal my 'management' identity. They requested, however, that I give a lecture to the entire artist community at the end of my 6 months with them. That lecture, *Artist as Leader, Leader as Artist,* was the first time I realized the profound overlap between my two worlds. Great artists and great leaders both have the courage to see reality the way it is, to see possibility, and to inspire people to move from current reality back to possibility.

Art gives me a vocabulary to express what is most important to me. Art allows me to bring beauty into the world. I no longer hide in my two soli-tudes. I have gone public with what is now known as leadership artistry. Legendary investment guru and Berkshire Hathaway CEO Warren Buffett seems also to have discovered the connection, asserting: "*I am not a busi-nessman; I am an artist.*"[8] That said, to this day, I never enter the studio thinking about leadership, management, or that I am a professor. I'm sim-ply drawn to making art.

Artistic processes help people to see possibilities that remain invisible to them when they limit themselves to using only words. In Banff's print-making studio, for example, I guided a group of design executives in mak-ing a collective, monotype print—a messy process that produced a somewhat chaotic result. After giving them a new way to see their cre-ation—by observing the details rather than just the whole—I asked the executives to find places of beauty within the rather ugly monotype. Transformation. When given the tools of an artist, the executives easily discovered beauty. Only then were they ready for words. Could they similarly find beauty in the chaotic situations that confronted them at work, in their communities, and in the world? Yes. Why? Because they now knew how to see beyond reality to possibility.

I invited another group to draw portraits of themselves 'leading beautifully', whatever that term meant to them. Colleagues then interpreted each other's renditions of themselves. All of us are sophisticated at hiding behind words, yet few of us are equally facile at hiding the truth behind color, texture, and design. Often inadvertently, the truth revealed itself in the self-portraits. Was the manager who drew herself larger than everyone else really as non-hierarchical, participatory, and supportive as she claimed? What aspects of her leadership really were large and most influential? What colors and textures does our current global economy need? What color would best support cross-cultural harmony? (One African executive answered, *"Beige. Because it recedes into the background and lets' others shine."*)

Art-making often exposes the powerful dynamics and unique opportunities that remain hidden when executives frame their perspective primarily in the logic of finance. In Switzerland, for example, creating collages representing their company's future allowed the most senior leaders—prior adversaries in a rather hostile Swiss-American joint venture—to identify a profound sense of purpose that subsequently guided their newly-merged company's mission and strategy. Art has the power to take us to a 'foreign land' and then brings us home to see ourselves anew. As T.S. Eliot eloquently expressed:[9]

> *We shall not cease from exploration*
> *And the end of all our exploring*
> *Will be to arrive where we started*
> *And know the place for the first time.*

To encourage managers to reflect on their leadership journey and thus to be able to come back home to themselves, I created *Leadership Insight*, a journal filled with art. *Harvard Business Review* highlighted the journal and the importance of arts-based reflection for high-level success.[10] My paintings have also been published in leadership books and journals, and, at the invitation of Sandy Fowler, editor of this book, on the cover of the *American Psychologist*.

I now create *Leading Beautifully Awards* to honor organizations, teams, and individuals not only for their accomplishments, but, more importantly, for the inspiration they bring to the future. Each *Leading Beautifully Award* is a one-of-a-kind ceramic artwork created specifically to reflect the aspirations and achievements of the organizations and people involved.[11]

My artwork has been featured in a number of exhibitions designed to bring the arts and leadership together. More than 5000 people visited my Montreal exhibit, *Reality in Translation: Going Beyond the Dehydrated Language of Management.* Press from around the world reported the story, using such titles as: "Teaching Business Leadership as Fine Art: Seeing the Company as a Blank Canvas, and Executives as Would-Be Creative Geniuses" (*Forbes*), "The Fine Art of Business" (*Times of India*), "CEOs Must Be Artists" (*Toronto Star*), "On Painting Beyond the Bottom Line" (*McGill Daily*), and "Bonding Beauty to Business" *(McGill Reporter)*.

BRINGING HOPE: GOING BEYOND OVERLY CONVENIENT FALSEHOODS AND INCONVENIENT TRUTHS

Perhaps my Artist Statement is the best way to bring this journey back to the present moment. As we all draw inspiration from our courage, creativity, compassion, resilience, and honesty, qualities I saw reflected in my mother's journey, we will have the courage to see today's world as it is, stripped of overly convenient falsehoods and exposing inconvenient truths. We will re-remember that we can do better. We will have the courage to imagine the possibilities that are needed to bring humanity together, even when others consider such aspirations naïve. We will have the courage to inspire each other to move from today's reality back to possibility. Perhaps my Artist Statement is the best way to bring this journey back to the present moment.

> In the midst of chaos, how do we see beauty? Surrounded by turbulence, how do we discover simplicity? Living together on one planet, how do we simultaneously celebrate our collective humanity and the unique resonance of each of our individual voices? Given the power of analytic understanding—driven as it is to claim life as knowable—how do we re-recognize the unknowable? Knowing all that we know, how do we surrender to the humility it takes to stand in awe of life's mysteries?
>
> Creation—whether on a canvas of words, visual images, organizational spaces, or the world's stage—is about giving birth to the possibilities inher-

ent in mystery. As an artist and a global leadership scholar, management consultant, and educator, I draw inspiration from many of the world's most influential artistic and societal leaders, including Marc Chagall. Critics acclaimed his paintings' striking humanity, and offered him their highest praise: "Marc Chagall gave this nihilist century a worthy concept: hope."[12] Art, and artistic processes, have the power not only to offer hope, but to guide us in rediscovering and creating beauty in our fractured world. Art does not dismiss science, rather it partners with all ways of knowing to go beyond what any one approach can produce on its own.

   In such ugly times, the only true protest is beauty
   Phil Ochs[13]

Nancy Adler has no conflicts of interest to declare that are relevant to the content of this chapter.

Acknowledgement This essay is dedicated to my mother, Liselotte Adler. This past year we celebrated her 100th birthday. Months later she left us. Her memory is a blessing.

NOTES

1. 1977. Albright's Words: Global task for the U.S. *New York Times*, June 6: Section A: 8.
2. Encounter described in Adler, N.J. 2025. Overly Convenient Falsehoods and Inconvenient Truths: Not What Leaders Thought They Would Learn. *International Business Review*, 34(1).
3. Earlier version presented in 2005
4. Found at https://www.goodreads.com/quotes/7713591-when-i-am-working-on-a-problem-i-never-think
5. Adler, N.J. 2008. *International Dimensions of Organizational Behavior*, 5th edition (with A. Gundersen). Mason, Ohio: Cengage.
6. Burns, May 19, 2024: https://www.youtube.com/watch?v=9n1OqPzIKH4
7. Earlier version published in Adler, N.J. 2015. Finding Beauty in a Fractured World: Art Inspires Leaders–Leaders Change the World, *Academy of Management Review*, 40(3): 480–494.
8. Buffet, as cited in Bryan, M. 1998. *The Artist's Way at Work*. NY: Harper: ix.
9. T.S. Eliot, "Little Gidding," *Four Quartets* (Gardners Books: 2001) Originally published 1943.
10. See Adler, N.J. 2016. Want to Be an Outstanding Leader? Keep a Journal. *Harvard Business Review*, January 13.

11. See, for example, the International Leadership Association's Leading Beautifully Award: https://vimeo.com/381842332

12. Riding, A. 2003. Anxiety and hope in a mystical fusion: Paris show offers Chagall's intense humanism beyond the *Joie de Vivre*. *New York Times*, April 22: B5.

13. Found at https://www.brainyquote.com/quotes/phil_ochs_205240

CHAPTER 3

Koi Memories from a Brackish Pond: A Third-Culture Kid's Search for Harmony

Clifford H. Clarke

An eleven-year-old boy jumped off the school bus to walk home three blocks up a narrow street over a bridge across the flowing creek. Just before the bridge from which he could see his home, just beyond the sandlot baseball field, a dozen young Japanese school kids jumped out of the shadows and surrounded him. Suddenly they began throwing stones to pelter this American boy to the point of injury while he was squatting on his haunches with his arms covering his head. The young students were all yelling loudly, *Yankee Go Home, Yankee Go Home* repeatedly, along with *Buta, Buta* meaning Pig, Pig. Seeing no other way to escape, the boy sprang up and took off running through the gang toward his home with the gang running after him yelling their chants closely behind. He finally got to his home screaming for his mom. Six months later the same 11-year-old and his brother were invited by these same Japanese boys to join their sandlot baseball teams, one on each team. How did such a transformation happen so quickly and influence this boy to pursue a life of bridging cultures?

C. H. Clarke (✉)
University of Hawai'i at Mānoa, Honolulu, HI, USA

S. M. Fowler, D. C. Yalowitz (eds.), *Creating the
Intercultural Field*,
https://doi.org/10.1007/978-3-032-01370-5_3

35

Initiating Adaptation in Two Cultures

As a five-year old boy from Atlanta, Georgia, I was transported with my family to a small Japanese community in Kauai, Hawaii. Barely three years passed when I was uprooted and taken to post-war Japan in 1948. Our parents transported a two-years' supply of dried foods in one shipping container for safe consumption in war-torn Japan. Memories of my first five years in the U.S. quickly faded and have remained elusive although memories of Hawaii remain vivid (Fig. 3.1).

From three years after the end of WWII my family lived in Tokyo for two years of language study. Following ten month's furlough in Kentucky, we returned to Kyoto where my parents initiated evangelical work. We lived in the eastern area of town where Dad had designed a large American ranch-style home, with a tiny aluminum-lined swimming pool deep enough to dive into and out of in one underwater arch. On that property today stand in two rows side-by-side 26 two-story townhomes. It became clear that Americans chose to carry their need for a lot of space even when local residents were satisfied with much smaller residences on very little land. This created a sense of privilege but also one of embarrassment. On the west side of our home was the community sandlot baseball playground where my older brother and I began our harmonious introduction to our local neighborhood, after the event of my stoning shared in my introduction, due to our baseball prowess.

From primary through high school, we attended the U.S. Department of Defense school in Kyoto in a large botanical garden filled with U.S. Army officers' families where 150 children lived. Until high school we were bussed to school but quickly learned the bicycle route to travel together each morning. After school I often rode my bicycle downtown to *Teramachi* Street to sit on a record store countertop with the son of the owner. We spoke in *Janglish* together and listened to music for hours-on-end. He was my first Japanese friend (Fig. 3.2).

One day in my 8th grade, Mary Nishimura, the secretary to the principal of the school, asked me if I would volunteer as an interface between the American students and the Japanese community when we went on field trips and to sports events. She felt that I had learned enough Japanese by then to serve in that capacity. I was honored and happily accepted the role. That was my first experience in having a role in building bridges

Fig. 3.1   Barefoot Cliff (Kiki) & Cole (Koko) in sugarcane field, Kauai, 1947

between Japanese and Americans. With practice a clearer focus was emerging for my future studies and career. I began to appreciate the distinctiveness of cultures and their similarities with equal appreciation.

Connecting with Family Roots

I struggled thereafter with feelings that I had about the Japanese because my parents conveyed a love for the Japanese couched in the conviction that they were lost and needed to be saved, which was in part their mission as missionaries. My Dad, also a Third-Culture Kid (TCK) and a missionary kid (MK), was raised in Kumamoto, Japan by missionary parents who served from 1898 to 1935. Also, my great-grandfather served as a

Fig. 3.2 Brothers Cliff & Cole with gym bags at Kyoto American High School, 1956

missionary in Nigeria for four years during the U.S. Civil War. He approached the Nigerian Yuroba people with a deep appreciation and gained multiple insights into their culture. He wrote about his experiences there in 1871 which he published in 1871 and 1972 (post-mortem) by J. A. Atanda (Ed.). I was deeply influenced by my great-grandfather's approach to people of another culture. This feeling was my inspiration to continue my studies after high school by majoring in World Religions at

Wake Forest University (WFU). Yet, at WFU, 1958–1962, I felt like a foreign student for four years.

TCK Challenges on an American College Campus

The training at WFU helped me understand the values and world views of the diversity around the world, a good foundation for intercultural communication studies. In those early days of intercultural communication, research focused primarily on international educational exchange programs of which I felt a part.

During those four years at college, I never stopped feeling like a foreign student adapting in a new culture. Like a Koi in a brackish pond, I had to learn to swim in either a collectivist or individualist world. I would often make mistakes as a typical TCK who lived with a global orientation, which caused me trouble one Sunday in 1960. I invited two Black brothers, sons of a preacher, my associates in the campus snack shop, to attend my White suburban Southern Baptist Church without thinking about encountering racism there. A sudden culture shock hit me when two Women' Missionary Union (WMU) leaders pushed me into the coatroom and told me I was not welcome with those Black boys. To worship with them, I should go to their church. So, that is where we went. We were exiled from the White church. These were the same WMU leaders who raised support for world missionaries, including my family in Japan. I never forgot that rejection, which woke me up to the dark reality around me. My empathy deepened for the Blacks who in 1960 were protesting their oppression at Woolworth's lunch counter sit-ins downtown in Winston-Salem, NC. Reflecting on those events I remembered my own experiences growing up in Japan where many Japanese similarly ostracized foreigners. Increasingly, my feelings of empathy deepened for all those feeling excluded or oppressed.

I recalled my experiences in the occupation days in Kyoto where the U.S. military occupiers demonstrated attitudes of the privileged class without engaging with Japanese. I never thought of myself as having privilege because I was too busy trying not to be excluded. I learned from my *Yankee-Go-Home* experience that it would take strategic efforts to gain some degree of inclusion. This task increases in difficulty in societies that project universalized assumptions, i.e., White privilege, a problem originating in individualist societies. I learned from Japanese that cultural viewpoints are very particular as collectively Japanese saw themselves as quite unique in global comparisons. A Japanese manager once told me *we can never expect a foreigner to understand us.* Having heard that saying many times it became a challenge to me to demonstrate that somehow it must be possible to understand diversities within and across cultures.

For four years in college, I never saw my parents in Japan nor called them due to costs. I treasured each letter from home. I had seven part-time jobs throughout my college years, including in the summers. In my first summer I dug foundation ditches for new homes alongside older Black builders. One day the oldest of them challenged me to a race in digging two parallel trenches of equal length for concrete foundations. I did not know he was champion of his group. You can imagine how badly he whupped me! I was reminded of the need for humility by the laughter and applause from the audience. I liked to think that part of their applause was for my efforts. The victor had twice my strength, was three times my age, and had been digging ditches for decades. I recognized some arrogance in my imagining that I could beat him.

I learned how differently I was perceived one day on campus, sitting alone in the student cafeteria. My custom when eating hot noodles in soup, to show my pleasure and to cool them, I would slurp them into my mouth without biting them off. I soon learned that I was isolating myself by doing so, much to my embarrassment and surprise. Hence, I was eating alone at a table for ten. From my childhood in Japan, I should have learned long before college in the United States to reflect the behavior in my environment to blend in harmoniously. My face turned red from the shame I felt, not the heat of the noodles, when a kind person told me how others saw me.

The greatest difficulty I had in adapting to life in the United States was in engaging one-to-one with college girls in social relationships. My interactions in Japan were all with groups of kids hanging out together. Dances were forbidden by my parents throughout school so I was heavily engaged in sports and other social activities. I was an absolute novice in American social dating relationships in college. I tried my best but was like a butterfly flitting from flower to flower throughout my four years in college, never losing a sense of embarrassing hesitancy and discomfort in such interactions, while trying not to be a prude. I tried not to reveal this to any other students, but I heard others describe me as *that shy kid from China.* They asked me if Japan was not someplace in China! This was 12 years after World War II! I felt that my experience as a TCK was of no interest to my fellow students. After my first year's registration as coming from

Kyoto, Japan, from the second year onward, I registered my hometown as Atlanta, GA, my birthplace. I thought this would help communicate my desire to assimilate with American friends rather than be isolated, like a stranger in a foreign land.

My U.S. college experiences grounded my learning about otherness in the United States. The next year in Japan was a time to enjoy being home and to reflect on my experiences in the USA. It was a different kind of otherness than what I experienced in Japan growing up where I was perceived as the minority, the outsider, the *Gaijin* or foreigner. In the United States otherness felt much deeper, even systemic, and more pervasive than in Japan, which I accepted as normal for a culture that valued individualistic independence. These diverse experiences helped me understand the feelings of exclusion and inclusion held by many minorities and why missionary kids (MK) from around the world often called each other cousins and their parents Uncle and Aunt in search of inclusion in a larger family as interdependent collectivists.

FINDING COMFORT IN BOTH CULTURES

I rushed home to Japan after final exams and before graduation ceremonies for my first job under Japanese management. Working under Japanese management for the opening year of Hotel Okura, 1962–1963, enabled me to feel included in a place I belonged and could make a contribution. Amidst a workforce of 1100 Japanese employees, I was given three opportunities of managing the swimming pool in their large garden, creating their first hotel magazine for guests from abroad that won an award for the Best Hotel Magazine in Tokyo, and teaching English to 350 employees. Today, I retain a deep appreciation for and affiliation with the staff of this 5-Star hotel that taught me so much about Japanese styles of management. They gave me an immersion experience for the work I would engage in later in life. I have retained my first name card which designates my membership in Hotel Okura's first year's staff over 63 years ago. I know other TCK who collected items reminding them of cultural transitions each time they crossed borders. There was always a deep sadness in leaving one culture, mixed with an eager anticipation of new experiences in my other culture.

Returning Home *or Leaving* Home?

My return to America for graduate school in pastoral counseling for three years at Duke University, my focus was on Carl Roger's client-centered counseling methods. I quickly became aware of how this counseling method from the 1960's Human Potential Movement was grounded in values of independence and individualism. I once again began feeling like a koi in a brackish pond, since I had just crossed The Pond (as expats in Japan called the Pacific Ocean) where I worked 14-hour days with interdependent collectivists. In my second year I changed my focus to Counseling in the Context of East Asian Thought. I made this change in recognition of significant differences between independence and interdependence. I wanted to build my knowledge and skills to counsel international students. However, the counseling psychology and training approaches in America were largely influenced by western culture, which presented co-dependent relationships as unhealthy. This assumption of an independent individualistic culture stimulated my curiosity to explore the psychology of East Asia where not co-dependency, rather interdependence and collectivism were more dominant in preparation for my intercultural career.

Discovering My First Professional Role

While in my 2-year internship in counseling at the University of North Carolina (UNC), I became acquainted with the Foreign Student Advisor (FSA) who helped me see the opportunities in international student counseling. There were few FSAs trained in intercultural student counseling. My empathy with such students was already strong. My thesis at Duke was a cultural analysis of Rogerian counseling. After finishing my studies and training at UNC with the student counselor and the FSA, I accepted a position at Cornell University in intercultural counseling.

LAUNCHING MY INTERCULTURAL CAREER

It was 1966 when my first paid intercultural work began in America. I was 25 and in charge of international student counseling and programing under David Williams' leadership. Programing involved planning outside-of-classroom learning activities for international students, which included those Americans with international interests. It also included advisory work with the many nationality clubs of students representing 81 nations around the world. These clubs sought to share their culture with Americans and to provide support for their own students.

One weekend in October, 1967, an experience at Cornell University launched me into the development of Intercultural Communication Workshops (ICW) for multicultural groups of Americans and foreign students to explore cultural diversities and similarities. In October, 1967, I invited David Hoopes, Director, Regional Council for International Education, to send five group facilitators of Cross-Cultural Communication Workshop (C-CCW) as he called them. I did not know they were trained to facilitate T-Groups (training groups) at the National Training Lab's (NTL) center in Washington, D.C. The NTL methods were grounded in independent individualistic cultural assumptions but they had recently engaged international students in workshops. I discovered that unknowingly they imposed their values across cultures by requiring adherence to certain group communication rules, based upon independent individualism, be practiced.

T-Group facilitation techniques had not been modified to include values and styles of foreign students or even collectivistic cultural groups within the United States. They practiced the communication rules of T-Groups, which included the exclusion of topics related to subjects outside of the circle of participants, explained as, only speak to what's happening here and now in the group. No there and then topics were allowed. Speak directly and take responsibility for your feelings about the group. Don't speak for others, only for yourself. Members were asked directly to share their feelings about others within the group. They were asked to respond to the life-boat exercise which was a situation of your ship sinking and you have one more seat in your lifeboat. Choose who in this group you are going to invite to save.

During a short break some students approached me to say that the facilitators were violating their expectations and assumptions of reasonable communication norms that they practiced. They could not continue participating if this continued without significant changes in facilitation styles that were more inclusive. I promised to inform the facilitators of their feelings in a mediator role since I was so familiar with non-U.S. cultures. I did so before the group convened again. The facilitator listened but his first words back in the group were, damn it Cliff, you've blown my leadership, as he slammed his cigarette case forcefully to the floor. He then told the group that they had violated his rule that participants must speak directly and not through a mediator in the group. I said, that rule and others were what blew your leadership. He excused himself from the group. Soon afterward, the majority of the students asked to close the workshop and some were in tears over being disrespected so directly. That is how the workshop ended. I felt terrible having responsibility in inviting them to such a cross-culture workshop.

The Birth of the Intercultural Communication Workshop (ICW)

A few days later, I invited the participants to gather again one evening to share their experiences and forty of the fifty came. The students were still upset and angry at the facilitators for what had happened across the five groups. I shared their feelings as they paralleled my own and we decided to develop a written critique of the C-CC Workshop to send to David Hoopes. We continued in constructive discussions of policies and practices of intercultural facilitators for a few hours. We had developed a substantial list of 35 guidelines for intercultural workshops and facilitation styles that we felt would be appropriate for multicultural groups. We chose to name the list the Intercultural Communication Workshop (ICW) Principles and Practices. I sent it to David Hoopes the next day recommending that without these guidelines the word cross-cultural should not be in the workshop title. I also wrote the students to ask if they would like to gather again to practice what we had discussed. Most responded positively.

Thus, the ICW at Cornell was born and Hoopes' response was very positive. He adopted the list and changed the name of his Cross-Culture Communication Workshop to ICW as I recommended. Thereafter, Hoopes began writing the periodic Intercultural Network Newsletter for the developing field of Intercultural Communication: Theory and Practice. David regularly published articles in his newsletter about the ICWs at Cornell. When he published the first Intercultural Readings in 1971, a description of the ICW and facilitative guidelines from Cornell were included (Clarke, 1971 and 1975a).

The INCAS (Intercultural Communication Association of Students) at Cornell was growing annually and conducting ICWs for multiple campuses around the northeastern United States. George Renwick, David Hoopes, and I worked for a couple of years to persuade NAFSA (National Association of Foreign Student Advisors) in Washington, D.C. to fund this growing movement since those involved were with International Educational Exchange programs. NAFSA's hesitation was grounded in fears that it would be like T-Groups. We convinced them there were major differences. In 1969 they began sponsoring regional and national programs to train facilitators from several dozen campuses. NAFSA sent two observation-researchers, Dante Scalzi and Cornelia Spring (1975), for a formal assessment of one ICW. David published their assessment in Readings in Intercultural Communications, the first of several Readings. From 1969 for three years, NAFSA engaged me as their first intercultural consultant to execute intercultural communication consultation projects on 22 university campuses to develop campus intercultural relations.

A fundamental learning from this early activity was that when independent individualists attempt to communicate with interdependent collectivists solely from within their independent world view with no sensitivity to context of interdependencies among collectivists, it may be called cross-cultural, but it is not intercultural. Intercultural communication requires sensitivity to differences of culture in perceptions, values, and communication styles, as Dean Barnlund (1976) said in his keynote address at the Stanford Institute for Intercultural Communication (SIIC). It required sensitivity to differences in perceptions and intentions, which was facilitated with the clear use of three communication functions: describe, interpret, and evaluate (D.I.E.) in that sequential order. Without the use of these process skills there may be misunderstandings, conflicts, and rejections. Facilitating these communication clarification processes, while withholding judgments, was essential to developing respect and understanding across cultures.

Refining the ICW Stages of Intercultural Development

To create the developmental model of the ICW, INCAS student leaders and I worked through our analyses of reflections on the life of TCK (Third Culture Kids) and others who feel they have successfully integrated into the holistic balancing of two cultures in one identity. This model evolved from 1967 to 1971 through recognizing the phenomenological steps over which we had stumbled with many failures along the pathways of our lives and within the ICW. Although these stages were manifested within groups through dialogue with others, we discovered new insights each time. These stages of development participants would experience to varying degrees as the facilitators grew in their skills with each ICW. Every participant would not reach the final stage of integration but some would or already had achieved integration prior to attending the workshops.

TCKs could describe integration as a synergy of two cultures in a context of finding comfort in appreciating both systems of values and communication styles in balanced ways as parts of a whole. A model for this definition is the eastern understanding of Yin & Yang within the same circle of identity. Japanese manifest this integration in their balancing of *honne* and *tatemae*, which are the private and public forms of speaking by which to maintain harmony. Nancy Adler and also Stephen Rhinesmith conceived of synergistic goals of intercultural communication, which Nancy shared with me in the early seventies. In an ICW no one was ever pushed or forced in any way to achieve any goal of integration. Many among TCKs choose not to resolve cognitive dissonance but to live within just one of their cultural heritages while sustaining an appreciation for the other. The following developmental stages are grounded in my personal life-time experience of integrating the two cultures that have influenced my personal and professional career. These were the evolving stages in developing my identity and I discovered that they also enabled a creative harmony in integrating the many diverse cultures represented in the ICW. I did not understand why until my graduate studies at Stanford University a few years later. Without having personal experiences through these developmental stages, facilitators could likely risk ineffectiveness. These stages of intercultural development evolved through dozens of workshops with trained student intercultural facilitators. These sequential stages are: (a) Awareness; (b) Mutual Respect; (c) Mutual Understanding; (d) Appreciative Acceptance: (e) Adjustment; (f) Integration.

Facilitators suggested that balancing the cultural and cognitive dissonance of two cultures is the experience of every TCK or any person who has chosen to sustain a feeling of home and comfort in two distinct cultures with different languages, values, and practices. Participants contributed their feelings and perspectives for the possibility of creating intercultural harmony. The challenges and opportunities within a life of balance have served as inspirations for myself and members from all cultures with experiences in ICW groups. Integration is not the goal of an ICW rather it is to engage in a communication process-oriented way of mutual learning in facilitated multicultural small group interactions for 3–4 days.

As facilitators we discovered a genuine opening among participants eager to share and learn more from each other without criticism or judgments as the discussions transitioned into multiple shared topics experienced by all, i.e., how respect is manifested and different practices in friendships. Facilitators guided the same processes often pointing out their observations of non-verbal gestures. They sought interpretations, maintained a balance of speaking and listening, explained why judgments are not helpful when they occurred, and offered other facilitative input to create safety, openness, and reciprocity. Their primary role was to attend to alternative cultural norms as conveyed by participants themselves. These facilitator functions were confirmed by NAFSA's observer-researchers who attended the 1969 13-State ICW in Cuddebackville, NY. We have also published them in more detail as *Intercultural Communication Facilitator Skills* (Clarke & Takashiro, 2019, pp. 273–274).

I felt very privileged to learn from facilitating ICWs for so many years because the process validated for me the utility of all my training and my natural style of supporting diversity as a TCK toward building inclusion in small groups and healing potential conflicts before they could begin in a safe and enjoyable process and environment. The participants' feedback continually provided a positive confirmation and appreciation for all those activities. The entire ICW facilitation experience stimulated my long-range desire to find some further graduate study program to explore further why these ICW processes were appreciated by so many. These thoughts matured while serving in various capacities at the Stanford (Bechtel) International Student Center (1971-1977) and studying at Stanford University (1977–1986) in the School of Education's Interdisciplinary Studies in the Social Sciences.

Advancing My Intercultural Career

Professionally growing from international student counseling and facilitating ICWs at Cornell for five years, I was invited by Lee Ziegler to transition to a similar opportunity at Stanford University in 1971. Stanford was the last of 22 campuses at which I served as NAFSA's intercultural consultant. Lee asked me to continue facilitating ICWs on the west coast as I had on the east coast. I also maintained my collaboration with David Hoopes in the further development of the blossoming intercultural communication field including theory and practice.

One such ICW was for California's universities and state colleges. We invited fifty students to gather for an experience in learning from an ICW. We also invited seven Encounter Group facilitators to be our co-facilitators from The Center for Studies of the Person, directed by Carl Rogers, who was the subject of my thesis at Duke six years earlier. I invited him to speak at the opening of the workshop. His subject was the universality of individualistic independence which fostered self-knowledge and comfort in supporting each individual's uniqueness disregarding culture. We had hoped to reveal the contrast between the two approaches to small group learning. Unfortunately, his trainers perceived no difference between their Encounter Group approach and the ICW. The experience taught me the power and validity of the expression that we all see what we wish to see through our culturally colored glasses. Our cultural perspectives act as blinders that create different perceptions of the same behavior across cultures. Through this California ICW I learned that dedicated individualists have a blindness toward diversities of cultures to which collectivists are immune. They assume cultural differences.

Conferencing and Research in Japan

While at Stanford I maintained an interest in applying the ICW learning model in professional settings for personal development purposes. In 1972 I appreciated an invitation from Jack Condon to join a panel at the Intercultural Communication Conference held at International Christian University (ICU) in Mitaka, Japan. I contributed my research findings on the panel's theme of Re-Entry following study abroad based on the 3-year summer workshops on re-entry I developed while at Cornell. The ICU conference was held with the traditional American professional academic conference format of presentations of multiple papers followed by brief Q&A. But time usually expired before many Q&A could be exchanged.

In meeting with David Hoopes at the ICU conference, I was inspired to consider another application of the ICW model. These discussions evolved ultimately into the Stanford Institute for Intercultural Communication (SIIC). But first, after the ICU conference, two Japanese ICU students joined my research on counseling of Japanese students in higher education, Akiko Endo and Chikao Kawakami. For a month we visited eighteen public and private universities across Japan to interview student counselees and counselors. I learned from my student associates how in-depth the meaning of silence could be in the Japanese communication style. I was awed by the length of silences that I was comfortable experiencing with them and the understanding that could be inspired by just focusing on each other's needs while traveling together for hours in silence. It was a memorable insightful experience I recommend to American friends.

From the 1972 research data I learned that 85% of student counselors in Japan employed Rogerian Client-Centered methods. In that research project I was hoping to investigate Japanese indigenous counseling methods, the *Naikan* Method and *Morita* Therapy. These were more reflective of Japanese traditional values but I found that these were used more by businesses for employees who were having social and performance difficulties. There is no doubt that the culture of Japan is always changing most frequently by western interventions, but lasting principles and values remain the same. These dynamics of changing culture were reflective of my developing identity along my path (Clarke, 1975b).

Nihonmatsu Workshops: Precursor to the Stanford Institute for Intercultural Communication (SIIC)

After returning to Stanford from my 1972 trip to Japan, I wondered how I could share the ICW model of learning by engaging multicultural professionals in intercultural fields in Japan. I discussed my ideas with Dean Barnlund, Dan Smith, David Hoopes, Paul Pedersen, Robert Moran, and others in Japan. We initiated a 12-person steering committee, six from each country. After a year of planning the event began in July, 1974 for ten days, including seven days for seven simultaneous intensive intercultural workshops, three in English, one in Japanese, and three in both languages. Each was facilitated by a professional Japanese and American leader in their field. Individual participants agreed not to change groups for the entire seven days. All participants had agreed to be research subjects in this event. In addition, we had a contract with Panasonic to use their video recorders and cameras to record the entire seven days to use for interaction analyses of each group. There were 74 participants, half from each nation, with a number of student assistants from ICU.

From our studies and interaction analyses of selected groups' video recordings, and a long time for deep reflections on this life-changing event as many participants have called it, I've surmised there were five essential assumptions we had in planning that were wrong and resulted in unfortunate consequences. These were: (a) That Japanese could commit to open discussions about diversities of age, gender, discipline, and profession; (b) That Japanese participants could be comfortable learning form each other for intense periods of time; (c) That senior professionals could serve as process-centered bicultural facilitators without shared training or much understanding of each other's culture; (d) That such facilitators could manage bicultural interactions including feelings about the atomic bomb in WWII: e) That bicultural members of various status groups could comfortably interact across disciplines with educators, counselors, business consultants, government agents, second-language teachers, translators, researchers, and practitioners. The benefits of this experience were deeply personal in our learning to question hidden assumptions and expectations we harbor within ourselves and to remain open to differences.

There were six publications that focused on the Nihonmatsu workshops and highlighted key lessons provided by the experience. The most revealing was by Paul Pedersen (2005) that he called *A Lesson in Humility*. I felt that we made a lot of mistakes in planning that event but conceptually it deserved another attempt in a different context.

The Birth of the Stanford Institute
for Intercultural Communication

During the 1972 ICU conference and the 1974 Nihonmatsu Workshops, I initiated conversations with David Hoopes about professional development programs that could be based on the ICW design. Our plans for the Stanford Institute for Intercultural Communication (SIIC) began in earnest in 1975 with the permission of Stanford's Graduate School of Education, Dean, Arthur Coladarci, I remained in the role of Associate Director of Bechtel International Student Center and added a teaching role at the School of Education after Everett Rogers invited me to take over his Intercultural Communication classes in 1975 as he was moving to another institution. I continued teaching two courses through the next eight years.

My original thoughts about establishing the SIIC were to incorporate lessons from the Nihonmatsu workshops in a renewed effort to provide intercultural professionals with a different form of development that would supplement professional conferencing focused on presenting papers. It would allow sustained learning interactions in small groups of professionals from different walks of life and provide a deeper dive into learning within a more holistic interactive process unlike academic conferences. I established principles that would guide the development of SIIC, such as, resource group leaders would: (a) Commit to supporting their groups throughout five-day workshops and further discussions sometimes creating 18 hour days; (b) Facilitate each member as a resource for mutual learning and respect with limited self-focus; and that (c) Participants would all commit to their first choice of workshops for the entire week to enable sustained relationships of mutual learning. The design provided for collective learning from experts' core knowledge in the field.

To facilitate core knowledge for all members, two three-hour seminars were given each week on Monday morning and Friday morning, Dean Barnlund on intercultural theory and concepts and George Renwick on evaluating intercultural interventions. On Wednesday evening participants were all invited to attend intercultural activities and learn experientially through simulations. The remainder of the week was dedicated to small group interactive learning. The original professions of focus in the first six groups were: University teaching; international educational exchange (IIE); multicultural education; international business consulting; health-care services; and counseling across cultures. Over 230 individuals attended the first year of SIIC at Stanford from multiple nations.

A significant lesson learned by all the invited leaders and staff was through an issue of the distinction between education and training processes. David Hoopes had received NAFSA funding to invite two regional representatives from each of the 12 NAFSA regions to be trained in ICW facilitation in the IEE workshop. Monday evening David presented his reasoning to the full staff/facilitators' group and focused on distinctions between the processes of educating and training. Training was distinctly focused on skills training for facilitating ICW's; education was focused on cognitive and emotional learning objectives, as he explained. So, what would become SIIC's learning objectives for the workshops? Challenging discussions ended in a vote. Except for David, all others agreed that SIIC should be focused primarily on educational objectives. Yet, there was enough flexibility in the group that David was supported in continuing to focus his IEE group on training objectives since that was the interest of the donor of the NAFSA grant. Also supporting him was the facilitator for the Counseling Across Cultures group.

CHANGING CAREERS TO JAPAN-AMERICA BUSINESS

Graduate Studies at Stanford

I chose in 1977 to enter Stanford's graduate program in Interdisciplinary Studies in the Social Sciences in order to understand why the ICW was such an effective process for learning, changing attitudes, and building communication skills to creating meaning in cultural diversity. I was determined to learn more deeply about six distinct disciplines; (a) social learning processes; (b) solutions to cognitive dissonance of the TCK from psychologists; (c) interaction analyses from social linguistics; (d) cultural change processes from cultural anthropologists; (e) attribution and social-comparison theories from educational psychologists; and (f) the varieties of approaches to evaluating educational curricula and training designs. For self-sustenance, I continued teaching two courses in intercultural theory and training while directing the SIIC for ten summers, 1976–1986. This was the beginning of my career change from academia to the global business context. At that time in 1977, SIETAR was still acting on its foundation of providing support to interculturalists in academia, business, government, counseling, language learning, healthcare, and all avenues of consulting in the intercultural world. However, before long in SIETAR 66 university faculty members withdrew to form the International Academy of Intercultural Research (IAIR), which is also interdisciplinary but with conference presentations that conformed to academic standards. SIETAR conference presentations had focused on academic research reports and reports of practical applications in training and consulting.

Entering the Corporate World of Japan-American Business

My dissertation research topic was Evaluating Intercultural Intervention Design Effectiveness on a Procter & Gamble Company's (P&G) Technology Transfer Project in Japan. Parts of it were published later (Clarke & Hammer, 1995). I worked for two years full-time as an internal consultant in P&G U.S. for 18 months and in P&G Japan for 6 months along with ten full-time associates demonstrating the effectiveness of our evolving designs as members of the Intercultural Relations Institute (IRI) which I founded in 1980. As this was my first dive into the global business world of technology transfers, it was a tremendous learning experience. My guide for each step in the design and execution of our plan was the value of the ICW process of facilitating mutual learning from personal resources of all members in a participant-centered process. I was also guided by my studies at Stanford and by George Renwick's strong support.

First, we had to experience and learn from our erroneous assumptions that nearly terminated our two-year contract of $500,000 during the first month. Our eleven-person team, was composed of myself as the executive coach (team leader), two intercultural management trainer/consultants (one Japanese and one American), two intercultural spouse trainers and supporters, two Japanese language trainers, three English language trainers, and one executive assistant.

We unashamedly began with the assumption that we were the invited intercultural experts imparting our wisdom to the working-class managers of this technology transfer project. Our two intercultural manager trainer/consultants delivered our comparative concepts of our two cultural values and norms we researched in preparations that lasted six weeks before the project began in June 1980. Within days the human resource director called me into his office to tell me that the participants could not figure out what relevance our presentations had with their need to transfer their skills to the Japanese.

Assignees were mostly strangers to each other, which we had basically ignored as keepers of the intercultural truth. (The first thing that we learned in business was that sarcastic humor was the name of the communication game the Americans played, which left the Japanese managers confused.) We received permission to take a week off and return with a plan that would be helpful. During the week I called Bob Moran at Thunderbird, read Harry Triandis on developing cultural assimilators, called George Renwick, and Harumi Befu (Stanford Anthropology Dean, chair of my Staford committee) to ask for help, in particular about the Cultural Assimilator development process through real-time critical incidents of work environments. This would become the first attempt at creating a Cultural Assimilator based on Critical Incidents in an operating binational workplace (Clarke & Takashiro, 2019, pp. 276–279; 2020, pp. 205–209).

At the end of the week, we decided to return as ethnographic researchers, as participant-observers and interviewers, to learn about our new environment in which we were privileged to work. Our focus became our client's members to whom we were committed for two years. Our first need was to learn about their needs for an organizational plan, a shared functional language, and the comfort of their spouses. Their context was tight time pressures of working for 16 hours a day with expectations to complete the transfer on schedule. Our task was to design developmental interventions in their processes that would enable their abilities to execute all of their managerial functions and supervisory functions with 400 new plant workers in Japan. We had 18 months in Modesto, CA, to achieve that goal. We were given an additional six months' contract to facilitate technology transfers in Akashi, Japan in real-time manufacturing processes. A genuine humility and effectiveness were essential for us to be accepted into their lives. It was essential for us to design shared goals and develop their total commitment to team success in building a bicultural corporate culture into our joint work processes and goals. We would succeed together by finding the way they could choose to integrate their cultures by facilitating their development of a bi-cultural organizational culture with unique intercultural communication skills in managerial function processes, including decision-making, teamwork norms, meeting leadership/participation standards, and six others.

Engaging in so many roles in various contexts with the same clients for 2 years, we became interdependent and we participated in their celebrations of success in operating the fastest start-up among seven other manufacturing plants around the world. We passed leadership over to the Japanese managers in two years from start-up of the plant, one year ahead of schedule. This saved all expat expenses for one year ($650,000 each) except for the remaining Japanese American manager who was their link to the General Offices in Ohio. The plant also celebrated the savings from having the highest quality, lowest scrap, fewest safety incidents, and highest productivity in P&G's paper-product plants' history. All of these results and benefits combined to save the company 32 times P&G's investment into our intercultural support for them. That was their internal assessment of their return on investment (ROI), an historical first for intercultural interventions, and an accomplishment that convinced them to become our greatest marketing partner as we grew to serve over 300 clients in 20 years entirely by our clients' word-of-mouth.

Our services for clients continued to evolve as did my learning and shifting between intercultural research, consulting, and training approaches with our clients' guidance. At every opportunity I sought to share our findings, processes, and challenges throughout the field in the United States, Japan, and Europe in professional conferences, licensing relationships, and publications (Clarke, 2017). Many of our 226 Clarke Consulting Group (CCG) members over 20 years were assigned to long-term internal roles in client organizations in Japan and the U.S. Our specialty was long-term projects that started from organizational research utilizing our nine research instruments followed by one CCG team serving as organizational development consultants, researchers, trainers, and executive coaches. Client-centered evaluations followed to measure our results and provide authenticity and accountability for the clients' investment in CCG.

Lessons from 300 Corporate Engagements for Interculturalists

There were three elements of my professional experiences that have brought me a sense of meaningfulness and satisfaction that I hope may contribute to contemporary interculturalists preparing for or serving in organizations in today's contexts of misunderstandings and conflicts across cultures. These three are: (a) My interdisciplinary studies provided me with 44 theories as foundations for my research, consulting, and training designs, which are holistic, realistic and effective in designing organizational interventions. An integrated assessment of organizations, teams, and individuals leads to discovering unproductive interactions and resolutions that enable results; (b) My foundation for facilitating productive interactions in organizations is research, which improves intercultural interventions by improving our designs, processes, and results of intervention projects and also benefits our clients with evaluation results that they care about and understand; (c) My approach was through enabling interculturalists to speak the language, recognize the operational processes, support the client's goals, and evaluate the results of their interventions in business terms that measured management's desired workplace results and corporate benefits. This required engaging management from the outset of the assessment of the project, in the intervention of the design, and in the design of its evaluation. The unexpected outcome of this process is that client managers often became interculturalists and entered the intercultural consulting field upon retirement, e.g., Larry Taylor, former President of Monsanto Japan and Michael Copeland, former HR Director of our P&G Akashi Project, and others. These three commitments were the foundations of my intercultural consulting career. My greatest honor amongst my peers was to receive SIETAR's Senior Interculturalist Award in the late-eighties for successfully pioneering the field by integrating the intercultural perspectives with the business world.

RETURNING TO ACADEMIA IN HAWAII AND HOME TO JAPAN

Changing Career Context Again

I returned to Honolulu, Hawaii in 2000 to continue serving clients in Japan until 2010. In addition, after earlier teaching at Stanford for eight years, I was excited in 2005 to be invited by Gary Fontaine at the University of Hawaii at Manoa in the School of Communication and Information, to teach three courses for five years in (1) Intercultural Communications Theory, (2) Intercultural Training and Other Interventions, and (3) Multicultural Organizational Culture Research. In the second and third courses, I used an organizational research process engaging six teams of five students each in exploring the organizational culture in 30 businesses over five years in Honolulu to give students the experience of such research from which to learn organizational culture. I published this as a case study in a chapter of a book to share with the field (Clarke, 2023). I was astonished by the effectiveness in terms of student engagement and learning outcomes, of integrating field work experiences into classroom courses in intercultural training and consulting.

Going Home *(?) ... to Japan*

Since leaving Hawaii for Japan in 2016 in retirement, I have dedicated my professional work to publishing. I regret never having had enough time to write while managing the growth of my businesses. My three daily challenges now are to continue learning from my Japanese spouse and environment, to continue coaching SIETAR Japan leaders and friends, and to maintain communications with family and friends in other lands.

When contemplating returning to Japan with my spouse and writing partner, Naomi, I remembered my parents' lives in the early seventies in Japan. One day at Stanford, I received an urgent telegram from my Mom in Tokyo. My Dad had just been stabbed 19 times in his throat and shoulders by an 18-year-old Japanese student attempting to assassinate him. Mom escaped the home at 6 a.m. and ran to the police box, leaving my Dad bleeding on the living room floor. He was taken to intensive care and his life was in danger. He had invited the son of members of his father's church in Kumamoto, Kyushu, to come to Tokyo for a relaxing week in their home while he was waiting to enter his first year at Tokyo University. After his attack when escaping, he forgot his locker number and storage key to the station locker where he stored his luggage. Police captured him when he came to get them that evening. My Dad was released after two weeks in intensive care in the hospital, to rest at home and the attacker was in police custody. But my Dad refused to press charges but released him into the care of his parents in Kyushu with confidence that God would bring him to repentance.

I wondered as Naomi and I were preparing to return to Japan in February of 2016, how my parents felt about returning to Japan for four years after a health recovery break at home to serve out their contract and receive their full pension benefits. I understood how they felt after such a horrible tragedy and came to understand why they retired in the United States, but I tried to understand why I wanted to retire in Japan as the first in my family of three generations in Japan to do so. Living the rest of my life in a wonderful intercultural marriage inspired me to go home in retirement to Kyoto. I discovered being in Japan brought me the harmony I sought all through my life. I know that I will always be longing to be with my loving family in the USA, especially at Thanksgiving and Christmas holidays, and especially as family members and friends begin passing away. Naomi empathizes with me since she was returning from 20 years in Hawaii away from her family in Japan. Together, sustaining a bicultural marriage inspired us to write on that subject too (Clarke & Takashiro, 2017) (Fig. 3.3).

As a TCK throughout my life I remember longing to be in the country I was not. One year I crossed the pond ten times eager to re-establish

Fig. 3.3 Cliff & Naomi on a river boat in Osaka, 2020

relationships on each visit. But my relationships always held a bit of ambiguity as I was often perceived as unpredictable in dialogue by friends and colleagues alike. Would I respond as a Japanese or as an American? I was comfortable with the ambiguity but one day at my Clarke Consulting Group office in California, a few associates came to my office door just to tell me that they could never figure out which style I was going to manifest in reaction to their thoughts and actions. I asked, weren't they the experts who helped others in business interactions to interpret styles of bicultural management? I also admitted that sometimes it was a mystery to me too. This koi in the brackish waters of two cultures has often struggled through the processes of clarification in my identification with Japan and America. The brackish circumstances of living in two cultures have presented many challenges in interpersonal intercultural relationships but I have tried my best to share my pathways across the pond while admiring the multicolored koi within it. There is beauty in diversity similar to the patterns of multi-colored koi. Perhaps a TCK's nature will remain a mystery even to this trained interculturalists despite my efforts to explain some of the challenges, motivations and dreams. There is always a role in today's world for anyone who lives between two cultures to function as a bridge builder between them. There is no longer a need to choose one or the other, as was suggested by psychologists who doubted the healthiness of those with cognitive dissonance. They were never able to find harmony in the dissonance of a bicultural identity. The world today needs admiration and appreciation of all the diversity on this Earth in order to avoid becoming more nationalistic with attitudes of racial or ethnic supremacy. We cannot survive without harmony between cultures.

Clifford H. Clarke has no conflicts of interest to declare that are relevant to the content of this chapter.

REFERENCES

Barnlund, D. C. (1976). *Multileveled, Multidimensional, Multidirectional, Multi-Coded Intercultural Communication.* Paper presented at the initial *Stanford Institute for Intercultural Communication* program (July), Stanford University, Palo Alto, CA.

Clarke, C. H. (1971). Intercultural Communication Workshops. In D. S. Hoopes (Ed.), *Readings in Intercultural Communication* (Vol. 1, pp. 73–79). The Society for Intercultural Education, Training, and Research (SIETAR).

Clarke, C. H. (1975a). Goals and Leadership in the Intercultural Communication Workshop. In D. S. Hoopes (Ed.), *Readings in Intercultural Communication* (Vol. V. 1, pp. 60–67). The Intercultural Network.

Clarke, C. H. (1975b). Personal Counseling across Cultural Boundaries. In P. Pedersen (Ed.), *Readings in Intercultural Communication, Vol. IV. Cross-Cultural Counseling*. The Intercultural Communications Network & SIETAR.

Clarke, C. H. (2017). Reflections on History: How Shifting Paradigms Created Intercultural Innovations, *Journal of Intercultural Communication*, No. 20, 1–26. Tokyo, SIETAR Japan.

Clarke, C. H. (2023). Multicultural University Students Learn Collaborative Leadership in Hawaii Beyond the Classroom: A Qualitative Case Study. In S. Egitim & Y. Umemiya (Eds.), *Leaderful Classroom Pedagogy Through an Interdisciplinary Lens*. Springer. https://doi.org/10.1007/978-981-99-6655-4_13

Clarke, W. H., & Atanda, J. A. (Eds.) (1871 [1972]). *Travels and Explorations in Yorubaland 1854–1858*. University of Ibadan Press.

Clarke, C. H., & Hammer, M. R. (1995). Predictors of Japanese & American Managers' Job Success, Personal Adjustment, & Intercultural Interaction Effectiveness. *Management International Review*, 35(2), 153–170.

Clarke, C. H., & Takashiro, N. (2017). Chapter 50: Sustaining Love and Building Bicultural Marriages Between Japanese and Americans in Japan. In C.-H. Mayers & E. Vanderheiden (Eds.), *The International Handbook of Love: Transcultural and Transdisciplinary Perspectives*. Springer Nature. https://doi.org/10.1007/978-3-030-45996-3

Clarke, C. H., & Takashiro, N. (2019). Transforming Shame to Collective Pride and Social Equity in Bicultural Organizations in Japan. In C.-H. Mayers & E. Vanderheiden (Eds.), *The Right Side of Shame: Transforming and Growing Through Practical Applications in Cultural Contexts, Chapter 18*. Springer Nature. https://doi.org/10.1007/079-3-030-13409-9

Clarke, C. H., & Takashiro, N. (2020). Chapter 14: Turning Bicultural Critical Incidents into Inclusive Bicultural Identities and Organizations in US Subsidiaries in Japan. In E. Vanderheiden & C.-H. Mayer (Eds.), *Mistakes, Errors, and Failures: Navigating Potentials*. Springer Nature. https://doi.org/10.1007/978-3-030-35574-6

Pedersen, P. B. (2005). Chapter 13: A Lesson in Humility. In J. A. Kotter & J. Carlson (Eds.), *The Client Who Changed Me: Stories of Therapist Personal Transformation*. Routledge.

Scalzi, D. V., & Spring, C. (1975). Value of the Intercultural Communication Workshop on Campus. In D. S. Hoopes (Ed.), *Readings in Intercultural Communication* (Vol. 1, pp. 54–59). The Intercultural Communications Network.

CHAPTER 4

Song of the Serendipity Road

John C. Condon

Serendipity has been explained as: *"a fortunate discovery made by one who is focused and alert, searching for one thing and comes upon something even better"* (Strogatz, 2015, pp. 103–104). There's no map to the serendipitous, except the one you retrace after you've traveled that unpredictable road, though my daughter, Christina, tells me that a Jyotish astrological birth chart would show that it all was foretold. In this song as I travel my life's road, there's a refrain: *"Little could I imagine..."* That's when we sense the serendipity.

JUST WEST OF CHICAGO

Just west of Chicago is the village of Oak Park where I lived my first twelve years. Then a lily-white suburb, now progressive, the village is best known for two former residents: architect Frank Lloyd Wright, whose home, office and a dozen of his earliest buildings draw visitors from around the world; and author and Nobelist Ernest Hemingway. When my older sister, Joan, was in high school there, her English teacher had been Hemingway's English teacher. "And he never let us forget that," Joan tells me. As a child

J. C. Condon (✉)
Jemez Springs, NM, USA

© The Author(s), under exclusive license to Springer Nature Switzerland AG 2025
S. M. Fowler, D. C. Yalowitz (eds.), *Creating the Intercultural Field*,
https://doi.org/10.1007/978-3-032-01370-5_4

61

I have no recollection hearing of either Wright or Hemingway but writing and architecture have been passions throughout my life—with my first contract for a book on mentalist magic tricks (and with a $60 advance!) when I was 16. Seventy years later I published my twentieth book, *It Goes Without Saying* (2025). And for the past thirty years I've lived in houses I designed (Fig. 4.1).

My father's grandfather was part of the "Famine Irish," among immigrant groups, the lowest of the low. My father's mother had emigrated from Germany and spoke with accented English. She lived with her youngest son, my favorite uncle, Erwin, who was blind. They lived in what then

Fig. 4.1   Jack Condon signing his 20th book: *It Goes Without Saying*

was a rural area, in a house without electricity or running water. Light was provided by kerosene lanterns, and even today the smell of kerosene stirs nostalgia for that home from long ago, that now lies buried beneath a runway at O'Hare International Airport. At Grandma's house, at age five or six I learned to prime the pump to pull up water from the well, and on Sundays, witness the spectacle of Sunday's dinner running around with its head chopped off. Years later I realized I had experienced what, to others, are just idioms.

Like many of his generation, my father never went to high school because then, when a boy reached adolescence, he was expected to help support the family. One of my father's early jobs working for his father, a cement man who built sidewalks and curbs in St. Louis, was, as the afternoon grew late, to go to the nearest saloon and bring the crew a bucket of beer.

My love of cities, their histories and neighborhoods probably began when I would accompany my father when he had work in Chicago. Driving on North Clark Street, he pointed out, "that's where the St. Valentine's Day Massacre happened. In 1929, the year your mother and I got married. Just days before the stock market crash." Along with stories of Al Capone were less exciting but more inspiring stories, like seeing Jane Adams's Hull House, and stories to increase my social consciousness. On a drive on the city's south side my father told me "Here's where the rumor of Mrs. O'Leary's cow kicking over a lantern that started the Great Chicago Fire. The Irish often got blamed." With few of the prejudices of that era, he would call attention to the ethnic neighborhoods we would pass through. At that time my father had a regular job as a buyer for Sears, but he was also an inventor for which he held several patents, none of which paid off. He was self-educated, and through him, I acquired my curiosity about words. He also taught evening classes on the ideas of Henry George (1879), the nineteenth century economics social justice writer whose book *Progress and Poverty* had an enormous influence worldwide.

My mother, a middleclass housewife frequently identified with women of that era, was shy, self-effacing, and like many other women then, had secretarial skills; she could type faster and spell better than I could. For years later when I began writing books, I used my mother's voice as a standard for how to write the way most people talked. For example, not using the word "self-effacing." My parents later moved back to

Chicago—my mother loved the big city—where she became a *temp* secretary, and lied about her age so she could keep working until she was almost 80.

In seventh grade the family moved to a much smaller community an hour away. DeKalb was then the home to a global hybrid seed corn company, a small motor factory and a state teachers' college that evolved into the enormous Northern Illinois University where I took summer classes that let me graduate from Northwestern in three years, saving considerable money. My ninety high school classmates were the daughters and sons of farmers, factory workers, and a few academics. Now I recognize that as a "multicultural" high school class, as considered by kinds of work and income, though the racial and ethnic diversity was scarcely different from that of Oak Park.

An Innocent Abroad

In 1956 at age seventeen I entered college at a small, relatively unknown school two thousand miles away. I wanted to go abroad, and had discovered that bilingual colleges existed, and learned there was a bi-lingual college in Mexico City. The father of a classmate had taught there. After a long conversation with him, he said, "why not give it a try?" I was persuaded. My parents were worried about their youngest going so far away. I told them I was interested in international trade, but in fact I had no idea of a major, but I wanted to visit a new land.

Many years later, visiting Harvard University, I had the pleasure of meeting sociologist David Riesman whose work I admired and had quoted in my doctoral dissertation. He asked me why I chose to begin college abroad, right after high school. My answer was not very interesting, but his comment was. He said that the initial college experience used to be very different from one's high school years, but no longer. And therefore, he believed the best time for a college experience abroad was the first year. "Junior Year Abroad is too late," he said.

I fell in love with Mexico, and it remains a first love. It was the best education, some in classes but mostly in ways that can't be formally taught: lessons in resilience, self-reflection, humility, and improvisation that have served me well throughout my life.

Mexico City College was a small school with fewer than a thousand students. Located at the edge of the city, high above the Mexican metropolis, the campus consisted of small buildings, several with mosaics designed by the groundskeepers. "A Jewel Box campus," one journalist called it. At that altitude, a chilly early morning class often began with the professor lighting a propane space heater to warm the classroom. The school had no dorms, so like many of the students, I lived in a large house in a fashionable part of the city that had been converted into lodging for eight or nine guests. My roommate, Gil, was an easy-going, serious Black student from Boston who was a paramedic. He was the first Black person I had ever met.

Classes were in English and Spanish. My favorite Spanish language professor, Enrique Anzures, was a gifted teacher with a droll sense of humor who was also an attorney. Sixteen years earlier he was the court reporter in the trial of Ramón Mercader, a Soviet agent from Spain who Stalin sent to assassinate Leon Trotsky in 1940.

The school published a bi-weekly newspaper, *The Collegian,* and I happily joined a cohort of witty and wise students all several years my senior. I think it was there that I learned to write. I became the paper's cartoonist and a reporter assigned to interview "interesting people" on campus, of which there were many.

Quite a few of the students from north of the border were able to be at this college because of the United States government program launched after WW II ("the GI Bill") that provided financial assistance to military veterans to attend college who otherwise would have been unable. That government program exerted an enormous social and cultural influence in the United States in the latter half of the twentieth century, democratizing higher education. At MCC, veterans received enough money to allow them to pay for tuition, modest living quarters, and maybe a liter of rum. Radical author William S. Burroughs, who had been E.T. Hall's classmate and friend when they were both thirteen, attending a private high school in New Mexico, had also been a student at MCC. Both became writers whose books, Burroughs's *Naked Lunch* (1959), and Hall's *The Silent Language* (1959), were published months apart.

Little could I imagine …that although I decided to leave Mexico at the end of that first year, I would return again and again. And for many reasons: for my doctoral research, on my honeymoon, as a guest professor at the *Universidad de Guadalajara*, to co-host traveling seminars, and, of course, to visit friends, and enjoy the simple pleasures of everyday life. There are many *Mexicos,* as they say, with extraordinary and ancient histories, a richness of indigenous communities and languages, sophisticated architecture and design, and a cultural depth often unappreciated by its northern neighbor that too often has not been a good neighbor.

U-Turn

Northwestern University, in Evanston, a suburb bordering the northern edge of Chicago, could not have been more different from that little school at the edge of Mexico City. The smallest and only private school among the "Big Ten" midwestern state universities with which it was typically grouped, its campus social scene, notably its sorority and fraternity social clubs, concern about fashion and status consciousness was especially puzzling to me. Along with other transfer students, as the school sorted out housing options, we were placed temporarily in the basement of a dorm. There I met international students and graduate students who, unlike many undergraduates myself included, were very clear about their goals. I always liked being among the youngest in groups. In recent years that has become more difficult.

Among the many advantages of attending a large university is the opportunity to meet people you've heard about and want to learn more. I realized that one evening in 1957, my first year at the university, when I went to hear a speech by Martin Luther King, Jr., in a small lecture hall only two-thirds full. I knew almost nothing about him, but his words revealed some of the realities I had missed growing up as well as the year living outside of the United States. His voice, strong, understated, and spoken with conviction, inspired. Afterward, I went up to the stage to thank him. Waiting as others did the same, the fragments of conversations overheard was a lesson about how little I knew about my own country.

Northwestern is known for small classes and outstanding teachers. An inspiration for me was Dean C. Barnlund, who later became a close friend and colleague. His focus was on communication theory, with his transactional model of interpersonal communication influencing the field of interpersonal communication. He was just completing his massive book, *Interpersonal Communication: Survey and Studies* (1968). Barnlund's intercultural communication work appeared years later. "Language and Thought" was Barnlund's popular introductory class where I was one of about eighty students. He called the classes "conversations." I think that class inspired me to become a professor. The class introduced me to the linguistic category *semantics*, in particular an applied version centered on the potential influence of language on behavior, General Semantics, which at that time was at its peak of popular interest. The next year I enrolled in Barnlund's graduate course on the topic and became friends with older and wiser and funnier students, several who became lifelong friends.

The person most identified with the General Semantics field was S. I. Hayakawa who also was editor of the General Semantics journal, *ETC*. For many years Hayakawa was based in Chicago, reporting for *The Chicago Defender*, a major Black newspaper. When I learned he had recently joined the Language Arts faculty at San Francisco State College, that news determined my next destination.

In 1959, the year I graduated, one of my professors showed me a new book and said, "You might find this interesting." Indeed: it kept me interested for the next sixty years. The book was *The Silent Language* by Edward T. Hall. *Little could I imagine then* that four years later I would visit Hall at his home in Chicago and begin what evolved into a friendship spanning four decades during which time we became colleagues at Northwestern, and much later, neighbors in northern New Mexico.

Let me step off my personal pathway and say something about Hall and that seminal book. For a decade after the end of World War II, Hall headed the United States government's Foreign Service Institute, primarily to help prepare technical assistance personnel going abroad to share their experience and skills in agriculture, medicine, public administration, and many other fields during that important era. It was a time of global reconstruction with entire nations newly independent from colonization, and new forms of government, while the United States promoted democracy in its competition in the Cold War. If people can be taught rudimentary foreign language competence, might not something similar be possible regarding "culture?" When Hall resigned after ten years the results were mixed, but it was then that he wrote his seminal book.

Hall told me that after *The Silent Language* was published "I was nearly driven out of the American Anthropology Association!" He had departed from orthodoxy, and perhaps worse, he wrote for a broader public. Members of that venerable organization created a panel to critique Hall's book at their annual conference. He told me "I could tell what they had planned for me when I walked into that room. I could see how the chairs were arranged." A quarter century later, in 1986, the chairs had been rearranged, and like the prodigal son, Hall was welcomed back into the AAA. I was honored to be one of the four people—and the only non-anthropologist—who was asked to speak for him.

Hall's work achieves what, in another context, physicist and Nobelist Erwin Schrödinger, describes what I believe characterizes Hall's goal and achievement: *"The task is. ... not so much to see what no one has yet seen, but to think what nobody has yet thought, about that which everybody sees"*.[1]

On my twenty-first birthday I arrived in San Francisco. Who wouldn't fall in love with San Francisco at the dawn of the 1960s? During the subsequent year I wrote letters to my friends and Dean Barnlund back at Northwestern about San Francisco, my new school and my classes. I sounded like a kid in love. Perhaps I was too enthusiastic, for the next year, just as I was planning my dissertation, my advisor, Dean Barnlund, left Northwestern to join the faculty at San Francisco State.

"Language Arts" sounded like a dream department, and for me it was. It inspired me to: write a short story that was published in a literary journal; write a novel (an independent study with author Walter Van Tilburg Clark, best known for his novel, *The Oxbow Incident*) that Prof. Clark read and that I tossed. I wrote a boring M.A. thesis that was also published. Most satisfying was working with the staff of *ETC. A Journal of General Semantics*, and also drawing upon Hayakawa's vast library for my thesis. Hayakawa, a charismatic speaker and personality, a second-generation Japanese-Canadian immigrant whose most famous book about how our language habits can influence our thinking and behavior, *Language in Action*, was a bestseller when published at the beginning of 1941, the year that ended with the bombing of Pearl Harbor. Bad timing for a book by an author named Hayakawa.

Hayakawa taught an evening class each week that drew a considerable audience. I facilitated one of the several breakout groups. I also joined the editorial team that produced *ETC*. We met at Hayakawa's home in a large basement office, adjacent to his extensive library in which I also wrote my M.A. thesis. For fun I would sometimes go for hikes in Marin County with two of the Hayakawa children, Alan, now a journalist, and his younger sister, Wynne, now a noted artist. Their mother, formerly "Marge" Peters, had a distinguished background as editor of the venerable *Poetry* magazine. Her brother, Wesley Peters, heir apparent to the Frank Lloyd Wright organization, made international news, marrying Svetlana Stalin, daughter of the soviet dictator. Years later Hayakawa went on to become president of the university, and not long after that, he was elected as California's junior U.S. Senator.

It was while I was at SFSU that I became politically active in opposition to the reactionary U.S. House Unamerican Activities Committee (HUAC). Most of the protest action was across the bay at U.C., Berkeley, where I was welcomed by one of the student protest organizations. The next year, in Chicago, I debated an FBI agent about a deceptive film that HUAC had produced that claimed to prove that the Communist Party had planned the student protests.

In reflection, the period between the Autumn of 1959 and the Summer of 1960 was among the most joy-filled and creative in my life. Perhaps most important was San Francisco offering my first glimpse of Asian, especially Japanese, values, beliefs, and culture. At a private Asian Studies institute, I took evening courses in Confucian Thought and on Zen Buddhism. I was so taken with what I was learning that I naively applied for a Fulbright grant to study in Japan. Prof. Hayakawa agreed to write a letter of support, and laughed, "Who won that war, anyway?"

BACK TO THE FUTURE

The Japan adventure would come later. Instead, I returned to Northwestern on a scholarship to pursue a Ph.D. I was sure it would be about U.S.-Mexican communication, but I didn't know exactly what or how. Nor was this incomplete topic immediately well received by the faculty because at that time most of the departmental dissertations were rhetorical studies. Barnlund and Frank Haiman, on the social science part of the department, supported of my ideas, but neither had done cross cultural research nor had any Mexican experience.

In search of an elusive something that could help me focus, I visited professors in other departments. All were generous with their time and suggestions. It was sociology professor Francis Hsu who told me: look at cultural values. That was the first time I had heard that concept. Later I realized that E.T. Hall rarely used that term, *values*. Once again it so happened that a book had just been published about an extensive study of variations in cultural values that gave me a template for what would shape my research in Mexico.

Mexico City was even more exciting to this 22 year-old than when I first visited five years earlier. Mexican scholars were generous in their help. Rogelio Díaz-Guerrero, head of the Psychology Department at the Universidad Nacional Autónoma de México, one of the oldest and largest universities in the world, was especially helpful and gave me access to the school's libraries. He also had published an article in *ETC.* on "interpersonal realities" and "objective realities," quite relevant to my research. Friendships formed during that time in Mexico have endured until today.

My studies introduced the first empirical research applying internationally Florence Kluckhohn's theory of cultural value orientations.

Kluckhohn's model was part of a multi-year, multidisciplinary research project headed by her husband, Harvard anthropologist, Clyde Kluckhohn. Only years later when I was teaching at the University of New Mexico did I realize the values research across five cultures had been centered at Ramah, New Mexico, just a three hours' drive from where I now lived. Among many books and monographs that resulted from this research, the best is *People of Rimrock: A Study of Five Cultures* (1967), edited by Evon Vogt and Ethel Albert. Professor Albert later held a joint appointment at Northwestern, in our department and in anthropology. Going from a class in anthropology to one in communication meant going from one culture to another, she said. Albert also directed one of the first ethnographies of communication, Gerry Philipsen's (1972) excellent study of "Teamsterville."

When the Dean of the Graduate School discovered I was in Mexico doing my research supported by a university fellowship, he ordered me to return home immediately or lose my Fellowship. An historian, he expected me to be in a library in the United States, and certainly not in Mexico where I suspect he thought I was having too much fun. When I protested that a study about Mexico might better be done in Mexico than Evanston, he sent me a stronger letter. "See here, young man! I will not allow you to indulge in sophistry!" If that seems strange, consider that instead of requiring me to pass the graduate school foreign language requirement in Spanish, I was required to pass the exam in French.

The dissertation was completed in 1963 when I was 24. It later formed the basis of four books, one on U.S.-Mexican communication published by Intercultural Press, and then a version in Spanish translated by my friend and former colleague, Carmen DeNeve, and then as the basis for what is credited as the first dedicated intercultural communication college textbook, *An Introduction to Intercultural Communication* (1975) in which I tried to encompass the whole sway of intercultural communication in terms of cultural values. A revised and adapted version that I wrote years later was published in Japanese. In 1971, Edward Stewart published an important book that used Kluckhohn's "value orientations" typology as a framework: *American Cultural Patterns: A Cross-Cultural Perspective.*

Little could I imagine that after receiving my Ph.D. I would be invited to become part of the faculty in my department. It took me a year to be able to call my former professors by their first names. Teaching in classrooms where previously you sat as a student gives a new perspective on both roles. When one has a model to follow it's easier to try new things that you imagine might engage the curiosity the students. In the summer of 1966 I wrote my first published textbook, *Semantics and Communication* (1967) based on the experience of being both a student and teacher in that semantics class.

Around this time, I married Camy Harland whom I had met when we were both students in one of Barnlund's seminars. Between the time she graduated and when we were married, Camy had joined a Catholic version of then-new U.S. Peace Corps, volunteering to work in Brazil. There she worked with educational theorist Paulo Freire and also Helder Camara, an archbishop beloved by the poor in northeastern Brazil. Camy's work was on a campaign to teach literacy via radio. But this was not literacy in the Portuguese equivalent of *"A is for apple;"* rather, it was *"J is for justice."* This was *conscientização* (*"conscientization"* or consciousness raising) through literacy, a radical departure from conventional pedagogy. After a military coup, the generals exiled Freire to Europe in part because they feared the impact of *conscientização.*

In Chicago where we would be married, the local bishop waived requirements conventionally asked of non-Catholics. Our reception was in a nearby settlement home where some neighborhood kids joined us. We celebrated with a piñata, and instead of wedding cake we served *baklava.* That cavernous old church endures; not so, the marriage.

To properly teach that Language and Thought class I thought that I needed to know something about a "non-Indo-European" language. Because Northwestern's anthropology department specialized in Africa, and with the rise of African American studies, Swahili was offered for the first time. Enrolled in that first Swahili class. I sometimes wondered if our pattern practice expressions were actually Japanese. The consonant-vowel pattern in Swahili often sounded to me like Japanese, which I'd never studied. *"Siagi haitoshi"* sounded to me like it could be the name of a Japanese pitcher just signed by the Yankees. In translation it means "not enough butter." Once again, *little could I imagine* that something I studied for one purpose helped to give me a year's leave from Northwestern to go to East Africa to study communication and nation-building in the newly independent Tanzania. At least that was the plan.

In the late 1960s, Tanzania, with a population of 12 million and 120 different tribes and ethnic groups, faced formidable challenges to their desired nation building. The capital, Dar es Salaam, then housed fewer than 300,000 people. In 2025 it is the size of New York City. What should be Tanzania's national language? Julius Nyerere, a former high school teacher who was elected Tanzania's first president chose Swahili, despite the paucity of books published in that language. He even translated Shakespeare's *Julius Caesar* into Swahili to demonstrate that Swahili was as good as any other language.

What could be more important than looking at the roles of communication in "nation-building," a vital goal and a widely used word at that time? Ten days after arriving in Dar es Salaam with a very pregnant wife, and a visa permitting us to stay there for a year, I was informed by the Tanzanian government that my research proposal was rejected.

Wondering how to make the most of my new situation I realized I could do a content analysis of the daily newspapers in Tanzania. There were two, one published in English, dating from when the country was a British colony. The other, a Swahili-language tabloid that featured poetry written by the readers. To help me with the project I hired two young men whom I'd befriended: Ezekiel Ngonyoni and George Shilaka, high school graduates with no research experience, but they seemed bright and understood what I needed help with. Ezekiel, who was about 20, was enamored of the Boy Scouts, and he often wore his scout uniform. George, in his thirties and dressed like he worked in an office, often carried a briefcase, with nothing inside. Occasionally he carried a camera attached to a strap across his shoulder. It was devoid of costly film, but it was a display of status and values. For me, this was a new lesson about intercultural communication in newly independent states, and more broadly I thought this might be the direction of my future research.

The improvised research project itself required measuring of newspaper column space and the counting of words. And, then characterizing and analyzing the content. It was a make-do project but not without value. The results were published the following year in *The Journal of Modern African Studies* (1967) published by Cambridge University Press.

As that project was coming to an end, I learned that across the harbor there was Kivukoni College run by TANU, the political party of this one-party socialist state. By ferry I visited the school and offered to teach a ten-month course on communication at no cost to the school. My offer was immediately accepted. It was the first such course offered there. In my class were women and men who were social workers, teachers, union organizers, district officials, and not a few "freedom fighters" from countries then still colonized, as well as from the powerful apartheid nation of South Africa. On average the students spoke four and a half languages. One spoke twelve. It was the most exhilarating teaching experience of my life, with smart, idealistic, experienced, practical-minded adults preparing to return to their positions with new competencies and a broader vision. Twice I lectured in my rudimentary Swahili. (And I never once said *"siagi haitoshi"*). Politely, the students told me they appreciated my effort but they preferred that I use English for the novel reason that most had been speaking English all their lives.

Five weeks after arriving in Dar es Salaam, my wife gave birth to our first child, our daughter. This was at the city's major hospital, Ocean Road Hospital, facing the Indian Ocean. That road was later re-named Barack Obama Road. I was present to witness the birth—rare for a man in this strongly Moslem-influenced land. We gave our daughter a Swahili middle name: Bahati. The next morning in my class, where many were parents themselves, I announced that the previous night I had become a father. Spontaneously, the class sang to me!

I can't describe the emotion I felt at that moment. It was as if a chorus echoed the joy I felt when I witnessed the birth. But it was then I began to appreciate what status that being a parent confers, as if one is not truly an adult until then. This is true in much of the world. Moreover, in East Africa, parents are popularly known by their first child's name: so now Camy was Mama Bahati; I was Baba Bahati. We were the only white family in the working class Magomeni section of the city, living in a newly-built, small two-room concrete block house that had electricity; water from the community well was delivered in metal drums.

Social life was largely outdoors, with dancing on the weekends, men dancing with men, women with women. And whenever Mama Bahati met other women in the neighborhood, baby Bahati would be passed around by the mothers because infants are blessings, and "It takes a village...." One afternoon as I was leaving the college, one of the older students said to me: "Say hello to my sister-in-law." I was puzzled. Do I know his sister-in-law? Then I realized he was calling me his brother.

I was able to do research on cultural values and nation-building, not what was originally planned, but still relevant. Thanks to Ezekiel and George, the research was conducted for two months, in the city and in villages upcountry as well. In a village they would call for people to "gather 'round:" then Ezekiel and George acted out a kind of debate, usually in Swahili, telling a series of short stories or anecdotes, and then posing choices of what to do or judge what is best among the values options offered. It was a theatrical questionnaire. At the end of each story, they would ask everyone—show of hands—which of the options they would choose, and the results were tabulated. The crowds loved this traveling show, at least those I witnessed seemed to. In 1967, in rural Africa, the transistor radio had just appeared; listening was almost always with many others.

Inevitably that magical year came to an end. Saying goodbye to the school, neighborhood, city, country, continent! Leaving a place we'd come to love, our daughter's birthplace that occurred not long after the birth of the newly independent nation, eager, proud and cautiously optimistic. Tanzania was the poorest of the adjacent former colonies, Uganda and Kenya. Many wondered if Mwalimu Nyerere's political philosophy, *Ujamaa*, could withstand pressures from the global powers, with the United States front of mind.

1968: A Terrible Year Until…

Returning to the United States after a year away, especially returning from a much poorer country is always a shock. I could relate back home when a local reporter asked a visitor from East Africa. "What has impressed you most about visiting the United States?" The visitor answered, "I think it's the size of your garbage cans."

The year, 1968, was a terrible year in the United States. Assassinations of Martin Luther King, Jr., and then Robert F. Kennedy, in a year when so many of my generation were protesting the war in Viet Nam, rioting in the streets, and in Chicago, clashes with police. News of yet more cruelty by reactionary powers but also more heroic gains in the Civil Rights movement. Nixon was about to be elected president. And that ill-advised involvement in the civil war in Viet Nam continued. Apart from the political and social tensions there were also personal tensions within. Everything felt wrong, and I'd never taught worse. In October I told the department Chair that I would be leaving at the end of the academic year, and I had no idea where we might go. By coincidence, if one believes in coincidences, four days later a letter from a Japanese university arrived that asked me: "Would you consider taking a leave of absence from Northwestern for one, or preferably three, years, to come to Japan to teach? We want to expand our communication department." It took less than a minute to decide "yes!" *Little could I have imagined* we would live in Japan for a decade.

We knew that we wanted to continue to live abroad and that for our children, maybe the only thing we could offer beyond our love, would be the gift of learning another language at the age when children learn a language effortlessly. Often it is only years later that a child recognizes it as a gift.

The brightest spot in a grim year was adopting our son. We asked at the Illinois state adoption agency, what very young children were most difficult to place? At that time, we were told that mixed-race kids, especially a child of Black and white parents, was the most difficult for the agency to place. Black families didn't often place children up for adoption; as in much of the world usually the baby would grow up within the mother's family. Endemic racism discouraged most white, potential adoptive parents from adopting "mixed race" children. We joyfully adopted our year-old son whose biological mother, we later learned, was from a very conservative, white, midwestern town and the child's biological father was Black. Both were college sophomores at the time. Christina was born in Africa, but her brother would identify as "African American" (Fig. 4.2).

Japan!

It was typhoon season when our family arrived in Japan. Fierce winds and a Niagara of rain perfectly fit the political and social conditions across the land. For the first weeks we were housed on campus where a student strike was underway. Japan's vaunted deference and respect shown elders and teachers that I had read about didn't match what I saw in the small college auditorium. I watched in shock as the university's white-haired president and other administrators sat stiffly in upright folding chairs as students in hardhats and red scarves berated them, marching up and down the stage, pointing and shouting. The *funso* (conflict) went on for many days. Classes that were scheduled to begin were on hold. It was the same across Japan. At Japan's most prestigious Tokyo University, the library was set aflame. No one in Japan knew how long this would go on or what to do. The faculty was split, hawks and doves. One of the first Japanese words I learned was *kidotai*, "riot police" who were called in to erect a metal wall around the main building. Students and faculty were forced to choose: come in for classes or resist and remain outside. The next week, classes began but among some of the faculty the memories never ended.[2]

Although there was faculty housing on campus, and much desired, we wanted to live in a Japanese neighborhood. Renting a house in Japan was expensive and complicated, especially when the prospective tenants didn't speak Japanese and were also illiterate in the language. But then we learned

Fig. 4.2   The Condon Family, 1968, in their Chicago Apartment

that the university librarian, Tane Takahashi, might be able to help us. Takahashi-*sensei*, who had studied at Bryn Mawr College during the war, became assistant to Elizabeth Vining, the person chosen by the U.S. Occupation authorities to teach English and manners to twelve-year old Crown Prince Akihito who would become the next emperor.

Librarian Takahashi also was the niece of the distinguished intellectual historian, Sokichi Tsuda, who had lived about two miles from the campus.[3] After his death the house remained vacant because a newly built four-story apartment building blocked out the direct sun, so important in Japan for refreshing the *futon* and drying the laundry. Long story short, we happily moved into that beautiful house.

Right across the narrow street from us was a small old duplex house, where the Kobayashi family lived. The family included two children, Hiroshi and Mariko, the same ages as Christina and Michael. The kids played together; absence of a shared language was no barrier. Camy and Mrs. Kobayashi developed a friendship as only young mothers can. We learned that their family would soon have to move because the owner of the house planned to tear it down to make space for a new, larger house. My wife thought we should invite the Kobayashi family to share our house—there was space for separate living quarters, and we'd share the kitchen and the bathroom. As she pointed out the many advantages, with my book knowledge of Japanese culture and intercultural communication, I explained why such an arrangement would never work.

Our families shared that house for more than the next nine years.

Soon, our children spoke Japanese better than their English. We were the only family in the whole neighborhood who was not Japanese, and in the late sixties and early 1970s, *gaijin* ("outsiders," but functionally "westerners") were a novelty in most of Japan. Out on the street, mothers would sometimes whisper to their children, "Look! There's a *gaijin!*" Strangers passing our children sometimes would reach out and touch their hair—what is it about hair? My daughter's red hair was a matter of public curiosity. Michael's hair seemed to attract even more touching to which he'd snap back, angrily. When they were a little older, Japanese kids passing on the street might giggle and say "This is a pen," or some other echo from an early English lesson, friendly but also a reminder that "you are different" to kids who didn't feel different. Camy offered English lessons at our house to kids from the neighborhood. Once, one of her students recognized me and when we passed, he greeted me: "Fine, thank you, and you?"

Looking back, a half century later, the children's memories of growing up in Japan are nearly all positive; Michael married a beautiful, tri-lingual, Japanese woman whom he met in Europe where she worked. Michael worked for a major Japanese corporation for over 20 years, rising to the rank higher than any previous non-Japanese in the massive organization.

Christina remains close to her childhood friends and returns whenever possible. That house we shared was torn down shortly after we left, and in its place today is a small park, marked with a plaque identifying the place as the former home of Prof. Tsuda and later, the Condon and the Kobayashi families whose kids grew up together.

Teaching at International Christian University (ICU). International Christian University (ICU), a bi-lingual, Japanese and English, institution, was established immediately after WW II. The enormous campus, then the largest in Japan, previously was the site of the Nakajima Aircraft factory that produced a WWII workhorse fighter plane. Truly, the Biblical invocation to beat swords into plowshares. It was unique in many ways: bi-lingual, a liberal arts education, a library open to all, student dorms and faculty housing on campus. The organizers of the 1964 Tokyo Olympics, after which Japan was welcomed back into the modern world, asked, unsuccessfully, the president of ICU to shut down during the Olympics so that the students from ICU, the only university in Japan with a Department of Communication, could serve as interpreters.

The students, as always, were my best teachers, often through observing how they worked together. In Japan, many things work better in groups than individually. Students who could be reluctant to raise their hand and answer a question because they had to consider context more than in the U.S.: why is the teacher asking this question? Who am I in this room—who is older or might know more? These considerations are part of the cultural context, implicit for any Japanese person, but not to an outsider newly arrived.

With my senior colleague, Mitsuko Saito, we began to plan what became the 1972 intercultural communication conference that involved 80 undergraduate students, with many presenting results of their thesis research, as well as a "Who's Who" of internationally known Japanese scholars with much to share that was relevant. Among the 1972 participants were: Cliff Clarke, who grew up in Kyoto; the University of Minnesota professor Bill Howell, who, uniquely then, taught a graduate class in intercultural communication. There was also Janet Bennett and Milton Bennett who had just completed their Peace Corps stint in Truk (Micronesia). Before the conference ended, Howell had persuaded them to join the University of Minnesota doctoral program.

Four years later, Clarke began the Stanford Institute for Intercultural Communication, and a few years later when he began his consulting firm, it was Janet and Milton Bennett who brought it to Portland where it thrived until 2018. Janet reminded me that at first Stanford gathering she was in my workshop on "Teaching Intercultural Communication." One of the first books in Japan on intercultural communication was the proceedings of this conference (John Condon and Mitsuko Saito, Eds.), *Intercultural Encounters with Japan: Contact and Conflict* (1974). A later international ICU conference was held in 1976, in which the recently retired E.T. Hall participated. The conference presentations were then published in the book, *Intercultural Communication for What? (J. Condon & M. Saito Eds,* 1976).

Down to Business

At the end of the 1970s, Japan was emerging from the postwar recovery and drawing interest, admiration, some jealousy and fear and hostility, and "Japan bashing." Joint ventures were being tried; many failed, but the presence of U.S. companies in Japan continued to grow.

I was asked by the American Chamber of Commerce in Japan (ACCJ) to do a needs assessment and offer a three-day training program for newly arrived managers.

The ACCJ collaborator in this was a manager of the Japanese branch of an American bank, and who, it turned out, had also attended Mexico City College. With Sheila Ramsey, a visiting professor at ICU, we interviewed expat managers about their experience in Japan. This led to three-day training programs that we were advised not to call them intercultural communication programs because that sounded too academic. Because we were offered the beautiful conference site just outside Tokyo that belonged to Mobile Oil, we used the name of their icon, Pegasus. For six years our program became "the Pegasus Seminars," an annual event for newly arrived managers until professional consulting and training companies had joined the chamber.

That experience and the increasing numbers of companies opening offices in Japan prompted me to write *With Respect to the Japanese* (1984). Glen Fukushima called the book "a bible for Westerners seeking to understand and deal with Japan, then considered the most competitive economy in the world." Later, this led to a revised edition by drawing from Prof. Tomoko Masumoto's research on the experience of North American interns working in Japanese companies, *With Respect to the Japanese: Going to Work in Japan* (2011).

As the 1980s approached Camy and I felt we had deprived our kids, nearly teenagers now, and their grandparents from really knowing each other, so we said goodbye to our friends and neighbors to return to our children's homeland they barely knew. A white daughter born in East Africa, a mixed-race son who was born in Chicago, and both felt culturally mostly Japanese.

Destination: A Land of Enchantment

We settled in a place none of us knew, the state of New Mexico, which on its license plates adds "USA" after the name of the state, because many think New Mexico is another country. I have lived in New Mexico longer than any other place, and taught at the University of New Mexico longer than at any other school. The school's mission was to serve the students in a state, economically poor, but culturally, none richer. Its stark natural beauty that drew writers and artists, like photographer Ansel Adams, a friend of Hall; and together they developed their photos.

I had almost always lived in or near big cities: Chicago, San Francisco, Mexico City, and the largest of all, Tokyo. Though I love the energy of big cities I love living at the edge of a town with fewer than 300 people. Driving ten minutes in one direction is the indigenous Pueblo of Jemez whose people have lived here for over a thousand years. Their language, Towa, spoken only here is, by intention, not taught outside of the village, and is not written. The oral tradition is alive here, and I am in awe. A few hours further south, at White Sands National Park, fossilized human footprints were found that date back 23,000 years, the oldest evidence of humans in North America.

Another benefit of living in a rural area is the rediscovery of the star-filled night sky. For most of the year the milky way arcs right overhead. I designed my house so that I can slide my bed onto the adjacent deck and fall asleep under the stars and with the sounds of the little river rising from the canyon below. Reminding that our relations with nature precede our intercultural relations.

It was here that I reconnected with Ned Hall who returned to his native Santa Fe after retiring from Northwestern. At the University of New Mexico when I arrived was Hall's former Teaching Assistant and doctoral advisee at Northwestern, Gladys Pilz. Miguel Gandert, an internationally acclaimed documentary photographer was recruited from a local television station, and he and I became friends and colleagues, and for many years taught advanced intercultural communication seminars together.

Graduate seminars were what I dreamed graduate seminars might be, usually meeting at my home. Several times Ned Hall joined us, and we would cook and share a meal afterwards. We would also have traveling seminars to site specific places, and an overnight. These included indigenous sites, and also a "border reality" experience, with conversations and overnights on both sides of the U.S.-Mexico border, centered on inextricable economic, political, health and social justice issues. Some grad students say it was a life-changing experience (Fig. 4.3).

Fig. 4.3   E.T. Hall at age 83 Delivering a Grad Seminar

As a doctoral student, Kathryn Sorrells, who met Hall in one of our seminars, coaxed him to come out of retirement and co-teach a seminar, the last classes Hall taught. With Richard Harris, originally from London, but with the decades of university teaching in Japan we offered seminars on a very Hall theme: space and place, exploring the subject with over-night fieldtrips. Getting out of the classroom and being in natural and built environments, meeting ordinary people in their communities: this was my goal in teaching that was finally possible. When Everett Rogers joined the department as chairman, his prestige and campus political savvy led the department to offer a doctoral program with an emphasis on inter-cultural communication.

From here I was also granted leave to teach at the University of Guam where Tom Bruneau was initiating an intercultural program. Another year I was granted a leave to introduce our field to the faculty at the *Universidad de Guadalajara*. I was privileged to be invited to consult at Southeast Asian refugee sites in Indonesia, Thailand and the Philippines. All the while I was able to reunite with colleagues and friends each July at the Summer Institute for Intercultural Communication.

On the 50th anniversary of *The Silent Language*, in 2009, I organized a Saturday seminar at the Summer Institute, to review and honor Hall's singular influence on the field he inadvertently created. A series of strokes cruelly had rendered him mute. With the encouragement of his wife, Karin, we phoned Ned, knowing he couldn't speak, but we said our thanks and said goodbye. Next morning I learned that Edward T. Hall had died during the night. Ours were among the last voices, some just meeting him, some in professions he inspired.

Hall's memorial service, at the historic St. Francis Auditorium in Santa Fe, New Mexico, where Hall embarked on his life's path, the eulogy and memories we shared were much like what inspires this book, a look-back on a life, to reflect, celebrate and ask what it's all meant.

The road, or path, is a sturdy metaphor, a horizontal line running from left to right, if that's the direction our literacy points us. But upon reflec-tion we know there's also the vertical metaphor of layered history. I look out my window and see the face of a majestic mesa that towers above. That chocolate-colored base is billions of years old. At the top compressed vol-canic ash from a mere few hundred thousand years ago, predating human life. The mesa encourages humility in our stories, remembering those who came before and those who will follow. And the question theoretical phys-icist Carlo Rovelli (2018) asks: "*Do we exist in time or does time exist in us?*"

NOTES

1. This famous quote attributed to Erwin Schrödinger is as evasive as his famous cat. There appears to be no definitive text or speech in which this first appeared. Scholars who have traced this find antecedent statements expressed by other philosophers, including Arthur Schopenhauer, and before. For more, see Ludwig von Bertalanffy (1952), *Problems of Life: An Evaluation of Modern Biological Thought.* University of Ottawa, 1952.
2. Linguistics professor at Georgetown University, Deborah Tannen told me that it was Hall's book that gave her the idea to publish some of her research findings for a broader audience and not limited to other linguists. Prof. Tannen's book, *You Just Don't Understand: Women and Men in Conversation* (1990) *was* on the *NYT* Bestseller list for three years and has been translated into more than 30 languages.
3. Prof. Tsuda was arrested by the Japanese fascist government during WW II, accused of slandering the imperial family. After the war Tsuda had been widely expected to become the next president of Waseda University, but in the academic political culture of the postwar years he was considered too conservative.

REFERENCES

Albert, E., & Vogt, E. (Eds.). (1967). *People of Rimrock: A Study of Five Cultures.* Harvard University Press.

Barnlund, D. (1968). *Interpersonal Communication: Survey and Studies.* Houghton Mifflin.

Bertalanffy, L. (1952). *Problems of Life: An Evaluation of Modern Biological Thought.* University of Ottawa Press.

Burroughs, W. (1959). *Naked Lunch.* Grove Press.

Condon, J. (1966). *Semantics and Communication.* Macmillan.

Condon, J. (1967). Nation Building and Image Building in the Tanzanian Press. *Journal of Modern African Studies, 5*(3). Cambridge University Press, pp. 335–354.

Condon, J. (1984). *With Respect to the Japanese.* Yarmouth, ME: Intercultural Press.

Condon, J. (2025). *It Goes without Saying: Culture as Communication.* Random Mouse Press.

Condon, J., & Masumoto, T. (2011). With Respect to the Japanese. In *Going to Work in Japan* (2nd ed.). Intercultural Press.

Condon, J., & Saito, M. (Eds.). (1974). *Intercultural Encounters with Japan: Culture and Conflict.* SIMUL Press.

Condon, J. & Saito, M. (Eds.) (1976). *Communicating Across Cultures for What?* SIMUL Press.

Condon, J., & Yousef, F. (1975). *An Introduction to Intercultural Communication.* Bobbs-Merrill.

George, H. (1879). *Progress and Poverty: An Inquiry into the Cause of Industrial Depressions and of Increase of Want with Increase of Wealth: The Remedy.* D. Appleton.

Hall, E. (1959). *The Silent Language.* New York, NY: Doubleday.

Hall, E. (1976). *Beyond Culture.* Doubleday.

Hayakawa, S. I. (1941). *Language in Action.* Harcourt, Brace.

Philipsen, G. (1972). *Communication in Teamsterville: A Sociolinguistic Study of Speech Behavior in an Urban Neighborhood.* Unpublished doctoral dissertation, Northwestern University, Evanston, IL.

Rovelli, C. (2018). *The Order of Time.* Riverhead Books.

Stewart, E. (1971). *American Cultural Patterns: A Cross-Cultural Perspective.* Intercultural Press.

Strogatz, S. (2015). *Sync.: How Order Emerges in the Universe, Nature, and Daily Life.* New York, NY: Hachette Press.

Tannen, D. (1990). *You Just Don't Understand: Women and Men in Conversation.* William Morrow.

Vogt, E., & Albert, E. (Eds.). (1966). *The People of Rimrock: A Study of Values in Five Cultures.* Harvard University Press.

CHAPTER 5

From Neo-Oedipus to Dora the Explorer: A Me-To-We Journey

Carlos E. Cortés

"On this earth there is one thing which is terrible, and that is that every-one has his own good reasons." That haunting line from Jean Renoir's 1939 film classic, "The Rules of the Game," captures the essence of inter-culturalism. Why? Because interculturalism explores the nature of *good* reasons as viewed from the varying and often conflicting perspectives of the world's diverse people.

REFLECTIONS ON INTERCULTURALISM

Interculturalism pursues understanding. But when I say understanding, I don't mean excusing, justifying, or exonerating. Interculturalism should not espouse neutrality. It should not function as an amoral get-out-of-jail-free card for every individual's or culture's action. Rather, it should foster a deep commitment to understanding why people, cultures, and nations do the things they do. They all have their reasons. Whether I personally

C. E. Cortés (✉)
University of California, Riverside, CA, USA
e-mail: carlos.cortes@ucr.edu

S. M. Fowler, D. C. Yalowitz (eds.), *Creating the Intercultural Field*,
https://doi.org/10.1007/978-3-032-01370-5_5

consider those reasons to be good or those actions to be admirable, accept-
able, or even deplorable is another matter.

For me, understanding reasons—of self and others—lies at the core of
interculturalist thinking. But I can't be certain. That's because I may well
be an intercultural imposter.

You see, I *discovered* interculturalism long after it began. I have never
taken a course on interculturalism, have read only sporadically about that
scholarly field, and have never earned a certificate, license, or degree in
anything intercultural. My very personal and sometimes skeptical understanding of interculturalism is based far more on experience, reflection,
and intuition than on scholarship or methodological indoctrination.

My learning method might be described as neo-Oedipus. Yes, the
Oedipus of classical Greek fame who killed his father and slept with his
mother. However, incest and patricide are not my guiding lights. Rather I
continuously try to emulate Oedipus the fearless detective who relentlessly
pursues evidence, whatever the costs, even if it leads to disconcerting and
uncomfortable conclusions.

In the Oedipal tradition, I think of myself as a *street interculturalist*.
That is, someone whose thinking about interculturalism has developed by
hanging around more grounded interculturalists, interacting with them,
and pondering the ideas that have emerged from those experiences. With
that in mind, let me invite you to my personal intercultural journey, a
journey that has occurred in three stages:

***Discovering interculturalism.
***Interculturally revisiting my life.
***Drawing on interculturalism to address specific challenges.

DISCOVERING INTERCULTURALISM

D. C. Discovery

1991. I discovered interculturalism in 1991. Sort of like Columbus discovered America in 1492. We both accidentally bumped into something
that was already there.

Columbus returned home proclaiming what he had discovered. Lost in
his arrogance was the fact that the Americas and their myriad cultures had
been there long before his "discovery." The same is true of my first

encounter with interculturalism. It had been around long before I got around to discovering it.

My accidental discovery occurred in March, 1991. I had been invited to be part of the three-person opening plenary panel at the 1991 Washington, D.C., conference of the late American Association for Higher Education. I arrived two days early so that I could get my fill of nearby Ethiopian food and, if in the mood, attend some pre-conference events. Glancing through the program, I spotted an intriguing-sounding workshop on interracial communication featuring a couple of people named Bennett. Why not? If I became bored, I could always slip out and head for the injera. However, boredom did not become an issue.

The Two Bennetts. Janet and Milton Bennett turned out to be a revelation. Their opening remarks on Black-White communication patterns managed to provoke participants, some of whom challenged the Bennetts with hostile comments. However, the Bennetts deftly managed what could have turned into a tumultuous and polarizing session and presented their arguments with calmness and dexterity. Afterward I hastened to introduce myself. The Bennetts subsequently attended my plenary discussion. Over the course of the conference we became friends. That friendship grew over the ensuing decades.

I learned that Janet and Milton Bennett were directors of something called the Summer Institute for Intercultural Communication (SIIC), then being held at Pacific University in Forest Grove, Oregon. They explained that the program drew hundreds of professionals from around the world for a curriculum of week-long courses on aspects of interculturalism. They invited me to SIIC to give the opening plenary talk for one of those weeks and to do an evening workshop on intercultural humor in July, 1992. Although I had been writing, giving lectures, and doing workshops on diversity for more than two decades, had chaired the Chicano Studies program at the University of California, Riverside, for seven years, and had been deeply involved in the development of K-12 multicultural education, I knew nothing about the field of intercultural communication. As a result, my 1992 SIIC adventure proved to be an experience in personal marginality.

SIIC Adventure. My keynote went well. Make that O.K. Drawing on my multicultural and diversity background, I thought I had given a good keynote. The talk received polite but tepid applause. This muted reaction challenged my overly-generous self-evaluation.

Then came my intercultural humor evening workshop for an audience of several hundred SIIC participants in a large auditorium. The presentation, which included the analysis of edgy clips from movies and stand-up comedy routines, provoked an active discussion about how different people and cultures could have varying responses to efforts at humor, including humor targeted at specific groups. Mission accomplished, I thought. But not for everybody. After the session a group of participants went to the Bennetts, told them that they were offended by some of the clips, and asked that my workshop not be repeated.

Long story short. My humor presentation ended up in the dust bin of SIIC history. I turned out to be Professor Harold Hill and, like The Music Man, I didn't yet know the territory. My showing of offensive media examples had proven to be *inappropriate* in this risk-averse setting emanating from a comparably risk-averse field. However, two decades later Janet Bennett invited me to write the entry on intercultural humor for her 2015 *Sage Encyclopedia of Intercultural Competence*, which I happily did. This time, no complaints.

My SIIC miscues notwithstanding, by 1995 I had become a regular SIIC faculty member. For more than two decades I gave week-long classes and evening workshops on various dimensions of diversity, such as Privilege and Inequities, rather than on core intercultural topics. For many of these classes I collaborated with Louise Wilkinson, an insightful and imaginative diversity and media specialist at Boeing. We had gotten to know each other when I served as a respondent for her doctoral dissertation research project and later met her in person at the Summer Institute.

My annual sojourns to SIIC initiated my street education on interculturalism. Discussions during meals, conversations at evening wine-and-cheese gatherings, and participation in optional evening sessions became my intercultural education. I also became marginally acquainted with intercultural scholarship, such as articles in the *International Journal on Intercultural Research*. Yet while I admired the thoughtfulness and erudition of intercultural investigation, that scholarship struck me as rather tame compared with most other social science and humanities fields. It lacked the vigor of heated scholarly challenges, bold disagreements, and clashing interpretations.

I ultimately concluded that, for me, the beating heart of interculturalism lay with personal experience and interactions rather than with published scholarship. From that experience emerged three principles that I personally found basic to the interculturalist project.

***a dedication to seeking the reasons that propel others—both individuals and groups—to think, act, and react the way that they do.
***a commitment to building bridges among diverse people, cultures, and nations.
***the courage to be an outsider, including taking individual responsibility for one's own actions even if this meant being unique, standing alone, and adopting public positions that go contrary to the mob (including the intercultural mob).

Almost imperceptibly, those principles began to influence my thinking. They also influenced my professional and personal actions. Consider the following example.

Dora the Explorer. In 2000, following the publication of my book, *The Children Are Watching: How the Media Teach about Diversity*, I became a consultant for Nickelodeon's new children's series, "Dora the Explorer," then in its planning and pre-production stage. At one consultants' meeting, the issue arose concerning the languages to be spoken by the characters. Most of the consultants championed the idea of having many of the characters be bilingual in Spanish and English in order to increase the amount of Spanish spoken in the show.

My interculturalist bent drove me in the opposite direction. I became virtually the sole person in the room who favored the idea of making Dora the *only* principal bilingual character. My reason: I wanted her to be uniquely intercultural, the one character who could use her bilingual language skills to build bridges of cooperative problem-solving, particularly when most other characters were English or Spanish monolinguals. I vigorously defended my position despite the lurking concern that this might lead to my getting dumped as a consultant. Fortunately, the producers ultimately agreed with me. The show publicly proclaimed Dora to be an intercultural bridge-builder. I ended up being promoted to the position of Creative/Cultural Advisor for "Dora" and its sequels, "Go, Diego, Go!" and "Dora and Friends: Into the City."

REVISITING MY PAST THROUGH INTERCULTURALISM

Birth of a Memoir

Pleasing Alana. Shortly after I began teaching at SIIC, my twenty-something daughter Alana made a simple but life-altering request. For years she had heard family stories, but fretted because nobody wrote them down. Would I? How could I say no?

So I began writing family stories. Lengthy sketches of my long-deceased parents and grandparents, including grandparent immigrants from Mexico, Austria, and Ukraine. Stories of growing up in Kansas City, Missouri, going to college at the University of California, Berkeley, and Columbia University, serving in the Army, pursuing a short-lived journalism career, returning to graduate school at the University of New Mexico, becoming a history professor at the University of California, Riverside, and launching a career as a diversity lecturer and consultant. Day after day I revisited long-dormant memories of my life. Almost effortlessly I found that I had completed a detailed 500-page family chronicle. Of course, it was for family reading, not for publication.

Reading to Alana. Rather than waiting to hand Alana this enormous manuscript, I read sections to her, sometimes over lattes on Riverside's Main Street promenade, other times in restaurants. Then came a startling day in a comfortable booth at Bob's Big Boy. I chanced to read her the story about my Mexican father's ill-fated attempt to become a polo player at Kansas City's Mission Brook Polo Club, a story both sad and hilarious. Throughout my reading I noticed the bobbing back of the head of a man sitting in the booth behind Alana. As soon as I finished, the man stood up, walked over to us, and told me how much he enjoyed the story. Did I have any more?

That incident triggered something. Maybe buried inside the detailed family chronicle lay a book clambering to get out. I returned to the manuscript, this time with the idea of identifying a core theme around which I could structure an actual book. The theme turned out to be interculturalism, revolving mainly around my parents' intermarriage, my growing up in a multiethnic, bi-religious, and tri-lingual home, and the impact of this experience on my personal journey. Consider the intercultural dimensions of the book's opening chapter.

"Dad was a Mexican Catholic. Mom was a Kansas City-born Jew with Eastern European immigrant parents. They fell in love in Berkeley, California, and got married in Kansas City, Missouri. That alone would not have been a big deal. But it happened in 1933, when such marriages were rare. And my parents spent most of their lives in Kansas City, a place both racially segregated and religiously divided. Mom and Dad chose to be way ahead of their time; I didn't. But because of them, I had to be. My

Fig. 5.1   Little Carlos

mixed background meant that, however unwillingly, I had to learn to live as an outsider (Cortés, 2012, p, 1)." (Fig. 5.1)

The book was ultimately published in 2012 as *Rose Hill: An Intermarriage before Its Time*. (Rose Hill is the Kansas City Jewish cemetery where my folks and my mother's parents are buried.) But before that happened, I took a major side-trip.

Memoir to Performance

Serendipity strikes. As I wrote my memoir, I looked for moments to read chapter drafts in order to get responses by various audiences. Fortunately my career trajectory provided me with ample opportunities. In July, 1994, at the age of 60, I had taken early retirement as a history professor at the University of California, Riverside, and then devoted full time to being a diversity consultant, writer, and lecturer. With some 75–100 speaking gigs a year, I sometimes volunteered to do a memoir reading as a side freebie at those gatherings. This included SIIC, where I would do an evening manuscript reading once during each week in which I taught a class.

Then, in July, 2003, serendipity struck in the form of Dawn Davies, a SIIC intern. After attending my reading, Dawn approached me with a bizarre suggestion. She enjoyed the reading and opined that it had the basis for becoming a good one-person play. A former theatre director, she offered to give me advice if I decided to give it a try.

I had taken part in amateur theatricals, but had never written a play. However, fools rush in where ... well, wherever. So I took up Dawn's idea. After many fits, starts, and miscues, this developed into *A Conversation with Alana: One Boy's Multicultural Rite of Passage*, an hour-long conversation between me and my daughter, Alana, represented on stage by an empty chair. The play (published in 2022) has proven so successful that I have performed it more than 150 times around the country. Post-performance discussions sometimes run more than an hour. At SIIC, in particular, audience members eagerly contributed their own sometimes-fascinating intercultural stories.

Interculturalism's role. Interculturalism informed both my memoir and my one-person play. Writing the memoir and performing the play deepened my understanding of my own *good reasons* and the *good reasons* of those with whom I interacted during my personal journey. The process also expanded my insights into interculturalism itself, particularly the importance of becoming more careful about making judgments, a dimension that I increasingly incorporated into my own consulting and workshops.

In particular, exploring my life in full view of audiences and readers helped me grow more comfortable with the unavoidable marginality resulting from my mixed background. But this went beyond comfort. I discovered that marginality actually brought me pleasure, even joy. My desire to belong declined. I realized that I really didn't give a damn about belonging in my personal life. If others didn't accept me as I was, that was their problem. In my professional life, I reveled in being a lone wolf, a skeptic, and a critic of orthodoxy, including intercultural orthodoxy.

Getting *Carled*. Maybe the best way to illuminate how intercultural-ism influenced the rediscovery and rethinking of my past is by providing two stories drawn from my play and memoir. The first is an abbreviated scene from *A Conversation with Alana*. It takes place in the fall of 1949 at the beginning of my sophomore year, when I switched high schools in Kansas City.

* * *

"On the first day of my first class the teacher calls the roll but not my name. I raise my hand.

> 'Excuse me, sir, you missed me, Carlos Cortés.'
> He reviews his list.
> 'I called your name, Carl.'
> 'But, sir, my name isn't Carl. It's Carlos.'
> 'That's not what the school records say.'

So in front of my new classmates I repeat, several times, that my name is Carlos, not Carl. Of course I didn't win. In fact, the teacher kicks me out of class and sends me to the principal's office. They call my folks. Dad storms over to school.

Now Dad didn't lose his temper often, but when he did...whhh. I'm afraid he's going to be furious with me for getting into trouble on my first day at my new school. But he's not. In fact, he's proud of me for standing up for my name, his name, our Mexican name.

Dad lectures the principal. 'My son's name is Carlos. His father's name is Carlos. His grandfather's name was Carlos. His great-grandfather's name was Carlos. And I'll be damned if you're going to call him anything but Carlos.' After that, they didn't.

Oh, I guess I ought to mention the class where this happened—Spanish (Cortés, 2022, pp. 15–16)," (Fig. 5.2.)

* * *

I now refer to such events as Carl Moments or Being Carled. Carl Moments are situations where people encounter obstacles to authentic inclusivity. When things happen that communicate to you that your inclusivity is con-ditional. You're welcome … but … or if … or sort of.

Fig. 5.2   Carlos in High School

I didn't like being Carled because of my name. I didn't like being ethnically marginal because of my mixed background in a racially-segregated city. I didn't feel good about having to lie about my religious background when I picked up dates at their homes (yes, in the good old days of the 1940's, protective Midwestern parents would often inquire about your religion). I had my own *good reasons*, but interculturalism helped me retrospectively come to grips with the *good reasons* of those with whom I interacted, even if their actions had made my life uncomfortable or even miserable. Interculturalism helped me adjust to and take pleasure in being uniquely marginal.

Basking in marginality. Sometimes marginality occurred in unexpected and ironic ways. This occasionally related to the fact that I had a Spanish surname and, through the dice roll of genetics, ended up with very light skin. Here is one incident that I wrote about in my memoir, *Rose Hill.*

Once I was invited to give a luncheon talk at a California statewide education conference. The invitation came from an Anglo who had never met me. On the day of the conference I introduced myself to him. His face fell. Caught off guard, he said something that others may have thought, but suppressed. "Uh, we were hoping for someone, uh, a little darker."

I was interculturally prepared. With additional help from Neil Simon's film, "The Goodbye Girl," I had a ready answer. "This year I'm working on younger. Next year I'll work on darker" (Cortés, 2012, p. 111).

Interculturalism has helped me deal with the unexpected, roll with the punches, and even take greater pleasure in life's ironies. The Anglo at the education conference had his own *good reasons*. Rather than getting angry, I focused on understanding those reasons. I didn't melt because he had committed a microaggression. I didn't accuse him of implicit bias. I didn't dissolve into a pool of intergenerational trauma. I simply smiled, shook my head, and enjoyed the ironic moment of his consternation.

Interculturalism encourages you to step back, take control of your own journey, and reflect rather than just react. Interculturalism encourages you to delay judgment rather than leap to immediate conclusions, to consider reasons rather than just responding to behavior. Interculturalism encourages you to self-moderate impact rather than rushing to accuse or blame. In short, interculturalism helps you draw strength from yourself and become more resilient through experiences with otherness.

My years at SIIC laid the groundwork by fostering my interculturalist street knowledge. The SIIC experience influenced the writing of my memoir and provided the impetus for creating my one-person autobiographical play. In the process interculturalism—particularly its emphasis on understanding the "good reasons" of others—became a deeper part of personal trajectory.

ADDRESSING CHALLENGES

Stages

Third phase. This brings me to the third phase of my intercultural journey. The 1990's had brought my "discovery" of interculturalism. During the first decade of the 2000's interculturalism influenced the exploration of my family roots and personal trajectory. As I moved through the 2010's and 2020's, I found myself increasingly drawing on intercultural principles in my professional life and other diversity-related endeavors. In particular, I drew upon such principles as personal resilience, intergroup bridge-building, and the dedication to the pursuit of understanding otherness. The following challenges exemplify this process:

***addressing the California Ethnic Studies controversy.
***writing the Riverside Anti-Racism Vision Statement.
***developing the UCR School of Medicine's Health Equity, Social Justice, and Anti-Racism curriculum.

California Ethnic Studies

UCR. In January, 1968, having just returned from two years in Brazil doing doctoral dissertation research, I joined the history faculty at the University of California, Riverside. My arrival doubled the size of UCR's two-person Mexican American faculty (the other, Eugene Cota-Robles, a distinguished UCR microbiologist, soon became my Chicano Movement mentor). In current diversity lingo, Gene and I were examples of institutional *onlyness*.

It was also a time when ethnic studies was beginning to take off at campuses around the country. Ivan Hinderaker, the UCR Chancellor, decided to get ahead of the curve. He formed a faculty committee to design an ethnic studies program. Obviously, the committee had to include our campus' two Chicano and two African American faculty members. This administrative request came at a personally inopportune time, since I was trying to complete my doctoral dissertation while also teaching a full load of brand new courses. The smart answer would have been no. I said yes. (I managed to complete my dissertation and receive my Ph.D. in June, 1969).

On July 1, 1969, UCR's Mexican American Studies Program (later renamed Chicano Studies) came into existence. Trained as a Latin American historian, I had never studied Chicano history. Yet in January, 1970 I taught UCR's first Chicano history class and from 1972 to 1979 I served as Chicano Studies chair. Ethnic studies was in my blood, but my scholarly and consulting interests ultimately drove me in different directions, particularly after I took early retirement in 1994 at age 60 and dedicated myself to being a diversity lecturer, writer, and consultant. **The Medina Bill.** Fast forward to 2019, when California State Assembly Member José Medina, one of my early UCR graduate students, proposed a bill to make ethnic studies a statewide high school graduation requirement. At about the same time the assembly passed a separate bill (proposed by a different assembly member) instructing the California Department of Education to create a model (not required) ethnic studies high school curriculum. Although the two bills were not legislatively connected, their fates soon became intertwined.

The Department of Education put out a call asking for applications to serve on the model curriculum committee. For a few seconds I considered applying, but common sense prevailed. I had not kept up with the field. I had also lost patience for the time-consuming, soul-shriveling horse trading involved in the writing of committee reports. At that moment, I had too many other fish to fry.

The too-large committee was formed (some twenty people), it drafted a proposed ethnic studies model curriculum, and the Department of Education posted the draft online for public comments. All hell broke loose. Within a short time the curriculum had received an extraordinary 21,000 posted public comments, 18,000 of them negative, sometimes exceedingly so. The controversy went public, with newspaper editorial writers and columnists weighing in, usually criticizing the curriculum for things ranging from its impenetrable jargon to its negativity to its selective inclusion (and exclusion) of ethnic groups in the appendix of lesson plans.

Although on a separate legislative track, the Medina bill to create an ethnic studies graduation requirement got caught up in the model curriculum controversy. Some assembly members who might otherwise have supported the Medina Bill refused to do so unless the model curriculum was thoroughly revised. The furor brought the Medina Bill to a standstill, as defenders and critics of the model curriculum dug in. The State Board of Education asked me if I could help break the stalemate. I could have assembled a team to address this challenge. But as had become my penchant, I decided to go it alone.

Applying interculturalist thinking. My approach was through intercultural bridge-building. Rather than wade into the argument by either criticizing or defending the model curriculum draft, I instead wrote a brief (twelve-page) document of eight principles for high school ethnic studies that I hoped could create a degree of consensus. Some of the principles reflected my intercultural thinking: working toward greater inclusivity; furthering self-understanding; developing a better understanding of others; and improving interpersonal communication.

I realized that my position statement would please neither defenders nor critics of the model curriculum draft. By going it alone and refusing to choose sides in the controversy, I had painted a universal target on my own back. Indeed, I received anticipated criticism from multiple directions.

But the gambit paid off. After months of effort and negotiations in which I was not involved, the model curriculum was modified. My position statement was included almost word for word along with some of the language from the original committee draft and myriad additions of lesson plans about ethnic groups that had previously been omitted. With the model curriculum in place, the state legislature approved the Medina bill and Governor Gavin Newsom signed it into law, making California the first state to require ethnic studies for high school graduation. My lone wolf document played some role in that success, although I have neither the time nor the interest to pursue the details.

Riverside Anti-Racism Vision Statement

George Floyd. In May, 2020, George Floyd, an African American, died the victim of a Minneapolis police officer. Riverside Mayor Rusty Bailey asked me if I would take charge of creating an Anti-Racism Vision Statement for the city. Since 1999 I had been serving as coordinator of the Mayor's Multicultural Forum, a quarterly public gathering open to all Riversiders to talk about diversity matters in the city. The Forum had conducted a number of projects, including writing the city's Inclusive Community Statement. Creating an anti-racism statement was more of a challenge.

This would be no leisurely walk in the park. The mayor's request came in July. He wanted to deliver the statement to the city council for approval in early October. No time to dawdle, hold multiple meetings, or rely on time-devouring subcommittees. Interculturalism to the rescue.

Multiple voices. To carry out this task, the Forum met by zoom for the first time in July. Several dozen strongly opinionated people participated. I mainly listened to them and took notes on their ideas, often conflicting ideas. It was up to me to create a document that would both reflect these myriad opinions and also have a chance for adoption by the ideologically-diverse seven-person city council. I had multiple bridges to build.

Based on the Forum's comments but working alone, I drafted a document, circulated the draft online, and asked for responses within three days. In they came. I took those responses, re-drafted the document within days, and recirculated it for another quick turn-around. This went on for numerous drafts, each time building more concensus, even though fissures remained.

For example, there was a division between hearts-and-minders (those who believed that the starting point should be capturing hearts and minds) and structuralists (those who believed that the starting point should be identifying and changing racist structures). I respected the varying *good reasons* and responded by building a verbal bridge between the two camps by titling one section, "Anti-racism begins everywhere (Riverside, 2020, p. 1)." The section included ideas offered by each camp.

When the Forum met again by zoom in mid-September, there was general consensus on the current draft. The meeting resulted in a few minor changes. We had created a strong, tight (two page), non-jargony document championing anti-racism enriched by intercultural thinking. Then it was off to the city council.

At the mayor's request, I presented the statement to the council and responded to questions. The report needed four votes to pass. It received six, the only negative vote coming from a council member who expressed concern that the statement might reflect critical race theory. The October 26, 2020, Los *Angeles Times* published a feature story on the Riverside statement along with a picture of Mayor Bailey, with a five-column headline announcing that "Riverside seeks a racial reckoning (Campa, 2020, p. B-2)."

UCR School of Medicine

Health equity. Simultaneous to the mayor's request, I received another call, this time from an associate dean of my campus' School of Medicine. He had a simple question. In the wake of Floyd's death, the medical school had decided to launch a new curricular initiative entitled Health Equity, Social Justice, and Anti-Racism. Would I be interested in working part-time as co-director of this new initiative? Let me establish the context for the dean's offer.

For several decades I had been giving talks and workshops on cultural competence, a fundamental precept of the intercultural field. This included health care cultural competence. Since the founding of our medical school in 2013, I had been giving an annual two-hour cultural competence presentation for all first-year students, so the school was familiar with my approach to diversity and health care.

But co-director of a new curricular initiative? At age 86, did I really want to take on this demanding responsibility in a field that I had never studied? The smart answer to the dean's question would have been no. But I answered yes. Five years later, I'm still there, partly thanks to interculturalism.

Fortunately I was paired with a superb co-director, a young pediatrics professor from Ghana named Adwoa Osei. Adwoa patiently mentored me in the intricacies of medical education while I reciprocated by mentoring her in diversity matters, including interculturalism. As we developed the content and pedagogy for the curriculum, interculturalism became one of our mainstays.

Enter Interculturalism: In particular, we drew upon interculturalism as we taught about doctor-patient relationships. This included the recognizing of differing *good reasons* of patients from varied backgrounds, particularly those who came from other health care traditions or might have had off-putting experiences with the U.S. health care system. We emphasized the importance of physicians developing greater intercultural understanding as a basis for building bridges to diverse patients. Topics covered a broad range, such as: an understanding of the capacity and impediments within the human brain when it comes to engaging diversity; medical perceptions of those with different types of disabilities; and challenges and opportunities for working with health care language interpreters.

Our curriculum is still a work in progress. It will inevitably remain a work in progress. Continuous health care research and the eruption of legislative action and judicial decisions on such topics as abortion and the treatment of transgender patients make it so. Ergo, the importance of addressing challenges through interculturalist thinking and action, while at the same time maintaining the humility of recognizing that interculturalism alone is no solution.

INTERCULTURALISM: MY JOURNEY

Transformation? This brings me back to a core topic of this book. Has my interculturalist journey been transformational? I'll address that question with less ostentatious language. It has certainly influenced me. Were it not for SIIC and the intervention of Dawn Davies in my life, I doubt that I would have ever written my one-person play and performed it all over the country. Likewise I would not have written numerous articles on interculturalism, such as my entry on intercultural humor in Janet Bennett's Sage Encyclopedia of Intercultural Competence.

Interculturalism gave me the opportunity to be part of the SIIC family and benefit from the SIIC experience. In turn, that experience has influenced the way that I address other professional and social opportunities and challenges, from consulting on scripts for Nickelodeon and Dreamworks ("Puss in Boots: The Last Wish") to medical school teaching. This includes the three interculturalist principles that I mentioned earlier in this article.

***I remain deeply committed to seeking *good reasons* for why people and groups do what they do, even when I despise their actions. Some interculturalists express a penchant for non-judgmentalism. Not me. I judge—both individuals and groups. However, as interculturalism encourages, I try to slow down when coming to conclusions, give others the benefit of the doubt, and remain sufficiently flexible so that I am capable of changing my views if new evidence or compelling arguments are presented.

***I almost reflexively look to build bridges when I encounter situations where there are widely-varying differences of opinion, particularly where polarization and stalemate have set in. However, in building bridges I try to avoid taking a mushy middle position. Rather I look for ways to reframe situations, as I did in the California Ethnic Studies Model Curriculum controversy, and to build consensus by providing alternate avenues rather than merely seeking compromise.

***I favor using my voice as singular rather than as part of a chorus. I almost always reject requests to sign group statements, because I seldom encounter a statement that doesn't conflict, in some respects, with what I believe. In the case of group projects, such as writing the Riverside Anti-Racism Vision Statement, I try to write the drafts so that I can make certain that they do not collide with my beliefs. Because of my commitment to *onlyness*, I often find myself in a solitary position, with critics coming from different angles, but so be it. I've been an *only* since childhood. Why stop now? (Fig. 5.3)

Diversity and Speech. Maybe the best way to conclude my examination of how interculturalism has influenced me is through my current

Fig. 5.3 Celebrating his birthday: 90-year-old Carlos with his wife Laurel, his daughter Alana, and two granddaughters Amaya and Tessa

major research project, a book-length study of the intersection of diversity and speech. As with many aspects of my life, this part of my journey began serendipitously. I was at the right place at the right time.

In 2018 the University of California launched a system wide initiative, the National Center for Free Speech and Civic Engagement. One of its first actions was to establish a fellowship program. It put out a call for proposals to conduct research on some topic related to the Center's mission.

I've never been a particularly enthusiastic proposal writer. Too structured, too detailed, usually too demanding of metrics. However, this one was simple: a brief essay explaining what I would like to investigate. No budget, no literature review, no elaborate research plan, no metrics. Just a simple, straight-forward essay. Perfect for a neo-Oedipal scholar like me. I wrote it, submitted it, and forgot about it. A couple of months later, while my wife and I were taking our second visit to Antarctica, I received notification that I had been named an inaugural fellow of the Center.

My proposal arose from a concern that had been developing, particularly over the previous decade. As a multi-decade diversity consultant, I had become concerned about a recent shift in some diversity thinking, with increased efforts to restrict speech. As a former journalist and a long-time member of such organizations as the American Civil Liberties Union, I proposed the following research question: why have so many diversity advocates become opponents of the hallowed American tradition of freedom of speech?

As it turned out, my question was overly simplistic and employed misguidedly dualistic thinking. Over the ensuing years I would continuously reframe my research project as I looked back at the half-century historical trajectory of the intersection of the post-civil rights diversity movement and American speech traditions. Part of that reframing involves rethinking the role of interculturalism within this story. Consider the following brief reflections.

Diversity Movement. During the 1970's, the diversity movement was characterized by joy, jubilation, and optimism. *We shall overcome* was more than a civil rights mantra. It reflected a manner of thinking. Overcoming was simply a matter of time, and the good folks were on the right side of history.

But two less-optimistic counter trends began to emerge within the diversity movement. The first was the rise of Critical Race Theory. (A note of caution: there was plenty of critical diversity scholarship prior to CRT and CRT does not hold a monopoly on criticism.) A formidable intellectual and social justice enterprise, CRT has provided many valuable insights into American history, culture, and structures. However, it has also contributed to a growing pessimism among some diversity advocates. Maybe we aren't going to overcome because such things as racism are too deeply embedded in the American trajectory.

Paralleling the rise of CRT was the growing emphasis on language. Always a concern among diversity advocates, language increasingly became the sole focus of some. This ultimately led to such tendencies as a concentration on microaggressions and the development of equity language lists. As with CRT, to some extent these approaches have provided valuable insights. However, some microaggression and equity language advocates have lurched into dogmatism and authoritarianism, complete with an intolerance of language mistakes (meaning what *they* judge to be mistakes).

Within the broader diversity movement umbrella, I view interculturalism as a framework that posits a more hopeful outlook on the human condition. Things can improve. We can help them improve even while recognizing structural impediments and sometimes-inequitable language practices. And we can do so by honoring good intentions and encouraging voluntarism through increasing intercultural awareness and the capacity for constructive intercultural communication.

Instead of moping about self-censorship, let's think in terms of speech self-restraint as an expression of common courtesy, with an added dimension of intercultural understanding. In this reframing, interculturalism emphasizes personal responsibility and the capacity to learn. In that sense it provides a healthy and constructive alternative to the dour, suspicious outlook of microaggression authoritarians with their accusatory penchant for finding fault.

Rethinking interculturalism. In a sense, my rethinking of interculturalism within the over-arching story of diversity and speech is a natural outgrowth of my professional journey. Within that reframing, interculturalism is not just a field of study. It is an optimistic, constructive, and futuristic way of living.

I began this essay with a quotation from a movie. I'll end with the opening line of L. P. Hartley's masterful 1953 novel, *The Go-Between.* "The past is a foreign country; they do things differently there (Hartley, 1953, p. 1)."

But the past is not the only foreign country. So is the future. Hopefully interculturalism will have more to say about the nature of that foreign country.

Carlos Cortés has no conflicts of interest to declare that are relevant to the content of this chapter.

References

Campa, A. J. (2020, October 26). Riverside seeks a racial reckoning. *Los Angeles Times*, p. B-2.

Cortés, C. E. (2012). *Rose Hill: An intermarriage before its time*. Heyday.

Cortés, C. E. (2022). *A conversation with Alana: One boy's multicultural rite of passage*. Bad Knee Press.

Hartley, L. P. (1953). *The go-between*. Harnish Hamilton Ltd.

CHAPTER 6

Falling in Love with Humanity: My Path to the Intercultural Field

Alvino E. Fantini

My grandmother, from a small town in central Italy, always had local wisdom to pass on. During my childhood, I remember her often saying: *Alvino, mi raccomando ... devi sposare una ragazza italiana ... bella, forte, e che non mangia troppo!* (Alvino. Be sure you marry an Italian girl ... pretty, strong, and one who doesn't eat too much!) Years later, however, I fell in love with a Bolivian woman. A cross-cultural dilemma! What to do?

MY EARLY YEARS

When asked how I became involved in intercultural work, I paused briefly to reflect, and my first thought was that perhaps I was born into it. This may sound presumptuous, but it occurred to me that perhaps most individuals enter a career in intercultural communications because of a key educational or professional experience. In my case, however, I began grappling with identity, acceptance, and adjustment to varied cultural

A. E. Fantini (✉)
SIETAR International, Dummerston, VT, USA
e-mail: alvino.fantini@worldlearning.org

© The Author(s), under exclusive license to Springer Nature Switzerland AG 2025
S. M. Fowler, D. C. Yalowitz (eds.), *Creating the Intercultural Field*,
https://doi.org/10.1007/978-3-032-01370-5_6

situations at an early age and, at the same time, I began to question my own identity.

With parents who immigrated from Italy (and a grandmother who spoke no English), I was completely immersed in Italian language and culture at home: we spoke Italian, ate Italian food, listened to Italian broadcasts, and read Italian newspapers (that is, until I was 13 when my grandmother passed away). Then things began to change. However, during my childhood, I felt discomfort with this identity with which I had been raised, which may explain my interest in associating with others who were different.

At an early age, when my buddies and I played cowboys and Indians (a popular game at the time), whereas most others wanted to be cowboys, I always chose to be an Indian. I am not sure what attraction I felt to others who were different from myself, but it may certainly have been my discomfort with who I was (as an Italian American). During my teens, for example, one of my best friends was Julia G., an African American I invited to our seventh-grade school dance. I enjoyed her company, finding her delightful and funny, and unaware that it was uncommon at that time to associate with a *person of color*. Two years later, I invited another friend, Judy G., to our ninth-grade school dance. Judy was also delightful and fun to be with. She was Jewish, however, and again it was also uncommon then to date individuals of other religious backgrounds (although I was unaware of this as well).

In subsequent years, other friends of diverse ethnic and religious backgrounds followed (again, perhaps it was their difference in part that attracted me). During my late teens, my girlfriends were a Mexican, an Armenian, and then a Greek, followed years later by a Bolivian (the only one I had ever met and the person who became my wife). Like many Bolivians, my wife, Beatriz, in fact, was not only of Spanish origin, but probably had indigenous blood as well and, surprisingly, also Sephardic Jewish heritage. And, incidentally, because her father was a diplomat assigned to Italy, Beatriz was born in Rome ... and happily, a cross-cultural dilemma was resolved!

Despite interest and attraction to individuals from diverse ethnic, racial, and religious backgrounds, ironically, I continued to be ashamed of my own ethnicity. This was especially poignant, I recall, whenever my grandmother came outside to call me home, shouting in her regional dialect: *Alvino, lascia di pazziare. Vieni a casa a mangiar'. Subito!* (Alvino, stop playing. Come home to eat. Hurry.) Given the presence of my playmates, this was always a source of embarrassment. And, I recall, now with some shame, how I rebuked my grandmother, saying: Nonna, why don't you speak English! But her English vocabulary consisted of only three words: Y*e-a*, *no-a*, and *a-maybe* (although her favorite word seemed to be *no-a*, *no-a*, *e no-a*).

The source of my shame at being Italian is not hard to explain. The early 1940s was not a good time to be Italian given that my early years coincided with World War II and Italy was initially on the wrong side. I recall words like *wop* and *dago* as part of my ascribed identity and unpleasant childhood experiences also come to mind—at school (where, European style, I still wore short pants in seventh grade), in the lunchroom (whenever I unwrapped my lunch from an oil soaked brown bag while others had neat sandwiches cut in triangles), and on the playground. Whereas these incidents caused me shame, they also taught me something—how it feels to be disliked and discriminated (although I acknowledge that my experiences pale in comparison with more pervasive and harmful discrimination often experienced by those of other races, religions, and ethnicities).

A Transformative Summer Experience

Participation in a summer exchange program upon graduation from high school in 1954, unexpectedly gave me a new perspective on my ethnicity. I traveled to Mexico with an organization known as The Experiment in International Living as member of a small, guided group. After a preliminary period in Morelia and Mexico City where we underwent *cross-cultural orientation*—my introduction to this term—we then went to the town of Xalapa in the state of Veracruz. There I was hosted by a family where I had seven siblings.

During the summer, it occurred to me to ask my host mother why she chose me from a group of twelve individuals. (Prospective host families receive photos and background information about group members prior to arrival to choose which person they wished to host). Her surprising response was that it was because I was of Italian descent, and she adored Italians! It was one of the few times in my life up to then that I had heard someone speak in positive terms about Italians.

During my stay, I learned that many other Mexicans also had interest in Italy, in Italian culture, Italian language, and in Italians, in general. Such views surprised me. I began to think that perhaps it might not be so bad to be Italian after all. That was one lesson. The other important lesson learned from that experience was how easily I adapted to a different way of life. I adapted with facility to my Mexican family, to their food and customs, and I learned Spanish easily (aided, I realized, by my knowledge of Italian). After identifying so closely with Mexicans and Mexican culture, I then thought that it might not be so bad to also be Italian after all and I now embraced three identities—American, Mexican, and Italian!

I gained something quite important from this experience: It was this new perspective of myself that made the experience so life changing. After returning to the United States and reflecting about the experience that just ended, I realized everyone must come to terms with whatever ethnicity, religion, or race into which we are born. And while an intercultural experience like the one I had in Mexico facilitated this realization, I now understood that we must all accept and embrace these aspects of our identity—whatever they happen to be. My Mexican family not only opened the world of Mexican culture and the Spanish language to me; it also inadvertently provoked a transformative experience that altered my perception, of others, but also of myself. A veritable paradigm shift!

LIFE AS AN ACADEMIC

Upon returning home, I entered college. Early in the semester, I was required to declare a course of academic study. Given my experience in Mexico, my interests gravitated toward Latin American Studies. Attending an Ivy League college (the University of Pennsylvania) proved to be another intercultural experience, one that I had not expected. At Penn, there seemed to be distinctive cultural norms—most students wore a certain brand and style of clothing (with patches on their jacket sleeves), they smoked pipes, and joining a fraternity was a top social priority. So, I followed along: I bought a jacket with patches on the sleeves, and although I didn't smoke a pipe, I did visit several fraternities. However, after participating in several events at frat houses, I felt repulsed by some of the behaviors I had observed.

An alternative to fraternities arose after learning about the existence of an International House (IH), located near campus, which sponsored social events for both foreign and domestic students. Given my interest in other cultures and international living, it was a more attractive place for me where I could socialize. And, after learning of its mission: to maintain a diverse and welcoming community and encourage understanding, respect, and cooperation among people from around the world—I knew I was in the right place.

Although the IH was not residential at that time, I was fortunate to be selected as one of four individuals to reside at the IH and to serve as hosts for social events. The other three individuals were students from abroad: my roommate, Chi-Ping Chung from China (who became my lifelong friend, and years later, Best Man at my wedding), Shmulik Lifschitz from Israel, and Antonio Rosario from the Philippines. Living at IH was a delight as I was able to meet both international and domestic students who attended IH events, as well as the renowned interculturalist and author, Pearl S. Buck, a member of the IH Board of Trustees. While living at IH, I realized that I was inclined to seek out individuals with international—and yes, intercultural—values.

My interests in Mexico and Latin America—and other cultures—expanded further, given my IH experience, and given the academic area that I pursued as an undergraduate student. Consequently, when later attending graduate school during M.A. and Ph.D. studies, I became fascinated with studies in Language Acquisition, Bilingual-Education, Sociolinguistics, and Anthropology, all topics which further enhanced my intercultural understanding and appreciation.

Years later, during graduate studies at the University of Texas, I was again fortunate when selected as member of a team of four anthropologists hired by the Hogg Foundation for Mental Health. This Foundation had undertaken a research project to study Mexican American culture (with findings later published by our project director (cf: Madsen, 1964). Whereas the State of Texas had established public health clinics along the U.S.-Mexican border (staffed primarily with Anglo health practitioners), they found Mexican Americans reluctant to use these services. Our research project, therefore, attempted to learn about illness and curing practices among Mexican Americans and to inform public health workers into reasons behind a reluctance to accepting gratuitous aid from local clinics.

During the project, I was apprenticed to a local *curandera* (folk healer), who provided me with a host of fascinating and distinctive views of life, both physical and spiritual. This intercultural experience, with practical consequences, reflected in some ways many of my childhood experiences given that many practices regarding illness and curing were reminiscent of my own upbringing. This fascinating experience, however, ended abruptly two and a half years later when I received a draft notice to enter the U.S. Army.

MILITARY EXPERIENCE AND BEYOND

My military experience turned out to be, nonetheless, another intercultural adventure. While not of my own choosing, it certainly provided a distinctive life experience. Upon completing boot camp, I was assigned to the Counterintelligence Corps (CIC). After completing training in Military Intelligence, my tasks as an Agent involved conducting security background checks for military and civilian personnel (i.e., DACs or Department of Army Civilians) with access to classified information, investigating security breaches on military bases, conducting interrogations, and various other activities. This was indeed a novel and distinctive cross-cultural experience and one that contrasted greatly with the type of personal interactions to which I was accustomed. My greatest pleasure when conducting background security clearances, however, was to conduct interviews in ethnic neighborhoods where I found that my investigative success was enhanced given my interest and ability to interact with ethnic diversity.

Although military service was normally a two-year requirement for draftees, due to the Bay of Pigs invasion which occurred in April 1961, my CIC status was extended for "an indefinite period of time" (which became an additional sixteen months). That event necessitated agents with my skills (knowledge of Italian and Spanish) to board ships with Italian or Spanish-speaking crews arriving from Cuba and to seek volunteers willing to provide intelligence information regarding their experience there. Military experience was possibly my most distinctive cross-cultural adventure (barring one other in Japan to be discussed later).

Upon completing my military obligation in June 1963, I traveled two weeks later to Vermont, the site of a student exchange organization, The Experiment in International Living, having applied for and been accepted as a group leader assigned to take students abroad for the summer. This was a highlight, especially since I was assigned to Italy, providing an experience in my parents' native country for the very first time.

My group was sent to Belluno, a town in the northern Veneto province (a short distance from Venice). There I experienced quite a different aspect of Italian culture from the one I knew and I also learned more about standard Italian language in contrast to the Abruzzese dialect from central Italy that we spoke at home. At the end of the summer when my students returned to the United States, I remained in Italy and traveled south to visit Isernia, my father's hometown, for the first time. There, I met many relatives, and I discovered something extraordinary: they all spoke just like my parents, ate the same types of food, and had similar mannerisms. The thought then flashed into my mind: Oh my gosh, my parents raised me (and my five brothers) as though we were still living right here in this small town in central Italy. The familiarity was pleasing but also both puzzling and revealing.

My work with The Experiment in International Living, it turned out, was quite the right fit for me. Given my background, my studies, my interests, and my experiences, I embraced the institution's philosophy, its activities, its emphasis on experiential education, and its approach to intercultural orientation and language teaching. Over the following years, I took additional summer groups to Spain and Greece, academic semester groups to Colombia and Italy, and I also directed (together with my wife) The Experiment's orientation programs held in Oaxtepec and Valle de Bravo, Mexico, for 16 summers. Travels with these programs were interspersed during the year with work with the U.S. Peace Corps, training volunteers for a variety of countries in Africa, Asia, and Latin America, a story which deserves a bit more detail since every effort involved intercultural preparation and language training.

In 1961, The Experiment had received some of the earliest contracts to train Peace Corps (P.C.) volunteers for their sojourns abroad. (Sargent Shriver had been an exchange student and also a group leader with The Experiment during the 1930s and, familiar with their orientation process and the experience which it provides, he engaged this organization to design and implement training for volunteers). From 1963 through to 1977, I served as Language Coordinator for Experimenters and also for more than 50 P.C. training projects destined for 36 countries. In this capacity, I worked with language instructors of over 36 languages whom we selected and hired from abroad and trained to teach in communicative approaches that differed significantly from traditional grammar-translation language teaching common at that time. The importance of developing intercultural *and* communicative competence (both cultural and linguistic) was stressed in training programs and results were reflected in volunteers who completed training successfully and went abroad (more on this below).

Orientation during these projects was a two-way process: Language instructors hired from abroad were oriented to our programs, teaching approaches, and U.S. culture, while assigned to prepare American trainees in their own languages and cultures. And we, the training staff, learned from our foreign counterparts while also learning more about ourselves through our work together.

On one occasion during my Peace Corps work, I recall an amusing (now, but not then) cross-cultural incident: Married only three weeks in early 1966, I was assigned to travel to Brazil to hire Portuguese language instructors. Given circumstances there, I had to request an extension to my visa permit and required to go to immigration offices in Rio de Janeiro. I explained to the clerk that I was recently married and I wanted to return home without delay and requested approval of my late departure to avoid further problems. His gleeful response was: *Eh, e não se preocupe. Nós temos muitas rapazes muito lindas aqui no Brasil.* (Don't worry. We have lots of lovely girls here in Brazil). A cross-cultural joke? I wasn't sure.

During my tenure of over 50 years with both The Experiment and its academic branch, the School for International Training, I traveled to many other countries to represent our organization at international gatherings (the U.S. Experiment was a member of an international Federation) as well as to conduct workshops abroad. Each experience around the world presented new challenges and provoked continuous reflection on my own abilities (learning from each new experience and from each new culture in places like Bolivia, Ecuador, the Dominican Republic, Ghana, Greece, Guatemala, India, Nepal, New Zealand, Romania, South Africa, Tanzania, and others). I also had the opportunity to teach at universities in Bolivia, Colombia, Mexico, and Japan, providing exposure to the culture of each country and also to academic settings and educational approaches at each institution. Not surprisingly, my experience in Japan was the most challenging and the most instructive (from a cross-cultural point of view) and deserves additional comment.

Beyond One's Comfort Zone

In 2007, I was surprised to receive an invitation offering a three-year contract from Matsuyama University (*MatsuDai*) in Matsuyama, Japan. The tasks cited were to develop a master's program in Intercultural Education, to direct the program, and to teach several courses. It required that I remain till graduation of the first cohort of students. Whereas the offer sounded exciting, it was also daunting—three years to leave my family and live as far away from Vermont as Japan!

I was surprised, however, when both my wife and my children, Mario and Carla (names chosen which remain the same in English, Italian, and

Spanish), encouraged me to accept—with a promise that my wife would visit each semester. Since both children had spent time in Japan as participants in the Japanese Exchange and Teaching (JET) Program, they were quite enthusiastic that I should also have an experience there. Given some hesitation, I responded that three years was too long but that I could accept a two-year contract, thinking they would certainly not accept. To my surprise, however, they accepted (and, as it turned out, I ended up spending two years and four months in Matsuyama which I absolutely enjoyed).

The new M.A. program at *MatsuDai* enrolled 12 Japanese students, individuals who spoke English and had had previous intercultural experiences living abroad. And, although I was the teacher and they the students, I am not sure who taught whom more since every day I encountered unexpected and novel experiences, inside and outside the classroom, which my students helped me to process.

As I entered the classroom each day, the students would immediately stand up (in unison) and give a slight bow greeting me with *Sensei, Sensei* (Teacher, Teacher) and continue bowing again and again (until I learned that as teacher and elder, I should stop bowing first). I also learned that the proper way to pass out papers to students was with two hands (and not simply toss papers on the desk in front of everyone). And I learned something especially important for use with my colleagues: When introduced to new individuals, it was appropriate to offer one's professional business card (in the proper manner) and to receive one from the other individual. After examining cards carefully (with attention to title and degrees), we then both had information to know how to properly address each other and who should defer to whom. All basic behaviors but unknown to me.

Each day I learned something more as I spent time in Matsuyama. When puzzled by some incident, I often questioned and sought advice from my students on some event that I experienced. I marveled at the fact that when I left my office and walked past the ballfield on my way to the tram station, I often found student athletes (members of the baseball team) scanning the sidewalk, assigned the task of pulling up any grass growing between cracks in the cement. When they saw me approach, they would immediately jump up and, bowing slightly (in unison), would greet me again with *Sensei, Sensei*. I marveled each day that I saw the same coin on the sidewalk that was not picked up. Since it did not belong to anyone, it was not touched. I also learned that as a new resident in my apartment building, it was appropriate to introduce myself and to offer a small gift to neighbors in apartments to my left and right. And so much more that I did not know about basic behaviors in this new culture. So much to learn as a *gaijin* that I wonder how many times I may have behaved inappropriately.

A frequent challenge at *MatsuDai* was attendance at our three-hour faculty meetings each Wednesday afternoon. Naturally, sessions were conducted in Japanese, so I always sought a seat next to an English-speaking colleague who provided brief comments to help me follow the topic under discussion. I observed several cultural differences: for example, when a controversial topic was discussed, once the opinion of the department chair became evident, others then adjusted their comments to fall in line with and agree with the prevailing decision.

I also observed a major contrast between my own custom and the Japanese approach to the timing deemed appropriate between speakers engaged in conversation, a contrast I learned about when studying sociolinguistics. This had to do with monochronic and polychronic speech patterns: Whereas speakers from an Anglo culture favor monochronic patterns (that it is inappropriate or impolite to overlap in speech when others are speaking). In contrast, most Latin cultures favor polychronic patterns in which overlap in speech is common and multiple speakers may even be speaking at the same time in a conversation—a pattern which is quite disturbing for Anglos. These differential speech patterns add an interesting dimension to knowing a second language (and its appropriate speech and interactional behaviors) when dealing interculturally. In Japan, I found monochronic speech not only to be the norm but also that Japanese speakers favor a greater degree of monochronism than Anglos such that a slight pause may ensue before another comment is made. Being unaccustomed to this speech pattern, I sometimes wondered facetiously why the lag or silence before another person spoke. Had someone forgotten what was just said?

Professional Engagement

My intercultural experiences and intellectual interests were enhanced and became definite career interests after learning about and joining the professional organization known as SIETAR International (The Society for Intercultural Education, Training, and Research). At the time, SIETAR International (SI) had member organizations in 35 countries, affording the opportunity to meet interculturalists from around the world. Attending

SI conferences each year in a different country and meeting colleagues from diverse backgrounds continued to excite me and to augment both my experiences and my knowledge. Unfortunately, SI has ceased to exist as such and SIETAR chapters in individual countries now hold national meetings rather than international gatherings.

As both a SIETAR member and as a professional educator, I valued being able to conduct hundreds of workshops abroad which also continued to broaden my experiences—in places like Ecuador, England, Ghana, Greece, India, Jamaica, Nepal, Romania, Spain, Venezuela, and many more. In addition, I served as consultant to two other exchange organizations besides The Experiment: CISV International (Children's International Summer Villages with headquarters in Newcastle, England) and AFS (American Field Service with headquarters in New York City) plus I conducted workshops at professional conferences and at the well-known Summer Institute for Intercultural Communication (SIIC) near Portland, Oregon. This involvement permitted professional discussions about the work members were engaged in and related to my continued work with The Experiment. Happily, my life experiences, my exchange sojourns in various countries, my academic studies, my professional work, and now my involvement with SIETAR, all added dimensions to my involvement, understanding, and on-going experience in the intercultural field (Fig. 6.1).

As a long-time member of SIETAR International, I served on its Governing Council whose meetings were held annually in different member countries. This experience eventually led to my election as SI President (a six-year involvement, with two years as Incoming President, two as President, and two as Outgoing President).

Remembering past experiences at Council Meetings, I picked up on something that I had observed at previous sessions. As a result, as President I decided to introduce a new approach at Council sessions in hopes of promoting increased equity and participation among members. Given that delegates represented each of the 35 member countries (and were often accompanied by national colleagues who sat behind them in a second row), I realized the challenge to participate fully for many individuals whose native tongue was other than English. Consequently, I decided to pause Council proceedings every 15 minutes or so to allow delegates a few moments to process what was discussed thus far during the session, together with their colleagues and in their own native language. Upon resuming the general session, delegates could then raise questions and ask

Fig. 6.1   With colleagues (Peggy Pusch and Marshall Brewer) at a SI Conference

for clarifications, if needed. This procedure recognized that although English was our *official* language, it was nonetheless a challenge for some international members to participate effectively in a second tongue.

THE ROLE OF LANGUAGE

These experiences—and most definitely, my own Japan experience—continued to impress upon me an important intercultural challenge, always present but often overlooked—the role of the host language as an important dimension of understanding another culture. I also began to value more my early exposure to two languages in childhood, as well as a third in my teens. And although I now speak five languages (Italian, English, Spanish, Portuguese, and Esperanto, as well as smatterings of French, Greek, and German), I found Japanese quite a challenge—unrelated to anything I knew and therefore difficult to access, in part because my work and contact with others in Japan functioned through English and my opportunities to study Japanese were limited. Nonetheless, I was quite aware that my lack of Japanese was a major impediment to fully accessing Japanese culture.

I remember listening to, and envying, Japanese children who at age five were already fluent speakers and I remembered (from my linguistic study) how all children have the capacity to develop native proficiency in whatever language, or languages, to which they are exposed (no matter their grammatical complexity). This ability, according to psycholinguists, unfortunately diminishes as we approach puberty. As children, we all accomplish the task of entering our native language and culture by an early age (becoming appropriate members of society in the process). However, when developing one language-culture and becoming a proficient *monolingual*, we also enter into a distinctive and *singular* view of the world, precluding other possibilities (all of which points to the value of adding a second language and culture).

As adults, on the other hand, to learn a new language we need the help of teachers, tutors, books, audio tapes, appropriate methodologies, and more. Yet, despite these assists, it is uncommon to develop native-like proficiency through these efforts and less so by simply being exposed to a new language in context (as with children). Whereas not all adults succeed in developing fluency in a second language (having lost the ability we had as children), struggling to develop proficiency in another language nonetheless is an experience that yields insights that elude us if we make no such attempts. As one author states: "…monolingual speakers miss out on the joys of bilingualism—the mental agility, better understanding of other cultures, and the endless surprises of a second language" (Dorren, 2018, p. 340).

When striving to express ourselves in someone else's tongue (at any level of proficiency), we experience the challenges, the difficulty, perhaps also the embarrassment and humility that often accompany such attempts. This helps us to understand and empathize with what individuals from other language backgrounds may experience when speaking to us in English. Moreover, increasing degrees of proficiency help us to attain something even more important—insights about how other languages offer new possibilities: new ways of conceptualizing, new ways of interacting, new revelations about the target culture; indeed, how other languages provide access to new views of the world.

So, one might ask (and we need to consider): how is this relevant to becoming interculturally competent? Or better said: to becoming interculturally *and* communicatively competent? This question is important for us to consider as interculturalists, for those of us who contemplate helping others to achieve such competence later in life—to transcend beyond a singular view of the world into other possibilities. Transcendence is enhanced not only by entering a new culture but also a new language and hence, another worldview! This topic deserves further elaboration.

Language: An Important Piece of the Puzzle

Back to Japan for a moment: There, given my limited knowledge of Japanese, I was delighted to discover that another ability—my ability to speak Esperanto turned out to be a great boon (yes, this is true) and that it also assisted my ability to enter the culture by meeting people ... in Japan, of all places! (Not the same as speaking Japanese, of course, but still useful.)

Esperanto, an artificially constructed language, created over a century ago, designed for international communication (a language which many think to be of little use and improbable), became my entrée into meeting and developing friendships with locals. At the time I did not know that two countries with the highest proportionate number of Esperanto speakers are Japan and Brazil, possibly because both countries have languages not commonly known by others, yet both are internationally involved.

Having consulted my Esperanto guidebook (listing Esperanto groups by country), I checked to see if a local Esperanto club existed in Matsuyama and found, to my delight, that indeed there was and that it met every Saturday morning. So, only a few days after my arrival, I attended the Saturday Esperanto session. I was enthusiastically welcomed by the Japanese members (in Esperanto) and instantly made new acquaintances, providing a connection with people and an area totally unknown to me, not in Japanese, not in English, but in Esperanto (although Japanese clearly would be better and would allow me to interact with still others). I will provide one early example of how my very limited Japanese affected me: One day, I entered the elevator of my apartment building and found a young man there who asked me: *Nan-kai desu ka?* (What floor is it?). It turned out that my apartment was on the tenth floor but I only knew how to count up to five. Hesitating briefly, I replied in Japanese: *go to go* (five plus five). The young man looked surprised but then turned and pushed the number five button twice. When the elevator stopped on the fifth floor, I got off, given my embarrassment, and then walked up five more flights to the tenth floor.

This experience in Japan and in other countries, and especially with many intercultural colleagues, made me reflect on an issue that has puzzled me over time: Interculturalists are concerned with helping others enter other cultures with sensitivity, respect, and understanding, yet I have known interculturalists (especially English-speaking interculturalists) who are monolingual. How is their understanding of other peoples, other cultures, achieved then? Only through English, through their own language? Through another language (even at low proficiency levels), one gains access to other ways of conceptualizing, communicating, and interacting; indeed, one steps out of one's habitual way of thinking and being in the world. Language is our ticket to membership into a cultural enclave.

As English speakers, we have the convenience that many people in the world learn our language and consequently our need to learn other languages is lessened. It eludes me, however, to understand how one can enter another culture appropriately and well (especially given my experience in Japan) without also grappling with the language of that culture since language is such an important medium when interacting with others (so, presumably that interaction, in order to gain an understanding of one's hosts, would best be carried out through the host language and not through one's own). Although monolingual interculturalists may excel in their careers, one area which monolinguals may fail to understand is how the ability to speak in a second language (especially the language of the culture under consideration) enhances intercultural relations, insights, and abilities.

Unfortunately, separation of language and intercultural studies is common. It is reflected also in the structure of academic institutions which establish separate departments of Foreign (or World) Languages and Intercultural Studies. This separation is contrary to what the study of *sociolinguistics* promotes, i.e., the nexus between language and behavior. These are inseparable and together contribute to the singular process of intercultural and communicative competence. This separation in academia is further substantiated in a study conducted titled "A Survey of Intercultural Communication Courses" (Fantini, 1993). Item 48 of this study asked questions regarding Language Development. The responses revealed that: *Few respondents address language in their ICC courses.* Item 49 asked questions regarding Bi−/Multilingualism, and responses indicated that: *The effects of L1, L2, L3 is the only topic in the survey which obtained no responses at all.* This important topic is further explored in the article "Language, Culture, and World View: Exploring the Nexus" in a "Special Issue of the International Journal of Intercultural Relations" (1995, IJIR, Vol. 19, No. 2) and in the section that follows.

Let me conclude this section regarding the importance of *language* for interculturalists by also commenting on the importance of *intercultural communication* for language teachers. For many years, language educators focused on language and grammar without addressing aspects of interactional behaviors that form part of communicating appropriately in the new language. *Culture* (in language courses) was primarily that of history and literature. The well-known interculturalist, Milton Bennett, addresses this deficiency in an article, "How Not to Be a Fluent Fool: Understanding the Cultural Dimensions of Language" (Bennett in Fantini, 1997, pp. 16–21). In recent years, however, language teachers are increasingly benefitting from the intercultural field and many are now expanding their focus to include other cultural aspects into their teaching approach. Both fields— language education and intercultural communication—need to inform each other as we look ahead. More on this in the next section.

Intercultural Communicative Competence

There are many reasons to expand the commonly used term *intercultural competence* to *intercultural communicative competence* so as to ensure that the *target language* is always addressed as an important dimension of intercultural abilities. This is such an important point that I will shift from my personal focus in this essay to a more academic discussion and introduce a linguistic construct to help depict how each language shapes and exteriorizes one's perceptions of the world (and how it in turn shapes one's internalized view in the first place). This construct, known as the input-output framework, follows (Fantini, 1995, pp. 145–6) (Fig. 6.2):

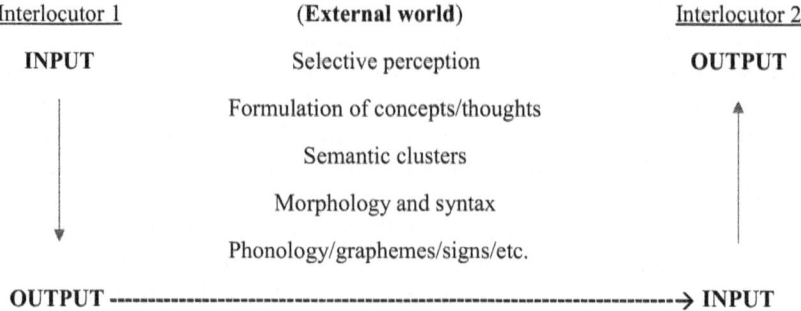

Interlocutor 1	(External world)	Interlocutor 2
INPUT	Selective perception	**OUTPUT**
	Formulation of concepts/thoughts	
	Semantic clusters	
	Morphology and syntax	
	Phonology/graphemes/signs/etc.	
OUTPUT --→		**INPUT**

Fig. 6.2 Input-Output Framework

To explain this framework further: At each moment we find ourselves in a given context (i.e., external world). In each context, an individual (in accordance with one's language, culture, and experiences) attends to (i.e., selectively perceives) aspects of that context. One's perceptions (apprehended through the senses) are formulated into thoughts or concepts (essentially a mental process). To communicate these thoughts to another person, of course, requires formulating them into some tangible manifestation (in accordance with one's language system). Hence, one's thoughts are organized sequentially in accordance with one's language syntax (since language is conveyed sequentially, i.e., one word placed after another), and words are *shaped* (according to one's language morphology), and then expressed physically (in sounds, signs, or writing). Chomsky called the mental aspect of this process *competence* and its physical expression one's *performance* (terms corresponding to deep and surface structures in linguistics).

This process illustrates how each language differs and mediates both competence and performance, and it provides compelling reasons to speak of *intercultural and communicative competence* (ICC). Although a longer term, ICC incorporates the language component, too often overlooked and not expressed in the term *intercultural competence* (IC), commonly found in the literature. Unfortunately, IC (rather than ICC) also serves as the conceptual basis in the design of several well-known and commonly used intercultural assessment tools which also omit reference to the target language and make no attempt to assess host tongue proficiency levels.

To counteract this oversight, one tool provides an alternative—the *Assessment of Intercultural Communicative Competence* (AICC). This form includes a section containing questions that attempt to assess the degree of proficiency one has attained in the target language *in addition to* other commonly acknowledged aspects of intercultural competence. This additional language component assesses three areas: the ability to establish and maintain relationships; the *ability to communicate* with minimal loss or distortion; and the ability to collaborate in order to accomplish something of mutual interest or need; plus, the four KASA dimensions: Knowledge, (positive) Attitudes/affect, Skills, and Awareness.

Research Interests

My education, work, and life experiences through the years have continued to inform my work in the intercultural field and what I felt should be shared with students and colleagues. Hence, my publication of the IJIR Special Issue (cited above) and various other publications and articles. However, my most intensive period of research (and what I consider to be my most important research contribution) took place from 2005 to 2015. This research project was significant because it examined ICC from *diverse* cultural perspectives, given that much of the existing literature about ICC was based on perspectives from a single culture (i.e., the United States) and in a single language (English).

Supported with grants from the Center for Social Development at Washington University, St. Louis, Missouri, and the Center for Educational Resources in Culture, Language, and Literacy, at the University of Arizona, at Tucson, Arizona, the research project took place utilizing the international structure of Federation EIL, the body that represents country members of The Experiment in International Living. This international structure enabled conducting and publishing two important studies under the title "Intercultural Communicative Competence in Educational Exchange: A Multinational Perspective" (Routledge, 2019). This ten-year project involved collaboration between researchers in eight countries (Brazil, Ecuador, Germany, Great Britain, Ireland, Japan, Switzerland, and the United States) and it examined three areas: (1) the nature of intercultural communicative competence (ICC), (2) ICC development in participants during exchange programs (both summer and academic semesters), and (3) the impact which intercultural exchange experiences had on the lives of alumni.

The study involved over 2,000 exchange participants to 36 countries plus over 200 host families (given that hosts as well as guests are engaged in intercultural contact), and it explored the significance and impact which such experiences had in transforming people's lives. The results, told in quantitative figures and qualitative narratives (provided by the participants themselves), identified relevant abilities toward gaining acceptance in a host culture, the role that learning the host language had on one's ability to engage in the host culture, and the impact which the intercultural experience had on one's later life (in terms of academic study and career choices) during an ensuing period of 20 years. In addition, the study identified specific program design components that most enhanced their intercultural experience, with participants citing family homestays and learning the host tongue as the most significant variables.

This study has been cited as a highly original contribution to the intercultural literature, basing its concept of ICC on literary searches spanning

50 years and conducted in five languages in addition to English in each of the six countries involved. This extensive approach provides a multinational perspective of ICC and formed the basis for developing the instrument used in the research (i.e., the *Assessment of Intercultural Communicative Competence* or AICC). It also assessed ICC development in exchange participants from multiple countries plus the impact on their lives. Following publication of the study (and the AICC Form provided in the Appendix), this unique assessment instrument has been continuously requested by (and provided gratuitously to) scores of graduate students and researchers conducting intercultural studies in countries around the world.

Intercultural Communicative Competence for Everyone

As I reflect on my path through an intercultural lifestyle and career (and wanting to share the excitement and rewards of such with others), I continue to review my own experiences. Whereas I originally thought that being part of an immigrant family (in my case) may have set the stage for learning to deal with two cultures early on, I now think that this cannot be the sole factor, especially since I was only one of six siblings to be so interested in people of different ethnicities, races, and religions. And in contrast to this curiosity and interest, I know individuals who may be uninterested or even repulsed by those who are different. Although being born into two cultures and two languages may have set the stage, I wonder how the experience of others, especially of those living abroad in another culture, may affect them. I wonder also about contrasts between those living dual cultural experiences with those who live in a single and dominant language-culture and who may never experience the pull and tug of adjusting cross-culturally daily and may never have experienced prejudice or discrimination.

Moreover, although one may choose an academic career to teach intercultural communication or to work in programs preparing individuals to go abroad, it may be possible that academic careers and knowledge about intercultural communication can remain primarily intellectual endeavors -- something taught in a classroom but perhaps without necessarily impacting one's life. Living interculturally (as in a bicultural household or living abroad) are indeed both *experiential* endeavors. They both present ongoing and continuous intercultural experiences as does marriage or relations with someone from a different culture. In these cases, in addition to

a career that *addresses* intercultural communication, one *lives* interculturally every day. Intercultural unions, for example, present unanticipated
issues on a frequent basis (serving as a constant reminder to live what one
teaches). Although issues may be trivial, even trivial differences need to be
resolved; for example: What are the roles and responsibilities of a male, a
female? Who is served first at the table—adults or children? What is the
seating arrangement? Who disciplines children? Which language should
we speak? And many other details that *might* not arise when both parties
are from a similar cultural background. In a bicultural household, two
cultures are constantly present while at home and perhaps a third when
one steps out the door.

On the other hand, thinking more broadly, I then began to think that
intercultural relations may also be a matter of degree given that absolutely
every relationship, especially when people live together in close contact,
presents differences between individuals that need to be addressed. When
one considers all such aspects of living together as well as of those when
interacting with others cross-culturally, differences and adjustments are
present in *all human interactions.* From this stance, intercultural interactions may be present in every relationship (*a continuum from interpersonal
to intercultural*), albeit to varying degrees—perhaps more extreme in
some cases, requiring more challenging adjustments the greater the diversity of ethnic, racial, and religious backgrounds.

So perhaps cultural duality (i.e., growing up in two cultures) is not a
guarantee that one will find an interest or an acceptance of an intercultural
world (especially if the duality is a negative experience). Is it then a question of nature or nurture? Or perhaps nature *and* nurture? Or even just
nurture alone? Additional intercultural contact in life (especially those of a
positive nature) help to experience, to learn how to interact, to understand, and to accept other individuals—from dissimilar backgrounds and
perhaps even those within the same culture. In my case, the catalyst was
clearly participation in an exchange program abroad, meeting people from
other backgrounds who had a positive influence upon me, and subsequently falling in love with someone of a quite different origin. So, being
born into an intercultural situation may not guarantee or provide enough
of a positive or transformative experience to produce a change of attitude,
of knowledge, of world view, of accepting others who are different.
Additional life experiences also affect one's trajectory.

Clearly, many events may provoke a paradigm shift. Whichever of many
paths may lead one to intercultural understanding and/or to work in the

intercultural field, of one thing I feel certain: Expanding my experience beyond my original cultures and languages (and providing the same for my children who have also benefitted greatly by accompanying my wife and me during many of our intercultural sojourns) has greatly enriched all of our lives, our knowledge of other peoples, and our comfort and enjoyment of diversity.

In the end, one must learn to accept one's own ethnicity and learn to accept (even better: to enjoy) that of others. And I believe that intercultural communicative competence also enhances and contributes to improving *interpersonal* relations. For these reasons, the field of intercultural communication is a most important, worthwhile, and exciting endeavor, a career path that enriches life, and one that contributes to better relations among people both *across* cultures and *within* cultures—a field of study and a career path that helps lead to acceptance of all people, of diverse races, ethnicities, and religions, and helps individuals to become better human beings. Indeed, the ultimate goal is for one to be comfortable in the world and to fall in love with all of humanity. I'll conclude with a phrase I have begun to see recently which captures these thoughts well: *Un planeta, una humanidad* (One planet, one humanity)!

Alvino E. Fantini has no conflicts of interest to declare that are relevant to the content of this chapter.

References

Bennett, M. (1997). How Not to Be a Fluent Fool. In A. E. Fantini (Ed.), *New Ways in Teaching Culture* (pp. 16–21). TESOL.

Dorren, G. (2018). *Babel: Around the World in Twenty Languages*. Atlantic Monthly Press.

Fantini, A. E. (1993, Aug/Sept). A Survey of Intercultural Communication Courses in Communiqué. SIETAR Newsletter.

Fantini, A. E. (1995). International Journal of Intercultural Relations, Special Issue: Language, Culture, and World View. Vol. 19, No. 2.

Fantini, A. E. (2019). *Intercultural Communicative Competence in Educational Exchange: A Multinational Perspective*. Routledge.

Madsen, W. (1964). *The Mexican Americans of South Texas*. Holt, Rinehart and Winston.

CHAPTER 7

Intercultural Opportunities: Catching On, Fitting In, Giving Back

Sandra M. Fowler

As Mae West purportedly said: "You only live once, but if you do it right once is enough." I'm not sure I did it right, but it has been a good life, filled with challenging work, a loving family, supportive friends and colleagues, loads of international travel, opportunities, and plenty of peak experiences. I hope all of that comes through in what follows.

GETTING STARTED

At age 4, I ran away from home. Maybe not running exactly—but the effect was the same. While my mother was gardening in the backyard I wandered to the front and saw neighborhood friends a year older heading down the hill. I joined the group and walked with them to Laurelton Grammar School. I went into the kindergarten room, felt like I fit right in, and sat down ready for school. In fact, I was convinced that is where I should be.

With my long blonde curls and looking a lot like Shirley Temple, people had warned my mother that I could be a target for kidnapping so I'm

S. M. Fowler (✉)
Carlsbad, CA, USA

© The Author(s), under exclusive license to Springer Nature Switzerland AG 2025
S. M. Fowler, D. C. Yalowitz (eds.), *Creating the Intercultural Field*,
https://doi.org/10.1007/978-3-032-01370-5_7

sure that crossed my mother's mind as she searched in vain for me in the neighborhood. The situation resolved when the kindergarten teacher realized I wasn't one of her students and in addition to my name, I was able to tell her my address and phone number.

Reflecting on my life, I realize that *fitting in* was a key concept for me because so often over the years I either felt that I didn't fit in or felt that I had to work hard to make it so. I was also very shy—and still am—which added to the challenge of making a place for myself in a lifetime of myriad moves and changes. Considering the meaning of *fitting in*, it seems that in the beginning I easily yielded to the pressure to adapt to the group. Most likely it was because my identity was still evolving. As I became more grounded in who I was, the recurrent tension between me as an individual and the individual who others wanted me to be (like them) became even more challenging.

Growing up in a peaceful suburb of Rochester, NY, my neighborhood had little drama and some diversity but not much. My mother, a former teacher in a 1-room rural schoolhouse, became a full-time homemaker when she married. My father was a broadcast executive by day and a musician with his dance band on the weekends. His instrument was the piano and his musical genre was the standards, or golden oldies. That meant piano lessons for me for 8 years at the Eastman School of Music in Rochester, NY. I could read music but did not have one iota of his incredible talent.

My ancestral background has always seemed plain-vanilla American because many members on both sides of my family immigrated to prerevolutionary America. My ancestors were English, Irish, and German but that early group arrived long ago and by the time I came along no one in the extended family spoke anything but English or remembered the old country.

When I was 12 my family moved into a new house just outside the village of Pittsford (a very white suburb of Rochester). So, in the middle of 7th grade, I moved away from friends I had known since before starting school to a place where the kids were a very close-knit group having had that same experience of growing up together. This was my first challenging experience of *fitting in*.

I loved school and was good at it, so it didn't take long to find a circle of friends and I became a leader in some ways. The Brighton-Pittsford Post invited me to write a column of school news for the local newspaper—my first publication and the beginning of my writing career. I joined in on all the things one can do in high school: co-edited the annual year-book for our senior class, had a lead in the senior class play, was a junior cheerleader and majorette, and represented the school both on the hockey field and for a city-wide organization. In 1956, I headed to the University of Rochester for my freshman year, planning to be a fine arts major and eventually open an art gallery in New York City or London. Feeling good about my prospects but not knowing tragedy would soon strike and change the trajectory of my life.

At the end of September, my mother had a massive stroke that put her in the hospital, and she never left. Mid-November after two more brain bleeds, she died. That began the emotional labor of coping with loss. It also played its part in my next life event.

The Next Phase

By Valentine's Day 1957, I was married and pregnant. Would that have happened if my mother had not died? Of course, we will never know but I had become emotionally dependent on the man I'd been dating, Bob Mumford, who was lovingly helpful and supportive. We discussed options which were scant in those days and decided to get married and continue the pregnancy. On Valentine's Day, we eloped to marry in the Presbyterian Church in Mumford, NY. We needed to keep the marriage secret since Bob was a senior in NROTC (Naval Reserve Officers' Training Corps) and all midshipmen had to sign an agreement not to marry prior to graduation. Another life change was on the horizon and the first of many domestic moves. Bob's first assignment was to the USS Valley Forge, an aircraft carrier, homeported in Norfolk, VA. That June I left my dad and sister, the three of us still grieving the loss of my mother, facing the challenge of *fitting into* a new life as a Navy wife and expectant mother—two things I knew nothing whatsoever about.

Living in the South, learning Navy lingo, figuring out how to establish a household, and preparing for Jim to be born in late October were indeed challenging. Also, I was only 19 years old compared to the other officer wives. What saved me was books. I have always loved reading and quickly found that a mobile library came to the parking lot of a nearby grocery store. Each week while waiting for the baby to be born, I would take out as many books as I could carry home and absorb them.

The importance of books. The very first book I took out of the school library in second grade was a geography book detailing various facts about a variety of countries. Writing that book report, I was awed by the variety that existed in the world. I read a dozen or more original Oz books losing myself in the land of Oz, that my dad had received from his parents for birthdays and holidays. I still have those books that started a love of fantasy and science fiction that continues today. My first adult book was *The Egyptian* by Finnish author Mika Waltari, quite inappropriate for a 12 year old at least in those days, These books that I so clearly remember presented cultures other than the one I was living in.

More fitting in. The Navy moved us every year or so necessitating more adapting and *fitting in* as we crossed the country several times. My daughter, Monica, came along in 1960 while we were stationed in Boulder, CO, making us a family of four. Navy life is a lesson in how to move, make friends, then leave them behind. It also forced me to become independent.

An event that stands out occurred when we were stationed for the first time in Washington, DC in the mid-1960s. As a volunteer for the Maryland Fair Housing Commission I stuffed envelopes and handed out pamphlets, including in my suburban Maryland neighborhood of Kensington. After our For Sale sign went up, a few neighbors came with an offer to "save the neighborhood" if we were to sell to a Black family. I was disappointed, shocked, and angry at that request. It was a transformative moment that led to lifelong support for fair and equal social justice.

My first time living in San Diego was busy raising two bright, wonderful children and finishing my bachelor's Degree majoring in psychology at San Diego State University. Because of the war, the squadron spent a lot of time in the waters off Vietnam and I learned a lot more about independence. Following that tour of duty, we returned to the East Coast, Washington, DC.

Another transformative event happened in March 1970 when I was diagnosed with stage 2 melanoma and the surgeon at Bethesda Naval Hospital told Bob that I had a 20% chance of surviving a year. That message paralyzed me at first, then made me begin taking one day at a time, trying to make it count. It also meant that I acted on a long-held desire to travel to other countries, so we spent two weeks traveling in Switzerland and France leaving me eager for more. I am so glad that I beat those odds.

MY CAREER PATH

Typically, people who become interculturalists have significant experiences living in a country other than the one listed on their passport that inspires them to create a career working interculturally. I lived in many places in the United States that were significantly different from each other such as Tennessee and California or Norfolk, VA and Boulder, CO—but not outside the continental United States. I don't have a second language other than high school Latin and French which I continued in college. They did show me how language impacts how one sees the world.

I entered the intercultural field primarily through research. My career arc can aptly be described as *research into practice*, a phrase Janet Bennett used a lot to describe what the intercultural field should be. It also fits with my psychology degree since *research to practice* is a hallmark of psychology as well. My career began in research, moved to practice managing the U.S. Navy's intercultural program, and finally transitioned to independent consulting and training. With each new job, I felt like a sponge soaking up whole new ways of seeing and understanding. I was seeing the impact of culture on norms, values, assumptions and language without having the conceptual background to recognize what they were.

Each of my early projects comprised the transformational learning that pushed me into the intercultural field. The cancer scare made me think about what I wanted to pack into the little time I might have left so I abandoned plans for a PhD realizing that I wanted a taste of the world of work. My first job was as *office girl* for an auto body shop. Fortunately, after a few months of that, I got a call from a friend at the Department of Labor informing me that the Applied Psychology Division of the National Bureau of Standards was hiring people with bachelor's degrees in psychology for a project. I applied.

Washington, DC (1970–1973)

The Bureau of Standards was created by Congress to do research for other government departments. It is perhaps best known for its work on measurements of all sorts, but for a number of years, it had an applied psychology division. My first project was a review of the world's literature on psychological aspects of underground mining for the Department of the Interior. Mining personnel go wherever the mines are, so over time they create their own multicultural lives and their own culture.

The research team leader hired a woman to do translations for us since she was fluent in 11 languages. Meeting Vera Forbes was transformational. Vera and I spent many days at the Library of Congress, searching the world's literature for articles and books that pertained to our research topic. An early lesson regarding language was when Vera asked that we not switch languages during the day explaining that each language has more than just the vocabulary, also a flow, rhythm, and world perspective. Vera would select a language, and I would explore the card catalog (a paper card search) for that country's mining literature seeking any title seemingly related to psychology. For the articles that piled up in our carrel, she would translate the abstract (which rarely was in English) then I would write a brief description of those articles that made the cut. Vera was an amazing woman.

Her story is worth its own book—as a young child, she walked out of Russia escaping with her mother during the revolution of Red October (1917). She opened my eyes to the very personal impact of culture, taught me a lot about language and she was my first mentor—we became friends.

The second Bureau of Standards project commissioned by LEA (the Law Enforcement Agency) was to analyze a survey of all law enforcement agencies in the United States regarding their experiences and perceptions of their equipment. Respondents included everyone from county sheriffs to urban police to state police and beyond. When we found an anomaly, we had to call the department and ask what was meant by their response. Yet another culture for which I learned the lingo.

My final Bureau of Standards project was on a Peace Corps contract. This was total intercultural immersion. I was on a team conducting a cost/benefit analysis of PRIST (Pre-Invitational Staging). At that time Peace Corps used Invitational Staging in which they vetted applicants based on their written information, phone calls to references, and with the candidate. If accepted, the person received a letter informing them that they were invited to a specific program in X country and had to report to a training location such as Ponce, Puerto Rico or Hilo, Hawaii on Y date. Peace Corps much preferred PRIST wherein candidates were invited to a location in the United States where staff did general intercultural training and had a chance to observe the applicants in person prior to assignment. Training had not yet moved in-country, so no one at Peace Corps headquarters had laid eyes on the candidate before they arrived at a training site such as Ponce, Puerto Rico, or St. Thomas. The extra step that PRIST inserted into the process cost more money, and Congress, with tightfisted fiscal oversight, requested that Peace Corps support the extra cost with evidence that it worked. I spent a lot of time at Peace Corps headquarters in DC, met interculturalists like Ed Stewart and Jim McCaffery interviewed trainees at the training site on St. Thomas, and on-site volunteers in Colombia. Our recommendation at the end of the study was to continue PRIST for the locations with high early return rates but go back to invitational staging for sites that had fewer early returns.

Did I know during my time at the Bureau of Standards that I was dealing with a series of cultures? Probably not because I was just learning the vocabulary to frame it that way. It was clear that the Peace Corps project dealt with culture, and although I hadn't reached the perspective that I have now—I was *catching on* to what culture means and its influence. As I look back, I realize that mining, law enforcement, and Peace Corps themselves were indeed cultures. Each one required learning something about their cultures including their "language" to *fit in* at least enough to manage the work. At the time, what I did know was that I was learning a lot about research and loved it. Most of my early projects were qualitative with some quantitative research mixed in. They provided a good foundation in analytical skills, team building, interviewing techniques, data collection, and organizational dynamics, focused on how culture affects getting the job done.

Mid-Career

Bob's next set of orders moved us back to San Diego. My boss at the Bureau of Standards connected on my behalf with contacts at the Navy Personnel Research and Development Center (NPRDC) so a job was waiting for me. After getting the kids in school, I enrolled in a graduate program at San Diego State University in organizational psychology. Working with multi-national organizations was my goal.

Working at NPRDC was a plum job for me. I already understood something about Navy culture, and I brought a research background to my first project in which I was quickly immersed: determining selection criteria for overseas duty. At last, I had a sense of *fitting in*.

San Diego (1973–1979)

During my 8 years of research at the Navy Personnel Research and Development Center (NPRDC) on Point Loma in San Diego, I worked on a variety of projects. The most major was the overseas duty selection process. When *doing* research, one *reads* a lot of research to find out what is known about a topic, in this case, *selection*. Unlike intercultural literature (which at the time was small) the selection literature was vast. The team closely examined the selection process for such organizations as Peace Corps and the State Department but none of them fit the military.

The Chief of Naval Operations, Elmo Zumwalt at that time, had established a program that homeported ships in places like Naples, Italy and Yokosuka, Japan. After several incidents in Piraeus between U.S. Navy individuals and Greek citizens, the Navy was eager to prevent such misbehavior. It was decided that a simulation of Greek culture could be used to assess how well enlisted and officers potentially stationed in Greece would do. The team I joined had found Garry Shirts and contracted with him to create such a simulation. About the time that he got started, an incident in Yokosuka required the research team to switch the focus to Japan. It was Garry who suggested that a culture-general simulation was what was needed since it could be used for anywhere in the world where U.S. Navy personnel were assigned. The outcome was the classic simulation game: *BaFa BaFa*.

My job was to develop behaviorally anchored rating scales for *BaFa BaFa*. The rating scales were to be used to score people while they were participating in the simulation game so that information could be added to their personnel files and used when they were being considered for overseas duty. I worked closely with Garry Shirts to ensure that the game was interculturally sound, and we were pleased when the Navy began using the game for training and dropped the selection idea. The simulation was welcomed by the training community beyond the Navy and since I was familiar with *BaFa Bafa* I began to get requests to run it. That was my introduction to training. I had no training to be a trainer, so I have to admit that I was not good at it. It took a while for me to learn to respond to questions during the game with "it's up to you" and mean it. Debriefings at first made me nervous so I either too lightly guided them or rigourously followed my set of questions with no exceptions. Fortunately, *BaFa BaFa* was robust enough to withstand my ineptitude. After running it hundreds of times, I got better at it.

The Navy dropped *BaFa BaFa* for selection going instead to a protocol to assess the level of sending an individual to an overseas assignment, i.e., we switched the focus from selecting who should go to identifying those who should not. Navy personnel are supposed to be worldwide assignable at all times, but realistically they aren't.

An example of a minor project for the Greek effort was to provide sailors with a *kit* that would help them understand Greek culture when they docked at Piraeus or were assigned to the base. The kit included a language slide card, a tape so the sailors could listen to how the words sounded, and a graphic story of Brent Folsom's (where the title of BaFa BaFa came from) experiences in Athens. That project led to meeting Harry Triandis, a respected Greek American author and researcher—another mentor and friend.

While working full time for the Navy I completed my Masters' Thesis using the Navy's humongous Human Resource Management database to create a matched sample of female and male officers. Much as I loved working for the Navy, there were instances of being disregarded as a petite, female civilian unless my ideas were expressed by a male uniformed colleague. I was a timid but ardent feminist, so I chose not to make waves.

One day in 1978, a female colleague at NPRDC said that she did not want to measure her life by the size of a stack of government reports on her bedside table. She had decided to take a year off and travel the world. I thought that was one of the bravest things I'd ever heard and began pondering those transformational words. My daughter Monica was graduating from high school and didn't have plans for what was next. We decided to buy an old VW van and began preparing to leave for a year of adventures while driving around North America.

What Monica didn't know was that had I had just heard that the head of the Overseas Duty Support Program (ODSP), previously known as the Intercultural Relations Program and then the Navy Ambassador Program before becoming ODSP, was leaving and the position was open for application. I jumped on it! But I was told that over 40 people applied for this intercultural job, so I wasn't sure I'd get it. As our plans for our year of wandering proceeded, I heard that I got the job and then I had to tell Monica I couldn't go. It took days to pluck up enough courage, but she was understanding and supportive. I packed my car, said goodbye to my two kids who would stay in San Diego (Bob and I had separated heading for divorce), and drove east looking forward to a new chapter.

Washington, DC (1979 to 1989)

Just before leaving San Diego, I had joined Running Psychologists because I had been running for exercise the past few years and had run my first marathon. I sent my application form to Ray Fowler; the founder and president of Running Psychologists who wrote back and suggested the next time he was in San Diego we might run together. I responded that I was moving to DC and gave him my phone number in case he ever got to DC. I had no idea that Ray Fowler was a fairly well-known clinical psychologist and was active in American Psychological Association governance, which meant that he came to DC often. Meeting Ray was a hugely transformative experience. We met in 1979 and were married on Cinco de Mayo in 1984. He changed my life and helped to make me a better person. Our 31 years together were life changing. We were well suited for each other, sharing many of the same interests. Our embrace of physical fitness through running (and ultimately walking) as well as other forms of exercise have allowed me to remain active well into my 80s. I don't remember how many marathons Ray ran but I did three. After his divorce, Ray's offspring were concerned that he would never find anyone suitable for him who liked to run, was a vegetarian, was involved in psychology, and had an international perspective. After my divorce, my kids worried that I would never find anyone who could handle me. We made both sets of offspring happy (Fig. 7.1).

As head of the Overseas Duty Support Program, I got to use my master's degree in Organizational Psychology every day. My goal was to expand the program in both scope and content and embed it within the Navy organizational structure. I organized the program according to an overseas transition cycle for personnel assigned to foreign duty stations. In addition, I contracted with Michael Tucker, then of CRE (Center for Research and Education) to create the Navy Overseas Assignment Inventory (NOAI), a pre-curser to the Tucker OAI, that we could use to assess the youngest sailors holding overseas orders but little experience. The NOAI was used for seasoned naval personnel as well.

Did I finally feel that I *fit in*? Not immediately. A group of government agencies had formed the Interagency Intercultural Roundtable that met monthly in person. I attended my first Roundtable meeting in my beige California pantsuit with a long flowing scarf. All the women at the meeting were in grey suits with skirts. I went shopping that weekend! The topic

Fig. 7.1 Sandy & Ray in Washington, DC

of that meeting hosted by Joan Wilson at the State Department was re-entry.

Upon arriving in DC in 1979 I had no idea what I would find. What I found was a buzzing hub of intercultural communication. It seemed that new programs were being developed weekly; generosity and sharing were unbelievable. It was like living and working in an intercultural stew. That meant that I could bring new ideas like re-entry to the Navy's program as I translated what I was learning into ways to help both uniformed personnel and family members destined for overseas duty as they transitioned to living in a culture other than the one on their passport. My focus at that time (as was true throughout much of my career) was on the application of intercultural knowledge, principles, and theories that could lead to both individual success and concurrently organizational success for the Navy abroad.

The intercultural field was so new that for trainers, both content and process were evolving and expanding rapidly. Trainers were adapting educational methods from other fields such as case studies from business and role plays from psychology to work with their trainees. New methods for intercultural training were also created such as the Contrast American exercise using an actor (very often Cajetan DeMello) to portray a businessman, boss, or colleague from a culture other than U.S. American. The Culture Assimilator took advantage of research and interviews to create Critical Incidents that provided answers from the perspective of the foreigner to questions about what happened.

There was a lot of sharing. I remember Bob Kohls spending several hours with Fanchon Silberstein and me showing us how he used newsprint on an easel to display his ideas and concepts in training. He was rather artistic and felt it was important to make his charts attractive. Yes, newsprint was the medium that we used most of the time along with an overhead projector to project one transparency at a time on a screen. I used a cocktail stirrer shaped like an arrow that they served with drinks on airplanes on the glass of the projector to point out things on the screen.

We often gathered when interculturalists visited DC, or for SIETAR DC meetings, the Interagency Roundtable, or other spontaneous reasons. At these meetings we grappled with such questions as: How do we know if what we are doing makes a difference? What can we use as a measure of success (the criterion question)? What is the best sequence and length of a training program? We examined every piece of what we were doing.

Learning from other interculturalists improved my ability to do my job since I was absorbing ideas, techniques, and experiences as well as how to talk with and question Navy personnel with overseas experience to discover their lessons learned and what could have helped.

Sitting in a Syracuse diner decades ago with Paul Pedersen (former SIETAR International president) he casually said that "people in other cultures are not wrong; just different." Why do I remember that? That example stands out in my memory, but as only one of many such ideas that came from talking with other interculturalists and reading Edward T. (Ned) Hall's books that opened the vast cultural dimension for understanding people. I believe that we were all trying to understand other people and the role culture plays in who they are.

Something else that affected how I thought about the intercultural field was the way interculturalists were using the bell curve (adapted from statistics) to explain differences and similarities between cultures. It fit my research perspective and allowed me to play with the statistics in ways that made so much sense in my thinking about norms, values, and stereotypes. It grounded my perception of culture in a visual way that both appealed to me and helped me understand better the relationships between cultures and intercultural concepts. I am a visual learner and like models and diagrams. George Renwick was adamant that people don't remember models and diagrams, so they help us trainers but not the people who come to our programs. I always felt that the models (like the bell curve) provided a framework to help participants remember the concepts I wanted them to know about. George and I never agreed but had lively discussions over the years trying to convince each other.

Those generous sharing times did not last. As interculturalism became more of a business, more proprietary materials and methods were developed. A sense of generosity and support still lingers but not to the extent it existed in the early days of the field.

The Later Career Years

After 18 years of working for the government, I realized that I was taking too much leave-without-pay to travel to international meetings with Ray. So, I gave notice and left my position with the Navy at the end of 1989 to try my hand at consulting and training which I thought would give me more free time for international travel (it turned out to be a false assumption). At about that time, Ray was recruited to head the psychology department at the University of Tennessee in Knoxville. As I searched for a project to keep me busy, Diane Zeller, who was the SIETAR International Executive Director, suggested that I update the *Intercultural Sourcebook: Cross-Cultural Training Methodologies* by David Hoopes and Paul Ventura (1972) that SIETAR had published. That suited me just fine and kept me very busy for the next 5 years as I reformatted the *Intercultural Sourcebook: Cross Cultural Training Methods Vol. 1 (1995) and Vol. 2 (1998)* changed the title slightly, and invited over 50 authors to write chapters, creating the 2-volume set. My editor was Peggy Pusch gave me a master class in editing, but her philosophy of editing was different from mine. She used a heavy red pencil, and I tried to keep the author's voice. We worked well together, both of us getting some of what we wanted, and improving both volumes.

International travel increased. Ray and I went to China half a dozen times starting in the early to mid-1980s as it opened to the Western world, and all over Europe and Australia for international meetings, to New Zealand for a sabbatical, and a lecture tour in post-apartheid South Africa. Consulting went well for a number of years until I became aware that I preferred finding the best person for a prospective client instead of doing the work myself. I *retired* while remaining professionally active, taking an occasional paying job but mostly referring other trainers and consultants.

I kept one client for 11 years: Dr. Simon Auster of the United States University of the Health Services (USUHS) which was the medical school that conferred MD degrees on graduates who were in the Armed Forces and public health. We did *BaFa BaFa* for the first-year students on the 1st day of classes for Simon's class. The debriefing was oriented toward their medical careers and the military context in which they would be working. For example, we devised a role play for the debriefing between an Alpha doctor and a Beta patient and vice versa. If you don't know the simulation game, this might not mean much except that you can imagine that Alpha and Beta were quite different cultures, so you would have an idea of how those role plays might go. Culture clash. Since there were over 170 students and Simon wanted the faculty to run the simulation, I hired a group of intercultural consultants familiar with the exercise to provide backup for the doctors. Simon used to say that organizing BaFa BaFa came close to Battle of Normandy proportions. After a few years, I invited Judee Blohm to join me as a co-coordinator which worked brilliantly, and gained importance after Ray and I moved from DC to La Jolla, CA. The consultants bonded and it went well until USUHS administrators decided to reorganize the medical training according to organ systems and canceled Simon's class. Simon Auster was a polymath and one of the most amazing individuals on my lifetime list of extraordinary people.

Giving Back

As I am reaching the end of my 80s, I realize there are several elements that wove together to create the tapestry of my career. Knowledge accrued as each job taught me so much and was a springboard for the next job. But a series of jobs isn't all there is to a career. Besides the jobs, the components that were important to me were: involvement in professional associations, training, fine art, and writing. The IJIR journal article Training Across Cultures (n.d.) wove together two important elements.

Professional Associations

Professional associations provide context for our work, they are great resources for networking, and they are a form of recognition that we are serious about what we do. I seem drawn to professional organizations: the American Psychological Association, the International Association of Applied Psychology, and as a member of the International Academy of Intercultural Research, I served for many years on their Membership Committee and more recently on the Ombudsman Committee.

SIETAR. I had heard about SIETAR while still in San Diego from some Navy Lieutenants who attended the first SIETAR conference in Gaithersburg to demonstrate *BaFa BaFa*. But at that time, I was much more interested in the North American Simulation and Gaming Association (NASAGA) and joined that group, attending some of their conferences and eventually serving on their Board of Directors and receiving their Ifill-Reynolds Award for Lifetime Achievement. I also wrote a column for their newsletter (*Simulation/Gaming*) that I titled *Beyond Sexism Through Gaming.*

It struck me that SIETAR might help figure out what I could do to improve and reconstitute the ODSP according to my vision. I talked my Commanding Officer into sending me to Mexico City where they were holding the 1979 conference, and it was a bonanza of people I needed to know It was total immersion in SIETAR. I also joined SIETAR DC, quite new then but now the oldest active Local Group in SIETAR's history. The conferences and meetings were a rich source of ideas for improving the Navy's program. I have attended every conference since 1979 except 2015, the year that Ray died.

SIETAR International was like coming home—finally the apotheosis of *fitting in.* Some lingering feeling like an imposter due to my lack of over-seas living experience was bothersome. One of the main things I felt was that SIETAR offers a professional identity. SIETAR is a professional group of interculturalists so to my way of thinking, membership in that group confers that identity. Of course, you must have the experience and knowl-edge to back that up.

SIETAR International and later SIETAR USA have had some very good years and managed to ride out the bad years. Balkanizing SIETAR International into smaller national and regional groups was a difficult period. Introducing DEIB (Diversity, Equity, Inclusion, Belonging) into the center of SIETAR USA did not go smoothly and still causes some unhappiness. I was one of the early resisters who thought SIETAR USA should be reserved for interculturalists since DEIB professionals have their own associations. My thinking changed as I saw the potential for SIETAR to be a bridge between the two disciplines. DEIB needs the intercultural approach which can work well to help people understand diversity and intercultural needs the DEIB content that we mostly ignored for many decades.

SIETAR has been helpful to me, so I wanted to give back to it and took on a variety of tasks for the Board of Directors. The list is long but provides examples of what kinds of activities one can be involved in with a professional association. An early responsibility was organizing a blue ribbon panel to explore the possibility of SIETAR International developing and conducting a certification program for interculturalists. We concluded that SIETAR International was not the organization to carry it out for an array of reasons. I've been an active participant and stalwart supporter of the Ethics and Awards Committee for both International and USA. I chaired the Election Committee several times, organized pre-conference workshops, and spearheaded the 1993 conference at the Omni Hotel in DC where I organized a separate day to highlight diversity and inclusion. I was honored to serve as the SIETAR International President in the late 1980s when the conferences were in Amsterdam and Ottawa where I got to sit next to Edward T. Hall at the final banquet. I was starstruck! (Fig. 7.2)

Peggy Pusch can be credited for forming SIETAR USA and I helped. We ran focus groups, developed a charter and by-laws, then later drafted the Standing Rules. I co-chaired the program committee with Robert Kohls for the year 2000 inaugural SIETAR USA conference in Fairfax, VA, chaired the 2003 conference in Washington, DC, then co-chaired the 2011 conference in Denver with Sue Shinomiya, and co-chaired with Janet Bennett the 2017 conference in San Diego. Organizing the preconference/Master workshops for five years was fulfilling. Serving as SIETAR USA President in 2019–2021 I started several initiatives, recruited a diverse Board that was very active resulting in an increased membership, and initiated a conference in Atlanta with the help of Karen Lokkesmoe as Conference Chair, followed by our first virtual conference in 2020. That provides an idea of the scope of my participation in my favorite organization.

Training

As my training skills improved, training became an important part of my career. Although I often worked by myself, I liked teaming up with other trainers, most often with Fanchon Silberstein. We designed training sessions for a variety of institutions and events such as SIETAR International

Fig. 7.2   Peggy and Sandy in Japan for a SIETAR International Conference

and SIETAR USA conferences, the Phillips Collection, and the National MultiCultural Institute and as a 3-day workshop for SIIC (Summer Institute for Intercultural Communication). Our mutual interest in fine art stimulated us to develop a number of training activities using fine art and at Janet Bennett's invitation, we took them to the SIIC for several years.

The Art Thread

Starting out as a fine arts major back in Rochester, I had put my interest in art on the back burner as I turned to psychology and then interculturalism. Working with Fanchon using art in training felt like returning to my

Fig. 7.3   Fanchon and Sandy at their SIIC art workshop

roots. It felt like I was picking up a thread that had dropped many years before (Fig. 7.3).

Returning one summer from our workshop at SIIC, I was talking with my husband Ray about how excited we had been at the response to our workshop. As CEO of the American Psychological Association (APA) and Editor in Chief, he instituted fine art on the cover of the *American Psychologist*, the flagship journal of APA, in their centennial year, 1992. At my request, he agreed for me to select artwork for the cover and write an essay to accompany the art. The Managing Editor liked what I did and asked me to continue. Ray agreed but he was concerned about the perception of nepotism, so he had me write the essays under Sandra Mumford.

After a few years, I was pleased to learn that Kate Hays, a performance psychologist in Toronto and someone I got to know during the 5K races at the APA conventions, was interested in writing some of the art essays. We formed a co-editing team that lasted until her death in spring 2022. I finished that year, but it wasn't the same without Kate and after 23 years of being the Art Co-Editor, I helped find successors and resigned. My work as the Art Co-Editor for the *American Psychologist* was always a joy especially when psychologists told me that *On the Cover* was the first thing they read.

Writing

Ikigai! My *aha moment* during an *ikigai* workshop with Sue Shinomiya was realizing I am a writer. As I understand, *ikigai* is the passion that fills your being. It is what you live for and how you contribute to the world. It is the strongest thread weaving its way through my life. While I am not one of the most prolific intercultural writers, I have published over a dozen intercultural articles and chapters as well as editing the two volumes of the *Intercultural Sourcebook: Cross-Cultural Training Methods.* I'm pleased with that record even knowing that does not come close to Craig Storti or Jack Condon's record number of publications—of which I am in awe.

Creating and contributing to newsletters was a recurring activity throughout my lifetime. For SIETAR International I wrote articles for their newsletter *Communique* while also writing the newsletter for SIETAR DC for several years. At the beginning of SIETAR USA in the year 2000, I edited its newsletter for several years before handing it off to Monica Marcel who at that time was head of LCW (Language and Culture Worldwide). Then in 2019 while president of SIETAR USA, I created a periodical called *The Interculturalist: A Periodical of SIETAR USA.* At the suggestion of Tatyana Fertelmeyster, we called it a *periodical* since it included serious content as well as news about what was happening in the organization. It was more than a newsletter, but it was deemed too long for current generations to read so we shortened the number and length of the articles and changed the name to *The "I": A periodical of SIETAR USA* and I edited that for another year.

Did It Make a Difference?

The world is a mess right now, some parts worse than others. Our goal to make the world a better place was a bit lofty, and we can't claim total success. However, between training and research and writing, I know that we have had some individual successes. Families who thrived overseas because of preparation they received at the Overseas Briefing Center for example, and businesspersons who were effective in running joint ventures with China because of George Renwick, and of course so many others. Making life better for individuals and families does count in the grand scheme.

Interculturalists have not had the opportunity to work with despots and autocrats, so we made no headway with them. However, as you read Steve Rhinesmith's autobiography and his work as a cultural ambassador to Russia, perhaps when he was allowed to do his work, it did make a difference.

Much of our work has had a ripple effect thus we have no idea how many people benefited from our training. I did not do hands-on training for Navy personnel assigned overseas but the Navy trainers who I trained and counseled were the boots on the ground and likely made quite a difference. Intercultural research informed the training and coaching so there was some effect from the work done by Richard Brislin, Milton Bennett, Michael Paige and many more. We don't know all the readers of our books and how the books might have influenced their lives and work. I like to think that our presence in the world has made some difference, maybe not as much as we hoped for but for the people who encountered us, perhaps a very big difference.

Are my thoughts rationalizations because it's too painful to think that everything I did counts for nothing? I don't think so. I remember the positive responses I received over the years and like to recall how good it felt to know that some people seemed to really get what I was trying to do to help make the world a better place for them.

Summing Up

Going through my filing cabinets to write this autobiography stirred up so many memories—so many people, so many projects in the intercultural field—so many lifetime friends and new friends spread across the globe. And so many opportunities that I grabbed onto as they charted new paths.

Nothing I did was done alone. The support of family, colleagues, friends, and—most of all—the interculturalists was the wind beneath my wings. Their warm welcome, generosity, caring, and willingness to share what they knew have been so characteristic of people in the intercultural field. It meant that I've had a good life and a most satisfying career. At the beginning of my career, I thought of myself as an organizational psychologist with a keen interest in international, multinational organizations but didn't start out to be an interculturalist. In the middle of the twentieth century interculturalism was just emerging as an academic and professional field. That is different now. Becoming an interculturalist is a clear option with educational programs, internships, and good jobs. It's now a choice and one that I would choose again!

Sandra M. Fowler has no conflicts of interest to declare that are relevant to the content of this chapter.

REFERENCES

Fowler, S. (n.d.). *Training across cultures.* International Journal of Intercultural Relations (IJIR).

Fowler, S., & Mumford, M. (1995). *The intercultural sourcebook: Cross-cultural training methods* (Vol. 1). The Intercultural Press.

Fowler, S., & Mumford, M. (1998). *The intercultural sourcebook: Cross-cultural training methods* (Vol. 2). The Intercultural Press.

Hoopes, D., & Ventura, P. (1972). *The intercultural sourcebook: Cross-cultural training methodologies.* SIETAR International.

CHAPTER 8

Regular Guy, Scientist, Bridge, Peacemaker… Interculturalist

V. Robert Hayles

Imagine a very diverse group of people from different locations stranded together in a cold place. Many did not trust or even hated others in the group. As night fell, one person gathered dry wood and started a fire to keep warm. That person asked others to gather wood and add it to the fire. Many refused saying "if I add my wood to the fire, my enemies will also get warm…so I refuse." Somehow one person was able to *lead* everyone to contribute wood to the fire.

I heard a story like this many years ago and it serves as an analogy for life and work. How my fellow contributors to this book came to demonstrate such extraordinary leadership is unique to each person. The story above is a vision that guides my work. Cultural differences accompanied by animosity, distrust, and hatred make this challenge both more difficult and more rewarding because it has significant positive effects on individuals and groups. In severe cases lives can be saved. This chapter describes the nurturing I received that enabled me to work effectively in this field. There are many paths to that end…this was mine.

V. R. Hayles (✉)
Manzanita, OR, USA
e-mail: rhayles@nehalemtel.net

151

NURTURING YEARS

I grew up in Wichita, Kansas in an all-Black neighborhood. The time was the 50s and 60s before civil rights legislation was passed and when public services (police, fire, schools, hospitals, etc.) provided limited, hostile, or poorly resourced services to its residents. Hypervigilance, caution, and self-sufficiency were paramount. My education was in public schools with K-6 being all-Black, 7–9 being 1/3 each Hispanic, White, and Black, and 9–12 being about 90% White.

As a youngster I hunted and fished with my Dad and uncles. As a teenager I had a passion for cars. When one started out of my sight and drove off, I could tell by its sound whether it was made by Chrysler, Ford, or General Motors. I could also discern the cubic inches and horsepower of the engine. Seeing less than one-fourth of a vehicle was enough for me to determine the year, make, and model. My favorite Christmas gifts as a child and young man were a chemistry set, microscope, telescope, encyclopedias, Winchester shotgun and a rifle.

Wherever I went in Wichita, inside or outside of the Black community, I was protected. Those protectors included a cousin (who carried a 45-caliber pistol), officer McAdams (the only Black police officer in Wichita), my Dad, uncles, Mom, grandmothers, aunts, school principals, and others. Without such shields I doubt that I would have survived. Many of my friends and peers did not make it to adulthood. While shot at as a teenager, I was never hit by a bullet or stabbed with a knife. Several attempts on both counts were made before I got past my teen years. There were also many offers of support/rewards for achievement. I graduated from 9th grade as the school valedictorian. The following stories provide examples of the above.

In my 7th grade Social Studies class, I received mostly A's on my papers and tests. I did receive one B+. It should be noted here for descriptive purposes (not for stereotyping) that the teacher was a White woman. The final grade for the course was a B+. At the graduation ceremony from Junior High (9th grade), the principal said there was one student in the school with all A's in all academic subjects. As he spoke, I wondered who had such a record. I certainly did not since I had a B+ in Social Studies. He called my name and asked me to come to the stage for recognition. I refused since I believed what he had said was not true. One of the coaches I had in basketball and track said "get your butt up on that stage." I did so.

I ran home after school to tell my parents that the honor I had just received was not earned, but I did not know what to do about it. My parents then told me about how they had taken off from work (at the end of 7th grade) to show the principal my tests, papers, and assignment grades. The principal called the teacher into his office and asked my parents to wait outside. They moved closer to the door so they could hear. When the principal examined my work and asked the teacher about the final grade...she said, "Negroes don't do "A" work." The principal said, "it looks like this Negro does." He overruled the teacher and changed my grade in the official transcript. Beyond having brave and supportive parents willing to take off from work and confront a school principal, this was an early lesson about what is often required to get justice when real accomplishment may be insufficient. One must also provide objective facts and details that cannot be denied without showing obvious malice of intent. That experience nurtured the diligent scientist within me.

During my first semester of junior high school, my parents, unbeknownst to me, also went to see the principal to have me removed from a full schedule of vocational classes and placed in a more balanced curriculum including math and science. I did learn carpentry, automotive repair, and other practical skills from my Dad, uncles, grandmothers and local African American tradesmen. I am an example of why a large village of caring people is required for children to be treated fairly and realize their full potential in prejudiced and classist systems.

I continued K-12 education (completion of 8th grade was all that was legally required in Kansas) and graduated from 12th grade as the Black valedictorian for the city of Wichita. The city annually selected the "top" Black student for recognition and support independently of the integrated high school designations. In those days being a good student garnered support from many quarters in the Black community. While the above protection, recognition, and support were necessary to help one survive and succeed, extremely high expectations and pressure to perform and contribute that can last a lifetime were also created. Unlike what has often been portrayed in the media, I did not experience peer harassment or teasing for academic achievement. I had peer support instead. They often praised my academic work and affectionately teased me about being "smart." They were also forgiving when I missed a shot on the basketball court.

Even though my academic performance was good, I have never considered myself an intellectual...just a regular guy whose parents purchased a set of the Encyclopedia Britannica (probably the only one in any home in our neighborhood) and the "All About" book series popular in the 1950s and 1960s. My parents (both college-educated) were working class and over the years were employed as teachers, a postal worker, a mechanic at Boeing, and a city/state/federal civil servant. They made sure that I was prepared for the world outside of our community. They transported me across town to art classes every weekend for a year after winning an art scholarship. Music lessons were provided on the piano, organ, bugle, accordion, clarinet, and saxophone. We went to museums, national parks, and even into Canada and Mexico. Their explicit goal was for me to be able to work and get along with ALL kinds of people. Those experiences made me more comfortable as the first and frequently only Black person in many situations. It also provided what my parents called "culture." That meant exposure to the kinds of places and experiences many European Americans but only a minority of African Americans had. They thought that would prepare me to be "successful" in the world outside of the Black community, giving me broader choices. While I did have many cousins, I was an only child and got a great deal of attention and support from my parents.

During my high school years, I worked for White people (description, not stereotype) that we considered to be "rich." The notation in parentheses is included here to pre-empt the notion that I held negative or stereotyped views of people because they were White. I did housework, grilling for large events, cleaned swimming pools, car care, lawn maintenance, chauffeuring, and other odd jobs. This was in the context of hearing many stories about my paternal grandfather who had no formal education but frequently responded to potential work opportunities with "I can do that."

One of my employers, Rick Clinton (a White man...description, not stereotype), guided me as I hired a group of high school football players to clear some land for him. Mr. Clinton, CEO of an oil company, taught me how to bid for a job, supervise workers, make a fair "profit" when hiring others to work for me, and a lot about how to be an entrepreneur. He also hired me to serve food and drinks at business social events where I listened for tips on how to manage money and invest. He helped me start investing in the stock market at age 16 and continued to teach me about financial matters for several years. After graduating, he hired my college roommate. He later revealed to me that he did so primarily on my recommendation. I grew up never even thinking about the possibility of being unemployed. If there was work to be done, there was opportunity. I have held that view ever since junior high school.

My story would not be complete without describing my parents and grandparents, who taught me a lot about life and the nature of work. Rosa was my maternal Grandmother and Mamie was my paternal Grandmother. Rosa did not complete high school and raised three children as a single mother. All three of her children went to college and had families of their own. She had a low tolerance for mistreatment of herself and her grandchildren. To back up her impatience with mistreatment she owned a pistol and said "I know how to use it. So don't mess with me or my grandchildren." One day she taught me a lesson about revenge. She and I (at about 4 years of age) were walking from her home to our home. The shortest route meant walking through a White neighborhood that bordered the Black community. It was thought to be dangerous for a young Black child to take that route, so my Grandmother accompanied me. We went past a house in the White neighborhood where a young White child was playing in the yard. He threw a rock at me and called me the N-word. I wanted to throw one back at him. She said "no" and called him over to her. She whispered something to him and walked a little further with me and said, "just wait." Shortly I heard a child being spanked and crying. Grandmother and I continued our walk as I asked her what she had said. She had told the child that the N-word was a very kind thing to say, especially to someone you love. She suggested that he tell the adult in the house that they were an N-word...and to do it with a smile. I do not endorse this approach and have not used it. I fully understand that my Grandmother, who was African American, poor, not well educated, female, an elder, a descendant of slaves, and had very little power of any kind, had very few options for protecting, defending, or striking back to protect loved ones or herself.

My paternal Grandmother was also a direct descendant of slaves and lacked a high school education. She had 9 children and raised 8 into adulthood. She was very religious, worked a minimum-wage job all her adult life, grew a very large garden along with fruit trees, and raised a few chickens. Working alongside her in the garden, I learned many valuable lessons about sustainable pacing for the day or a lifetime, dealing with tragic losses (three of her children died before age 30), generosity and sacrifice (my college graduation gift consumed all of her wages for about a month), getting along with the sometimes difficult spouses of her children, and watching her children being harmed by racism. Both Grandmothers gave me perspectives and insights that enabled me to accomplish much while hopefully remaining kind, decent and humble. My maternal Grandfather, Richard Bass, lived in another part of the country and died in his 60s. My paternal Grandfather, Champion Hayles, had no formal education and worked on river boats on the Mississippi River and was a waiter on pullman railroad cars across America. He served the President of Mexico on one trip. When the President left the train, he tipped Grandfather a dime and told him "when you come to Mexico, call me and I'll give you a good time". When Grandfather did visit Mexico, the President entertained him at his home overnight. He told the grandchildren many fascinating stories about his travels. He drove from Kansas to New York at 80 years of age, and lived independently until his death at 103. We learned from him that we could do things that we had previously thought were forbidden or not possible for African Americans.

My Mother—Nancy

She was college-educated and an accomplished pianist and organist who accompanied well-known singers (including Marian Anderson) in the 1940s. She had exceptional observational powers and nurtured my intuition about people. One afternoon I brought a girl (teenager) home after a trip to the local amusement park. I walked my "date" home and when I returned, Mom asked me if I knew that she was pregnant. I did not and had no clue as to how Mom knew. From that day forward I started paying much closer attention to how she knew things that did not seem discernable by me or many others observing the same situation. What I learned from her saved me from big trouble many times later in life. She could often sense when someone had hostile intentions towards me or others. I learned to heed her warnings. It also led me to be aware of opportunities that were far from obvious.

My Dad—Robert (Sr.)

While I learned many skills from my Dad, one of the most important lessons was how to build trust with people who are different and possibly biased. He often talked about his work experiences for a wealthy family during the 1940s. At the time of our discussions, he had worked for one for less than a year. In those days cash transactions were common. One day that family directed him to deposit ten thousand dollars in cash at a local bank. For perspective, my parents paid fifteen hundred dollars for the home where I grew up. We had many long conversations about why they would trust a Black man with ten thousand dollars in cash. Understanding how that happened and the qualities of my Dad that enabled such outcomes served me well. Many years later that ability enabled me to convince a White male (noted because earning the trust of someone different can be more difficult than earning the trust of someone more similar) agency head to give me authority regarding how a million dollars in research funding should be allocated to Historically Black Colleges and Universities.

COLLEGE

Because I did not know what I wanted to do when I grew up, I pursued an undergraduate education at the University of Kansas that opened multiple futures. That included pre-med, pre-law, a minor in chemistry, and a major in psychology. During school breaks and summers I worked for DuPont as a chemist. My project was to develop a new analytical system using infrared rays to analyze products during production. This technique would allow adjustments during production and avoid having to discard non-compliant products afterwards. Looking back, this was an incredible opportunity for an undergraduate student. While I enjoyed scientific work, I especially liked the process of getting workers to implement new technology during production that I had developed in the laboratory. Ultimately, I resonated more with human and organizational development than chemistry. Psychology won out over both law and medicine. I decided on a graduate education in psychology. Medicine was a close second. Later in life I married a woman whose father was a physician. He and I had a close relationship filled with mutual love and respect. His daughter, my spouse, and I attended the same college, but did not meet then. To this day I believe that if she had taken me home to meet her parents while we were in college, I would have an M.D. instead of a Ph.D.

During college my parents moved from Wichita to Topeka, Kansas. Dad got a job with the State of Kansas Employment Service and Mom got one proofreading for a publisher. They purchased a home in a suburb of Topeka. The seller, Mr. Schwartz, was a Jewish man. Being Jewish is noted here because he was also a minority in that neighborhood. It was a lovely home on a corner lot in an otherwise all-White neighborhood. I was attending the University of Kansas in nearby Lawrence at the time. Dad asked me to come home one weekend shortly after they moved in. We had a private conversation about the fact that they had received death threats and that someone had driven a jeep through the yard and caused significant damage. His job involved travel to other parts of the state such that he would have to spend several nights each month away from home. Mom would be alone during those trips. While Dad and I had hunted together for many years, we had never discussed the use of firearms for self or home defense. He asked if I could/would come home when he travelled, sleep with a loaded gun nearby, and use it if necessary to protect Mom and our home. He said he would respect my decision. At this time in history, police protection could not be counted on by African Americans. While Mom never said anything about this situation, I'm sure she knew why I was sleeping at home and commuting to school when Dad traveled. This experience, as is true for many other vulnerable or oppressed populations, deepened my understanding of what it is like not to feel safe or have protection by official authorities. It also meant that the option of being a conscientious objector would not be available to me.

Coincidentally, Mr. Schwartz introduced me to the CEO of a book bindery in Topeka, Kansas which led to a good summer job after my freshman year.

Military Service

I graduated from college in 1970 during the Viet Nam war. Rather than being drafted, I joined the Army National Guard. I went to basic and advanced infantry training at Fort Polk, Louisiana as an enlisted person. During this time, I met another supportive White man with power. During a leave of absence for rest and relaxation at a town near Fort Polk, the proprietor of a disco refused entry to several soldiers because he said that "there will be fights if I let the "N-word" and "S-word" come in." When word of this got back to the Post Commander, he immediately put the offending establishment on the "off-limits" list. This meant that no military personnel were allowed to patronize that business. A major reduction in revenue was certain to follow. The owner of that disco immediately went to the Post Commander and showed him a photo of a sign displaying "We welcome ALL military personnel." Later during military service, I was asked to be a race-relations officer. I hesitated and resisted (uttering a few expletives quietly) but was assigned that role anyway. When I asked what I was expected to do, I was told "you have a background in psychology...figure it out." No doubt being Black was also an unspoken determinant. I applied what I knew about behavioral and organizational change to this challenge. Since I was given carte blanche by the Commander, I initiated many fun and scientifically grounded actions. They included applications of theories about the effects of multi-cultural teams having common goals, creating reward structures for group achievements in multi-racial groups, setting up training where diverse team members each brought elements required for excellent team performance, providing feedback to leaders for what years later were called "inclusive" behaviors, and so on.

Looking back, this was my first "intercultural" job. I demonstrated the superior performance potential of multi-racial units. So-called race was the only issue on the table at that time. So-called is used here because I learned later that race was only a social and not a biological variable.

Because of my individual performance and test scores during the first few months of military service I was directed to go to West Point to become an officer. I refused, which made my Commanding Officer livid. He called me names that are not appropriate for repeating here. The Army needed and wanted more Black officers, and he would have gotten credit for recruiting one. While the opportunity was supposedly based on my performance, I did not like the feeling of being recruited even in part because I was Black. I served the rest of my time in the military as an enlisted (regular guy) person. Six years seemed like enough to be considered a good and patriotic American. During my service years I became the Honor Graduate of an Army Non-Commissioned Officer Academy. My Dad and uncles (most of whom served in the military) had advised me to learn every skill possible and get out as soon as possible. I followed their advice and started graduate school in Psychology after being honorably discharged from active duty.

Sidebar. The personal experiences in this chapter speak to some of the ways I learned to work with ALL kinds of people as a peer or leader. If one can talk comfortably about matters important to a range of individuals, from hunters to trades people, businesspeople, scientists, teachers, athletes, members of hate groups, religious practitioners, atheists, etc., it might be possible to get people from many walks of life to put their wood on the fire, even though everyone around it might get warm. The above experiences also show how one can learn about healthy uses of power to make things right for those who are unable to do so for themselves.

Graduate Education

During the 1970s many people helped me in significant ways. A few are noted here that were particularly influential in the broadly defined intercultural sphere. Dr. Stuart Cook (Professor at the University of Colorado) was well-known for his research on prejudice. He influenced the Supreme Court's decision regarding school desegregation (Brown versus Board of Education). As a graduate student in psychology, I was very fortunate to have him as my advisor. He met one-on-one regularly with each of his graduate students and gave authorship credit to any student who made significant contributions to a publication. This was not true of all senior professors and showed me how one could/should behave as a mentor. In one of the courses that I took from Dr. Cook, he had students read several journal articles before each class. When they sat down for class, Dr. Cook would select an article and randomly assign one student to attack the article and one student to defend it. The debate started immediately without an opportunity to consult notes. His teaching style and approach to advising taught us how to debate and persuade. I used and applied many of his teachings and lessons in the years to come.

I knew that having a doctoral degree would allow me to help more people and have more career options. My Ph.D. thesis work demonstrated how Black students with average high school grades and entrance exam test scores who valued achievement did as well in college as those with high grades and high entrance exam test scores but lower ones on achievement values.

CAREER POSITIONS (DREAM JOBS)

My first job after graduate school was as a Research Scientist for the Battelle Human Affairs Research Center in Seattle, Washington. While working there primarily as a social scientist, my hard sciences background supported working with physical scientists doing research on energy generation and conservation technologies. There were also opportunities at Battelle to address multi-cultural mental health research.

While working at Battelle, I went to Washington, D. C. seeking funding support from the Office of Naval Research (ONR). ONR was established in 1946 to "plan, foster, and encourage scientific research" and "support science and technology research that benefits both the naval services as well as the nation."

During that research prospecting trip my last interview before going back to Seattle was with Dr. Robert V. Guthrie at ONR. He funded and managed research on intergroup relations and organizational effectiveness. After my discussion with him about the research I wanted ONR to fund, he closed the door and shared his personal plan. His home was in San Diego, California and he was about to accept a position in San Diego as a scientist at the Navy Personnel Research and Development Center. He thought I would be a perfect replacement for him at ONR and asked if I would be interested. The thought of managing millions of dollars of research on issues dear to my heart was appealing...and doing so at 28 years of age seemed unlikely. I said yes, applied for the job when Dr. Guthrie left, and accepted it when offered. Even before he knew I would get the job he shared his advice for success. He said, "do excellent work in a pleasant manner." He knew this would be essential, particularly for the only professional person of color in that office.

In this process I experienced another insight regarding how insidious racial bias can be. My first supervisor at ONR, Dr. John Nagay, shared a reference I had received from Battelle as part of my application. The last line of the reference said "Dr. Hayles is not the right person for this position." I asked why I was hired anyway. Dr. Nagay told me that he knew the person providing the reference and believed that he was trying to retain me at Battelle. I was the only Black scientist on staff and the possibility of losing me possibly motivated the provision of a bad reference. Dr. Nagay believed that it was assumed that because I was Black, I would get offered the job. This was an unsettling realization. Fortunately, he did not think that way. He put competence first and mentored me in ways that made the opportunity a dream job.

Office of Naval Research

I was allowed to make funding decisions, manage research conducted by some of the best researchers in the U.S., publish, consult to Navy and Marine Corps organizations, testify before Congress, be an Adjunct Professor of Engineering Administration at George Washington University, be active in professional organizations like SIETAR and the Association of Black Psychologists, participate in international meetings with NATO allies, and be a guest lecturer at military educational institutions. That included the Naval Postgraduate School, Air Force Academy, and Defense Systems Management College. When traveling as a civilian scientific officer for the ONR, one is treated like a high-ranking military officer, including the use of a diplomatic passport. As a former enlisted person in the Army who had only been outside the United States to Canada and Mexico, this put many smiles on my face.

During the late 70s and early 80s, while managing research for the ONR, I corresponded with Dr. Jehuda Amir, well known for his research on the *contact hypothesis*. It describes the conditions under which prejudice is most likely to be reduced. He was addressing Israeli-Palestinian relations and trying to move both groups towards peace. He shared what he was learning about "contact conditions" and I shared U.S.-based research on intergroup relations. I applied his theory to our military and civilian personnel and organizations. He applied our learnings to his work in Israel. While the scientific knowledge base regarding which conditions of contact are most likely to reduce prejudice has grown substantially since the 1970s, applications of that knowledge still seem lacking today.

Scientific findings in medicine and physical science are often slow to be translated into applications...the same thing happens in the behavioral sciences. Part of the joy of working at the ONR was the opportunity to expedite the translation of basic research into application to improve the lives of people and the effectiveness of organizations.

During my time with ONR the Navy updated its training on equal opportunity. At ONR, we were positioned as scientifically grounded subject-matter experts and were available to the Department of Navy and Marine Corps for consultation. A Navy Commander came to see me one afternoon asking how to design an updated training program about equal opportunity. I offered him coffee and treats as we sat in my office and casually talked about what a good program might contain. I mentioned things like having cognitive, affective, and behavioral components, compliance with adult learning principles, sequencing the components to build understanding, opportunities to practice what was learned, etc. I also suggested immediate and longer-term evaluations following standards published by the American Society for Training and Development. He thanked me and left. That was an enjoyable afternoon talking with a smart and eager student.

Two weeks later he returned with a thick binder saying that he had designed the program "as per my specifications." I put on my poker face while thinking "what have I gotten myself into". I had failed to understand how the military dealt with scientists, perceiving their "suggestions" as guidance. I reviewed the program thoroughly with him. It was outstanding and contained everything I had "suggested." I dropped the poker face, got excited and recommended that the program be delivered by two trainers for each session. Those trainers should be diverse in race and gender for some classes and homogeneous for others as the first few sessions were rolled out. The learning outcomes should be examined as a function of trainer demographics. We did so and very simple statistics showed that participants learned significantly more when the trainers were diverse in race and gender. It was likely that seeing individuals who are different working together helped reinforce the academic lessons about the merits of equal opportunity. After the pilot sessions it became Navy policy that all teams delivering this training be diverse in race and gender. I quickly began to understand the potential of what one could do in this military environment.

Later at ONR I used the style that I had learned from my ancestors and teachers to negotiate, often behind closed doors, for new research initiatives that addressed or benefited Navy families, Historically Black Colleges and Universities, young researchers, women on Navy ships, and multidisciplinary research teams.

A bit more should be said about Navy families. In deciding to fund a body of basic research, it was usually required that potential applications of that research be specified along with a *sponsor* for those applications. I was able to acquire funds for research regarding the impacts on sailors of the availability and use of support for their families. In general, when the family is supported, the sailor does well. I was very fortunate to find Sandy Fowler in her role leading the Navy's Overseas Duty Support Program. She became a sponsor for Navy family research and evaluation. More details on this arena can be found in Sandy's chapter in this book and in Ann O'Keefe's book *Launching The Navy Family Support Program* (2019, pp. 258–275).

In 1977–1978, David Hoopes, Paul Pedersen, and George Renwick edited a three-volume series titled *Overview of Intercultural Education, Training and Research*. They asked me to write a chapter called "Inter-Ethnic and Race Relations Education and Training". That led me to review the various theory-based approaches to training on intergroup relations. It was my first formal opportunity to catalog and draw on intercultural models and tools as well as those that came out of work on race relations. Intercultural work was strong on dealing with cultural differences. Race-relations was strong on dealing with prejudice, discrimination, racism and hatred at the individual, group, and organizational levels.

Synergy and symbiosis between intercultural and diversity work were starting to develop within me. The job at ONR was to sponsor research on
intergroup relations, scientifically determine what measurably improves
those relations, and put proven theory into practice in civilian and military
organizations in the Department of Navy. Because this was done with
public funds, the knowledge was made available free and without restric-
tion both domestically and throughout NATO countries.

In the late 1970s my involvement with the Society for Intercultural
Education, Training, and Research (SIETAR) increased along with learning more about "intercultural." It was also a time of much international
travel, and the associated growth opportunities. After helping facilitate a
SIETAR International meeting in Europe, a contingent of mostly Germans
took me aside privately and remarked that "while we appreciate how well
you help run the meetings, we are curious about why we have to use "your
rules." It took a while before I was able to communicate that a guide used
in the United States for running meetings was titled "Robert's Rules of
Order" (first published by Henry Robert in 1876). Clearly there had been
some 2-way intercultural learning. Stereotypically, Germans would have
confronted me publicly and I would have had to attempt a public diplomatic and face-saving response. The Germans chose a private conversation
where I could be direct in my response. While I constantly modified meeting processes to fit the multi-national mix of SIETAR International Board
participants, they remained affectionately known as Robert's rules. Over
time I learned to say things like start times will be British, the schedule
generically European, breaks with German punctuality, rules of order will
be modified American ones, etc. Initially the best ideas for each aspect of
our meetings were taken from specific national cultures. Over time, meeting processes were creatively designed to suit the whole of SIETAR.

In the early 1980s there were opportunities to use diversity and intercultural skills as I helped the Defense Systems Management College
update its curriculum for teaching military and civilian executives involved
in the acquisition of large military systems how to be effective leaders and
administrators. In the mid-1980s those skills were used while working in
the Office of the Secretary of the Navy. In that role I administered all the
research and development for the Department of the Navy. It was an
opportunity to manage a large diverse cluster of people and organizations
with an annual budget of about a billion U.S. dollars. In the 1980s that
seemed like a lot of money. To me intercultural/diversity meant working
with military, civilians, political appointees, career civil servants, scientists,

warriors, academics, business professionals, members of Congress, Americans, NATO people, as well as the infinite variety of men and women with diverse identities. Research was sponsored on things not typically thought of as being associated with the military. That included applications of lasers to manufacturing technology, development of blood plasma for universal use across blood types, high temperature lubricants for civilian use, computer-adaptive testing technology for use in education, improved weather prediction, smaller computer memory devices, deep sea exploration technologies, and more. This was an exciting time and fitting way to begin to close out my time with the government.

Digital Equipment Corporation

In 1988 I went to work for Digital Equipment Corporation in Sales, Services, Marketing, and International. My position was "Valuing Differences Manager" responsible for helping people work together across ALL differences. It was an application of much of what I had learned to date from my ancestors, teachers, and experiences. My nickname in that role was the "hired gun for valuing differences." When a human resource manager identified a line manager or executive who was not supportive of Digital's Valuing Differences initiative, I was called to meet privately and confidentially to strongly encourage them to get on board. My track record, according to many human resource managers in Digital, was exceptional. Digital was one of the few companies that moved beyond equal opportunity and affirmative action to valuing differences in the 1980s. They also went beyond race and gender to include many of the ways in which humans differ. Both general diversity and issue-specific work were done at Digital. It was also both domestic and international, reflecting what was known in the intercultural field as well as the burgeoning diversity field. Many of the best practices put in place at Digital in the 1980s remain effective in the twenty first century.

Final Corporate Job: Pillsbury and Grand Metropolitan

My time with Digital was wonderful and brief. Two years later I went to Minneapolis to become the Director of Human Resources for the Technology Center of The Pillsbury Company. That was my official and primary job. Beyond what one might expect with that title, I was also brought in to help make peace between American leaders in The Pillsbury

Company and British leaders in Grand Metropolitan. This required inter-cultural work in the context of distrust and misunderstanding.

In contentious situations reframing can be powerful. Manuel Ramirez III conducted research funded by the ONR and changed the vocabulary used in social psychology to describe people who are significantly affected by the physical and psychological context from "field dependent" to "field sensitive." Using less pejorative language can be a healing force.

In support of this new role, I had the great blessing of being married to a woman who had exceptional international and intercultural abilities. She coached me and facilitated success particularly in this aspect of what the company needed. Two written resources suggested by her were instrumental in building bridges between American and British executives at Pillsbury/Grand Metropolitan. *Painted in Blood: Understanding Europeans* by Stuart Miller (1987) and *Brit-Think, Ameri-Think* by Jane Walmsley (1987). They became required reading during my tenure. I also conducted workshops where each group was required to say what assets they saw as being brought by the other group. Retrospectively, I believe lasting peace did occur in this organization. For me, the blend of science and human resources once again caused me to feel that I was in a dream job where I could happily spend the rest of my career.

The human resource role also allowed me to lead diversity work within the Technology Center. We developed a group of internal employees who worked at all levels and in a diverse range of jobs. They were affectionately known as "the Cadre." I conducted several weeks of education and train-ing on how to be a diversity trainer, advocate, and problem-solver. The Cadre became our internal trainers/champions and conducted general sessions on diversity as well as issue-specific workshops on age, race, gen-der, sexual orientation, style, and more. Every employee received this training and education. The Cadre was created in 1989 and continued to function not only after I left the Technology Center in 1991, but also after Pillsbury was acquired by General Mills in 2001.

As of 2025 I am still in touch with former Cadre participants who con-tinue to lead diversity work wherever they are. Along the way, and rein-forced many times over, I learned the power and durability of creating an internal group of talent to conduct diversity and intercultural work. A dear colleague and major teacher along this line was Dr. Janet M. Bennett (Executive Director, Intercultural Communication Institute, Portland, Oregon). I had also learned a great deal about conducting effective large-scale training by working with Sandy Fowler as she orchestrated a large scale BaFa BaFa experiential learning session in which I was part of her team of facilitators.

In 1991 I was asked to lead diversity work for the entire Grand Metropolitan Food Sector on a worldwide basis. Grand Metropolitan owned all of Pillsbury (Burger King, Haagen Daz, Pearle Vision, Alpo, Green Giant, Food Service, and the baked goods business), International Distillers and Vintners, and Grand Met Foods Europe. Just like I wanted to tell the Army Commander many years before "no thank you" to being a race relations officer, I was not interested in leaving the Technology Center. I was very happy as the Director of Human Resources. My boss, human resources staff, and scientists in the lab were ideal colleagues given my personality and skills. My physical science background allowed me to sit in for the Senior Vice President of Technology when he was away. My work-life balance was healthy, and the company was very supportive of my professional and personal well-being. I was in heaven and not about to give up my wings. As my maternal Grandmother would say, "All good things must come to an end." The CEO of the Grand Met Food Sector *required* me to accept the position of Vice President, Diversity for the Grand Met Food Sector. "Required" meant making my boss an offer that was difficult to refuse and me an offer that opened powerful doors through which I was hesitant to walk. The *regular guy* was not excited about an office next to the CEO, access to the corporate jet, frequent trips across the Atlantic, suit and tie instead of a lab coat, executive social events, and so on. The CEO was Scottish and had risen to that level in a British company. He understood dominance and discrimination by virtue of his own personal experiences. He approved corporate officer status and made me a financial insider with full access to ongoing financial performance data so that I could see which businesses might benefit from intercultural/diversity help to improve their financial performance.

During my tenure with Pillsbury/Grand Metropolitan the company let me take a short leave to serve on the transition team for a U.S. President. This president happened to be a Democrat. I agreed to help staff his administration on the condition that competence was the primary criterion and party affiliation was secondary. He agreed that if the person was competent and supported his agenda, at least one Republican would be welcome as a member of his cabinet. Other Republicans would also be welcome in other positions. This was an exhilarating experience. Today I continue to advocate this philosophy. Competence must come first.

Diversity and culture can then add value by bringing a synergistic mix of assets to bear on the tasks at hand.

After a couple of years in this role my responsibilities were expanded beyond worldwide diversity to include line human resource responsibility for the tax, treasury, and technology organizations. I was in line for a top human resource job at one of the company businesses somewhere in the world. It was either that or leave the company. After some company-supported professionally facilitated soul searching, I decided to leave the company and start an independent consulting practice. The company treated me well by supporting the completion of a book co-authored with Amida Mendez Russell, *The Diversity Directive* (1996), and became one of my first clients.

"Teach and do it on your own nickel." This was advice given to me by James R. Behnke (former supervisor as the Senior Vice President for the Pillsbury Technology Center) as I was trying to decide whether to become an independent consultant or accept a top human resources role for one of Diageo's businesses.

"Someone different from you can help you see things about yourself and your situation that you are less likely to notice". This was advice from my spouse about what I was experiencing at work and in life. She and Jim were instrumental in making the decision to work independently.

V. Robert Hayles, Effectiveness/Diversity & Inclusion Consultant (1996–)

This turned out to be another *dream* job and likely my last. Consistent with my ancestral origins (60% African, 30% European, 10% Native American), family history, and personality I chose the above description. I am not President, CEO, Principal, Owner, or Chief. I am just a consultant who does what he believes in and loves to do. My Native American identity compels me to do only what I can do well. My European roots provide insights into the lives of those who don't look like me. My African ancestry results in having many minority experiences and lessons.

Passion

Sometimes passion for what an organization does supercharges the work. As a person committed to civil service and democracy, I was fired up to work with Dr. Janet Bennett to consult with several public agencies. As a car enthusiast working with vehicle manufacturers (e.g. Ford and Mercedes Benz), I was thrilled to help them make better products with more satisfied employees. Co-consulting with Steve Hanamura to the Seattle Mariners was both fun and highly successful. After training all their internal and game-day workers, the season that followed had zero reported "diversity" incidents. Steve's extraordinary knowledge of and passion for baseball made this possible. My love of science made working with pharmaceutical and high technology companies (e.g., Abbott Labs, Johnson & Johnson, Medtronic, Litton Bionetics, DuPont, Honeywell, and Cray Research) joyous. I was blessed to work with more than 150 clients in 15 different countries.

Ten Principles that guide my consulting practice

1. My scientific mindset requires evidence-based strategies and tactics to improve how people and organizations function.
2. The proof (commitment) of my practice is in personally owning stock in every publicly traded client. This fact is also shared with those clients. Some even made me an insider requiring legal clearance before making stock trades.
3. My drive for efficiency and durability/longevity means developing, partnering, and using the internal resources of clients to the greatest extent possible.
4. The pursuit of excellence means providing clients with the best resources available for the work that needs to be done. If I do not personally possess the needed expertise, I find and refer it without costs to the clients or finder's fees from the other consultants.
5. Diagnosis precedes prescribing strategies and tactics. Follow-up evaluations are part of the plan.
6. Start with senior leaders.
7. Trust must be sufficient for me to be treated like an insider. This helps focus the work where it is most needed and maximize the benefits of the consultation.
8. Do not provide consultations to competitors in the same industry at the same time. This applies to most corporations and rarely to public, educational, governmental, and non-profit organizations. This supports confidentiality and builds trust.
9. Diversity and intercultural work are woven together.

10. Inclusive definitions of diversity and culture are mandatory. All forms of unfair and inappropriate behavior and practices are to be addressed both individually and systemically.

Lessons Learned

Later in life I realized that I had absorbed through observation and experience, how mothers, aunts, teachers, and women who cared for "their" children as well others' children, develop trust by being trustworthy. Those lessons from these women about building trust, along with those exemplified by my Dad, uncles and Grandfather, taught me what I needed to know about dependability, integrity, and trustworthiness. This later opened the doors to being a financial insider (whether working as an employee or as a consultant); seeing confidential business strategies that enabled me to provide help with measurable outcomes; and being a personal coach and confidential advisor to executives making difficult and far-reaching decisions about their people and businesses. Gifts from my ancestors, advice from my colleagues, and coaching from my spouse helped me persuade many to put their sticks in the fire and keep everyone warm.

As I reflect on what is happening in 2025, I take refuge and comfort in watching our son. As a teenager, he swore he would never work as hard as I did. As a parent, I tried not to push or pull him into doing what I did, but to create his own path. He did. He is a physician (double board certified and a post MD fellow), scientist, teacher, and father who creates music and art. Ironically, he works harder than I did. It is delightful to hear his music and see his artwork, especially given my own truncated musical and artistic pursuits earlier in life. He and many of his professional colleagues are committed to making life better for those most in need of care. While I worry about their well-being in these times, I celebrate their ongoing commitment and feel the potential warmth of more sticks being added to the fire.

V. Robert Hayles has no conflicts of interest to declare that are relevant to the content of this chapter.

REFERENCES

Hayles, R., & Russell, A. (1996). *The diversity directive: Why some initiatives fail & what to do about it.* Co-published by Chicago, Irwin Professional Publishing and Alexandria, American Society for Training & Development.

Hoopes, D., Paul Pedersen, P., & Renwick, G. (Eds.). (1977–1978). *Overview of intercultural, education, training and research* (Vol. 1–3). Society for Intercultural Education, Training and Research.

Miller, S. (1987). *Painted in blood: Understanding Europeans.* Atheneum.

O'Keefe, A. (2019). *Launching the navy family support program: A heartfelt blend of history and memoir.* Amazon Kindle Direct Publishing.

Walmsley, J. (1987). *Brit-Think, Ameri-Think.* Penguin Group.

CHAPTER 9

Living an Intercultural Life (And Not Realizing It)

Stephen H. Rhinesmith

I should say now that I never thought of myself as an interculturalist, I was just working internationally my whole life, but of course that is part of the definition of an interculturalist, especially since I had decided that my life's mission was to help people deal with an increasingly global world with which they were not familiar. This became the defining purpose of my personal and professional life.

EARLY YEARS

I didn't think anything of growing up in a community where most of my friends were Black, Catholic or Jewish—and then there was me. It seemed like a normal community in the 1950s on Long Island where everybody returned from the war and settled into small Levittown houses. I went to Westbury public school system from K-12 and had a great experience. I had a lot of leadership opportunities, and life was rolling along until May 14, 1960, when I was a junior. "How would you like to go to Germany?" I heard someone say over my shoulder as I was in band practice one

S. H. Rhinesmith (✉)
Portsmouth, NH, USA

© The Author(s), under exclusive license to Springer Nature
Switzerland AG 2025
S. M. Fowler, D. C. Yalowitz (eds.), *Creating the
Intercultural Field*,
https://doi.org/10.1007/978-3-032-01370-5_9

afternoon. I had applied to the American Field Service (AFS) program months before and hadn't been informed I was accepted. I turned around to see the school principal, Mr. Kickham, standing there with a letter he had just opened from AFS saying they had placed me with the family outside of Nürnberg, Germany, where I would live for the summer after my junior year.

For some context, I had never known anyone who had been overseas. This was before international exchange programs were popular and before school trips abroad were commonplace just 15 years after the Second World War had ended. Naturally, I was stunned and excited. I ran home after school to tell my parents. My mother, who was cleaning the basement, almost had a heart attack, but my father—who was more adventurous—said he thought it was wonderful and that I should do it. A month later, in the middle of June, I boarded my first plane flight from New York to Montreal to meet the MS Seven Seas—a small, converted combat ship from the war that was now taking students back and forth to Europe.

From an intercultural perspective, I remember writing home to my parents that there were people on board from California, Utah, Texas, and places that I had never thought of. It was a good trip over with orientation language to the country that we were going to. There were 1500 of us all going to different countries throughout Europe. I boarded a train to go from Dusseldorf to Nurnberg where I would stay for eight weeks with my new family. As an only child, I now had three brothers: Christian, Traugott, and Heinz. I asked Christian what people called him, expecting him to say "Chris", but instead he said emphatically "Christian." This first cultural encounter taught me the lesson not to expect to be calling people by nicknames or shortened names.

I had a pleasant summer. My family did everything they could to keep me happy. I was homesick, and it was difficult to be alone in a village without any other teenagers. We did go once to visit one of Christian's cousins, where I had a second cross-cultural experience. Christian said "we're going to visit one of my cousins. "Great," I said. "What are we going to do?" He looked at me and replied, "What do you mean what are we going to do, we're going to visit my cousin." I repeated, "Yes I understand, but what are we going to do?" He repeated that we were going to visit his cousin. He then with a very frustrated voice said, "You Americans, why do you always have to do something, why can't you just be." I learned many years later, in studying intercultural communication, that it was said that

"Americans were not human *beings*, but human *doings*." I didn't understand at the time what that meant; I have since learned very well. In the middle of August, we all gathered again to take a chartered ship back to New York. That was convenient for me since my parents could pick me up and take me back to Long Island. I had been intrigued by the whole experience and *my mindset had been changed*. After my time in Germany, I seriously wanted to explore a larger world and other ways in which people live. Before Germany, that had not been a goal for me. *This was the major transformation of my life*, which set me on course to explore the world through practical programs and experiences.

College Years

The AFS experience had such an impact on me that I decided I wanted to go to a college where I could continue my interest in foreign affairs and culture. I was accepted at Wesleyan University in Middletown, Connecticut for a very unusual program. It included German language training and a semester abroad. Naturally, given my AFS background in high school, I selected Germany. However, little did I know, I would experience much more than a journey. I studied for three months at a Goethe Language Institute outside of Munich. Then I was free to drive anywhere I wanted. I chose Berlin and spent time there consuming a reading list of 50 books in German that we had been given to read to get back into Wesleyan for our junior year. It was quite a demanding program since we also had to write a paper in German reflecting on what we had learned from the 50 books we had read!

Nevertheless, I did not let this tough academic assignment keep me from wandering. I wound up driving to an area south of Oslo, Norway, where I lived with a Norwegian family for a month or so and worked in a factory. From there I drove all the way south to Gibraltar and then up the Spanish, French, and Italian Riviera, before traveling back through Switzerland and Austria to Munich. This, plus another trip I made from the Normandy coast of France to Dubrovnik in what was then Yugoslavia, enabled me to cover almost all the countries of Western Europe and drive 20,000 kilometers throughout Europe by the age of 20. It provided an incredible foundation for my future international work.

This experience also inspired me to go on to graduate school where I could continue to study cultural diversity. Cross-cultural relations was a new field of study in 1965, which was developed through President

Kennedy's creation of the Peace Corps in 1961. There was a great deal of interest in how to prepare young American college students to work for two years in a country that, in some cases, they had never heard of. I discovered the Graduate School of Public and International Affairs at the University of Pittsburgh had a concentration in cross-cultural relations. I also was accepted at the Columbia Graduate School for International Affairs, but this program was more focused on politics and law, which was not my primary interest. I was accepted to Pittsburgh with a Heinz Fellowship.

During my college years at Wesleyan, I worked summers at AFS headquarters in New York. It was located across from the United Nations and the perfect spot for the work that we did. It was also a perfect spot to find a life partner. My wife and I joke about the fact that we had an "arranged marriage", because our parents had known one another for many years (both being Methodist ministers). My father had met Kathe during a summer camp that he attended as a counselor. The summer after my junior year at Wesleyan she also took a job across from the United Nations. My father suggested that I call her and have lunch and we were married a year later in 1965.

I could not have made a better choice for a wife or a graduate program. I spent four years becoming a true interculturalist earning a master's and Ph.D. in International Affairs with an emphasis on the theory and practice of helping people from different cultures and cultural backgrounds learn to work together. I studied with Professors Michael Flack, Marshall Singer, and Edward Stewart, three of the pioneers in the intercultural field. Dr. Stewart and I traveled around the world visiting hospitals of the Order of Medical Mission Sisters, a Catholic-based medical order from Rome. The Sisters received training after six years of working with the local people as their colleagues and patients. Dr. Stewart and I developed training modules to help them understand things that had happened due to cultural influences and intercultural dimensions that affected their work with patients. This took us to visit remote hospitals in India, Bangladesh, Kenya, Malawi, Uganda, and Ghana where we learned what impact our training modules had on their experience.

During these years at Pittsburgh, David Hoopes, Director of the Regional Council for International Affairs, and I connected with Cliff Clarke from Cornell to develop the Intercultural Communications Workshop (ICW), which we ran for international students coming to the University of Pittsburgh. This was one application of intercultural theory that I found very helpful in developing a greater understanding of the challenges and solutions for intercultural adjustment. It was so influential that I was stimulated to write my Ph.D. dissertation on managing across cultures conducting original research at the bush hospital that Ed Stewart and I had visited in Ghana. The objective of the research was to analyze the challenges that Western medical personnel from the Medical Mission Sisters had in working with local Kenyan staff, patients, and relatives.

During the end of my doctoral studies in Pittsburgh, Kathe and I started a family with the birth of our son, Christopher. I was doing quite a bit of consulting for Peace Corps and when he was only 8 months old the Peace Corps asked if I and my family would move to Kenya to live in Nairobi for three months during the summer of 1971. I was there to design and develop a three-month cross-cultural program for the Americans who had just arrived in country for their two-year assignment. In addition, I was asked by the Peace Corps to design and facilitate cross-cultural staff integration programs for locals and Americans in six other African countries. Toward the end of my Ph.D. program, I was spending quite a lot of time in Africa. A littleunpublished paper I wote for Peace Corps on *Integrating a Multi-Cultural Staff* (Rhinesmith, 1996) got a lot of attention within and outside of Peace Corps.

At one of these programs, I met David Berlew, a Harvard University professor who ran the Behavioral Science Center in Boston for Professor David McClelland, head of the Social Relations Department at Harvard and the famous researcher who had conceptualized the idea of *achievement motivation* as a driving force in American economic development after the war. When I graduated from Pittsburgh in 1969, David offered me my first full-time job in Cambridge where I had a chance to expand my knowledge of cross-cultural relations to the area of interpersonal relations in general through McClelland's achievement motivational psychology.

THE AMERICAN FIELD SERVICE (AFS)

While in Nairobi, I received a letter from AFS announcing that the current president of the AFS World Organization was retiring, and they were interested in whether I had any ideas for a new candidate. I replied that I did not know anyone of the stature for the position since the retiring President had been the Dean of Admissions at Yale before being selected for the job. When I returned from Nairobi, AFS held its first World Conference of representatives from the 60 countries in the AFS system.

At that time students were exchanged primarily between the United States and these countries although it gradually developed to be exchanges from any country in the system to any other country.

I attended this conference as the President of the AFS USA Alumni Association. When it was over I wrote a synopsis of it for the Alumni Association Board, which fell into the hands of the Board of Directors of AFS International. I shortly thereafter received a call from the Search Committee asking if I would consider being nominated for President and CEO of the AFS Global organization. At 28, I thought the request was incredulous, but this was 1971 when we had a generation gap in the United States, and they were looking for someone young enough to deal with the 10,000 high school students who were on the program each year. On December 7, 1971, the Board of Directors of AFS elected me to become the President of AFS International with 60 countries, 300 staff, 5000 volunteers, and 10,000 students a year to care for. This transformation placed me squarely in the intercultural field and a marvelous 10-year leadership opportunity.

It was during this time that I worked with David Hoopes to create SITAR, which I served as one of the first Presidents in 1982–1983. After that, my participation in SIETAR (the "E" in recognition of the educational members) diminished as my responsibilities at AFS grew, and I moved on to other boards and organizations in the international exchange field.

My Board at AFS was extremely generous and understanding when I informed them that I needed to see AFS operations around the world. This led to a policy that was developed, which allowed my wife and me to travel around the world each year at company expense. Over the years I had the opportunity to see and talk with people from 60 countries. In addition, I ran a series of conferences each year to meet with the representatives from each country. In September we would meet in Europe with all the Europeans and those in the Middle East and Africa. In October we would meet in Latin America with all the heads of the Latin American organizations, and in November we met in Asia with all the heads of the Asia Pacific countries. From these three meetings we developed an agenda for the coming year that I presented in January to the AFS Board of Trustees, which was made up of some 30 people from around the world. Our staff would write policy papers and recommendations for priorities, and the Board would vote on how we should implement our organization's priorities during the coming year. It was a reasonably fair way to set the annual agenda for the organization worldwide.

As President of AFS, I saw the organization as an instrument of peace in the world. I believed that people who better understood each other across cultures would be less prone to engage in warfare. I was therefore anxious to ensure that countries that were not involved in AFS, but were important politically, participated. For this reason, I opened a program in Israel, Egypt, China, and the Soviet Union. I also tried to increase the diversity of our program with South Africa.

At the time our South African program included whites and colored (primarily Indians), but no Blacks. In 1976, during one trip around the world with my wife, I arranged to visit with a group of principals of high schools in Soweto, the Black Township of Johannesburg, to explore Black African participation in the program to the United States. I explained the AFS program, and the idea of bringing students from South Africa to the United States to live with families for a year and then return to Soweto, hopefully with a more open mind and experience. To my great surprise, the principals opposed the program unanimously. They explained that students who spent a year in the United States would have enormous reentry problems back in Soweto. The shift from living with an American family of any class to living in Soweto was too great for young people to bear. I was unsuccessful in persuading them to even attempt this programmatic idea. Two days after we left Soweto, it blew up in an explosion of frustration against the apartheid system.

Nevertheless, over the years that I was President, I was happy to be able to increase the diversity not only of countries participating in AFS, but also within countries. I remember being besieged by reporters on my first trip to Australia. When I got off the plane their first question was why we did not have greater representation from the indigenous peoples on our programs. We faced the same situation in New Zealand with the Māori, and I am happy to say that by the end of my Presidency, both groups of indigenous people were represented as students we brought to the United States.

HOLLAND AMERICA CRUISE LINES

At the end of 1979, at the age of 38 and having spent 10 years at AFS I felt that, while I could be there for the rest of my life, I needed to look at the for-profit world. I managed to persuade Peter Drucker, the well-known management consultant, to provide me with advice as I sought a career change. He suggested that I become the President of the American Management Association, a not-for-profit organization training managers all over the United States. At the same time, a member of my Board at AFS, John Berry (not the Canadian psychologist), was being promoted from President of Holland America Cruise lines to CEO. He approached me and asked whether I would be interested in succeeding him as President and Chief Operating Officer.

Both jobs would be a challenge since I was unfamiliar with management training on a national basis, and as I used to say the only thing I knew about the cruise business was that the "pointy end of the ship should be going first!" I chose Holland America but discovered a week after I became President that there is an additional caveat in shipping. This is that the pointy end should go first—but not down! I had the fastest indoctrination to a new job that one could imagine as one of our ships caught fire and sank in the sea off Alaska. Fortunately, the Canadian Coast Guard, US Coast Guard, and several nearby ships were able to rescue all 650 passengers and 350 crew without any deaths. The ship, however, rolled over and sank as it was being towed back to Alaska for repairs.

The reason the owner had asked me to become President was to improve ship—shore communications. All the ships were manned by Dutch officers, Filipino engineers, Indonesian servers, hotel workers, and British cruise staff. This truly was an intercultural assignment since there were communication challenges across the cultures and languages on the ship, and between the Dutch officers and the New York headquarters. As president, I was responsible for all officers and crew providing the best experience possible for international guests from around the world. Unfortunately, that first year was even more difficult than the ship sinking. It was the time of the 1980 OPEC oil embargo, and it threw the finances and planning of the corporation into the unknown.

In addition, we had a strike in Bermuda and a poor season in the Caribbean in 1980–1981 which further hurt the company's bottom line. All of this resulted in the need for a total review of our strategy and direction. The owner did not feel that I had the experience to conduct the strategic review (and he was right). In response, he brought in a new CEO to deal with the strategy of the company. The two of us did not see the future the same way (which often happens between senior officers of a company), and since he was CEO, he decided it would be best if I moved on. While I was disappointed to end an experience that I thoroughly enjoyed with the crew and officers, this is a good example of where inter-cultural skills don't equal strategic management skills in a particular indus-try. Moving on was the right move and I did it. After a few years of consulting, I received the true opportunity of a lifetime for anyone inter-ested in cross-cultural relations.

PRESIDENT REAGAN'S U.S.-SOVIET EXCHANGE INITIATIVE

For my generation, having grown up under the U.S.-Soviet nuclear threat, I had never known any positive relationship between the United States and the Soviet Union. In 1980 Ronald Reagan was elected presi-dent and for four years embarked on a military program (known as "Star Wars") to outspend the Soviets. However, in 1985, after a quick succes-sion of the deaths of three Soviet Chairmen of the Communist Party, Mikhail Gorbachev became the President of the Soviet Union and Chairman of the Communist Party. The American government was divided on how much Gorbachev could be trusted. The State Department was cautiously optimistic, but the Defense Department was suspicious of what it meant for U.S-Soviet relations. Gorbachev made it clear that the Soviet Union was in trouble economically. He was looking for a new approach from the United States.

At the first summit meeting between Reagan and Gorbachev in 1985 the Americans decided to make a proposal that would test Gorbachev's true interest in a different kind of relationship. We proposed and the Soviets agreed to a U.S.-Soviet citizen-to-citizen exchange program, which would bring citizens from each country to visit the other to begin to get to know one another better. This was the first time there had ever been such a broad exchange approved by both sides in the history of U.S.-Soviet relations; in the exchange field, it was seen as a breakthrough. The negotiations in Geneva also agreed that the program would be run by a Coordinator from each country with the diplomatic rank of Ambassador. I was selected by the head of the U. S. Information Agency, Charles Wick, and President Reagan to take on the job as Coordinator for at least six months. I wound up being there for almost 2 years in one of the most interesting and important diplomatic roles that I have been privileged to have.

The Summit meeting took place in November 1985, and I was to start in January 1986 with a trip to Moscow with Director Wick. Naturally, the intelligence community was at a loss to figure out who I was since my work with Peace Corps and other not-for-profit organizations had always been non-political. I was quickly of great interest to the KGB, FBI, DOD, NSA, and CIA. This intelligence community overseeing people coming in and out of the United States from the Soviet Union was at a loss as to who this new Ambassador was. That led to a series of actions that I will not go into here for security reasons but to give you an idea Admiral Poindexter (who at the time was the National Security Advisor to President Reagan) appointed me as the head of an Inter-agency Intelligence Exchange Task Force. The explicit objective was to ensure that the exchanges I allowed would not be used by the Soviets for intelligence gathering. I found myself in the paradoxical position of running an interagency task force of the intelligence community to ensure that the program I was running would not be used for Soviet and KGB intelligence gathering. It was an interesting time—to say the least.

I was appointed not only because of my 10 years as President of AFS, but also because I had written the first book on international exchanges which was used by 2500 volunteers in the United States to understand the exchange process. The government also was aware of this book and wanted to use it to try to expand high school exchanges with the G7 countries. This was a particular interest of President Reagan's since he was concerned that the postwar generations did not have the same feelings about the Transatlantic Alliance as the generation that had fought the Second World War. He believed that exchanges like AFS could be expanded in the G7 countries to ensure that the next generation would continue to appreciate the special relationship of the former allies.

President Reagan gave me the highest appointment in the U.S. Government's Senior Executive Service (SES) and the title of U.S. Ambassador to enable me to work with officials and others in the Soviet government of equivalent rank. This included the Ministerial and Executive levels. I also had three bosses: Charles Wick, Head of the U.S. Information Agency as primary, with a dotted reporting line to Jack Matlock, Director of Soviet Affairs for the National Security Council. and Mark Palmer, the Assistant Secretary of State for Eastern Europe and the Soviet Union. This began a journey that took me from Washington to Moscow every other month and resulted in my becoming acquainted with some 25 Soviet ministries and associations.

When I was in Moscow, I used to stay at Spaso House, which was the residence of the U.S. ambassador to the Soviet Union, Ambassador Hartman, a career foreign service officer, was at that time the

U.S. Ambassador. One night as we sat discussing the situation between the United States and the Soviet Union, he said to me "Steve, you know more people in the Soviet government than I do. You have more access and a broader range of understanding of the government than is possible for anyone else. I hope you take advantage of it for us and the Soviets."

I did my best. During the time I was in the position, we facilitated many exchanges of different kinds. The ones that were most recognized were Billy Joel's first trip to the Soviet Union, Vladimir Horowitz's triumphant return after many years away, and a large conference of 125 Americans and 125 Soviets who met in Riga, Latvia, then again the next year in Chautauqua, New York at the famous Chautauqua Institution for discussions of U.S.- Soviet relations and to have a chance to get to know one another better. All of this was under my supervision. This two-year period from 1986 to 1987 was a particularly good time for U.S.-Soviet relations. Gorbachev was going through *glasnost* and *perestroika* and was searching for new ideas. The Americans were intrigued by his interest and were doing all that they could to take advantage of the opportunity to enter the Soviet Union with business opportunities as well as other initiatives. By the end of 1987, I had stayed long past my initial six-month appointment and decided it was time to move on. The exchange initiative had been established and was taken over by professional Foreign Service Officers from the United States Information Agency and the State Department.

Globalization

After this time in government, I returned to a theme of my study in graduate school and became interested in what was happening in the private sector in the development of people for international assignments. Businesses were beginning to globalize, and managers were now working for global corporations. Most managers had no idea what this meant. I did some research on the subject and wrote a book at the point when many companies were in the process of globalization. This led to a book tour and interviews not only here in the United States, but also in Japan and a consulting contract with the Ford Motor Company to acquaint their senior management to global management skills. Over the course of five years commuting between New York, Detroit, and around the world, I paired up with William Ury, to work with some thousand senior Ford managers to develop a more global mindset.

During these years, I met two clinical psychologists who were also interested in training executives to become more effective in their interpersonal relations. All this activity was facilitated through Professor Warner Burke, professor of leadership at Columbia Teachers' College in New York. He had developed a program for improving executives' self-awareness and asked me and the other two trainers, Dr. Peter Cairo and Dr. David Dotlich, to join him in the early 90s in a major contract to train the partners in the Arthur Anderson auditing and consulting firm throughout the world. This program was a four-day format with each manager assigned a coach to help them internalize the material on becoming a business partner. Since we taught it all over the world, there was also a segment on cross-cultural communications and developing a more global mindset for which I was responsible.

In 1998 Peter, David, and I had an opportunity to develop our own business (CDR International) running global leadership programs for corporations. Our first and major client was the Bank of America, which asked us to train their top 1500 executives over several years. By that time, we had also been asked by Merck to train their top 1000 Leaders and by Novartis (a Swiss pharmaceutical company) to run a program in global leadership for their middle management group. This program continued from 2000 to 2015 and involved over 4000 managers. The Merck program went from 1998 to 2004 and other engagements had us traveling the world for at least half of our working days. Spending 150 nights overseas per year running Global Leadership Programs would continue for 25 years. It was truly an extraordinary and transformative experience. We conducted Global Leadership Programs for companies in Eastern and Western Europe, the Middle East, Asia/Pacific, and Latin America. Interestingly there were no programs in Africa since at the time American businesses had not established themselves and African executives on a level that they felt it worth the investment. Other than those companies mentioned, we had significant contracts with Mitsubishi in Tokyo, the Civil Service Center in Singapore, the Young Arab Leaders in Dubai, and Banco Santander in Madrid. There were also many other speaking engagements throughout the world during this time.

One company that stands out for me is Merck. Merck is a complicated company in that there are two Mercks, one in the United States and one in Germany. The company in Germany is the original Merck founded in 1668 and is still a family company. Merck in the United States was created in 1918 after the First World War as a reparation from Germany. It incorporated itself in the United States and became what most people in the United States know today as Merck. However, Merck in Germany owns the name in every country in the world except in the United States and Canada. This did not matter for 100 years until people started googling Merck on the Internet and many times wound up with the wrong company. This remains a problem between the two companies, but Merck in the United States has adopted the name MSD for use internationally and the original German Merck operates under different names for its different businesses in the United States and Canada.

Behind all of this, however, is the Merck family in Germany, now in their 13th generation of ownership of the company. I've had the privilege for the last 12 years of being a leadership advisor to the Merck family and the senior leadership of Merck KGaA. I also spent 15 years with the senior leadership of Merck in the United States. Fortunately, it has all worked rather smoothly. Amazingly, I started in Germany as an exchange student at the age of 17 and I am continuing my career in Germany at 82.

Russia and China

I feel the need to say a few additional words about my intercultural experiences with Russia and China. In both cases, I was present for the biggest evolution of two societies that existed in modern times. I was also one of the earliest Americans to visit the Soviet Union in 1962 and China in 1978 just four years after Nixon's visit to open relations between the two countries.

Russia. I remember my first visit to Moscow under the old Soviet Union in 1962, which at the time was a very drab city built from Stalinist concrete. It was impossible to tell apartment buildings and stores from one another. One thing I do remember, however, was that there were special stores for foreigners and normal stores for Soviets. Of course, these special stores were not easily identifiable, and you had to show your passport to get into them. They also had better quality products than could be found in normal stores for Soviets. The second thing I remember was that in the Soviet stores many times you would stand in line because you had heard that there was something to buy. The Soviets would not know what it was, but they were anxious to buy anything they could use to barter with somebody who had what they wanted. This was the state of consumerism in all old Soviet times from Stalin through Brezhnev.

This was the first of 57 trips to the Soviet Union and Russia between 1962 and 2005. From my responsibilities with the government in the 1980s, and other opportunities to witness the Soviet Union collapse after Gorbachev was purged through Yeltsin's seven-year tenure to Putin's appointment as President in 2000, I was witness to the changes. But I could feel myself becoming increasingly irrelevant after Gorbachev. During the last part of the 1980s American consulting firms and businesses began to open, and I became less and less cutting-edge in my knowledge. It seems hard to believe while I was an Ambassador who had given presentations in the United States about the Soviet Union as a Soviet expert. That expertise was quickly overcome by foreigners who lived in Moscow, spoke Russian, and were exposed to the latest evolution under Gorbachev and then Yeltsin.

I continued to visit Moscow for some years after I left the government. The major reason for my visits was that the Vice Chancellor of Moscow State University arranged for me to meet with the Chancellor to discuss the possibility of starting a new department of organizational sociology at the University. It was a fascinating experience. The Chancellor at the time was a physicist who resembled the Wizard of Oz. I met with him in his huge office and worked through interpreters. He told me he wanted me to set up a new concentration of organizational sociology in the sociology department that would be a challenge in organization change for students (and professors) to adjust to some of the changes that Gorbachev had been trying to try to introduce through *perestroika*. This was an extraordinary opportunity, and I now became intrigued with the new Russia and its development under Yeltsin.

I accepted the offer and was given an office in the Moscow State University "wedding cake" building that so many people identify with Moscow. I was told that I was the only foreigner who had ever been head of a department at Moscow State University (and that that remains true today). I was given my Soviet University ID card and a faculty salary of $15.23 a month, which I decided not to collect (and which I saw dissolve under Yeltsin's transformative economic policies). I remember the first day going into the University's smoke-filled corridors and seeing how many students would show up in my classroom to hear about this new area of study. I worked through my longtime friend, colleague, and interpreter Sergei Filonovich, who eventually became Chairman of the department and carried on its work for some years. I was informed a few years ago the Department was still functioning after 25 years and continues to have a great deal of student interest even now during Putin's time. Naturally, I no longer have any affiliation with the department, but I feel that I contributed to some cross-cultural understanding in its establishment.

Another significant experience during my time in Russia was trying to establish a high school exchange program for AFS. I requested a meeting with the Minister of Education whom I had gotten to know during my time with the government. The Soviets (like the Chinese) had traditionally not been interested in any international exchange student exchange programs except for graduate students and technical experts who could advance their knowledge by coming to the United States. They saw little reason why a young high school student should live with a family in the United States and did not appreciate the cross-cultural side of their learning.

Nevertheless, I managed to gain a meeting with the Minister. I told him what I was proposing, and I got the standard answer "Why in the world would we send young people when we don't know what their future is going to be?" I told the Minister again what the impact could be on students' mindsets and expanding their view of the world and its possibilities. He thought for a long while and then looked me straight in the eyes and said "OK, I will do it, but I want you to know that I am doing this for *you*, not because I think it's such a great idea." Based on my personal relationship, this exchange of students was born in 1995 and continues today. As it turned out, in 1982 my family and I hosted a Muslim student from Indonesia for a year in our home. It turned out to be a classic AFS experience with contact still today. We have visited him and his family in Jakarta, and his father, mother and others have come to visit us here in the United States over the years. One recent weekend. Indra (now 62!) came with one of his sons who is applying to MIT. Indra still calls my wife and me "mom "and "dad ". I was talking with his son who asked me what he should call me. I asked him what does he call his grandparents back home? He said, grandpa and I said well you now have another grandpa and I have another grandson. This is another way to lead an intercultural life which is just normal and we love it.

China. It was December 2nd, 1978, and Mao Zedong, the nemesis of the United States, had died just two years before. Six years earlier, in 1972 President Nixon made his historic trip to sign an agreement to establish diplomatic relations between the two countries. In China at this time a power struggle emerged among the "Gang of Four" as to who should succeed Mao and continue his legacy. I was sitting on a Pan Am plane from Washington to Beijing after being briefed by the State Department regarding what we might expect. The *we* were 20 leaders from various civic organizations in the United States who had been invited to spend three weeks touring China, because the Chinese felt we could be useful in communicating a better understanding of what Chinese life was like, since very few Americans had been there since the Second World War.

Donna Shalala and I, both in our 30's, were probably the youngest of the group. I had been selected because I was President of AFS and Donna was a young Assistant Secretary of the U.S. Department of Housing and Development in the Carter administration. The group also included the Head of the League of Women Voters, the Executive Directors of the World Affairs Councils in San Francisco and Boston, and other similar civic leaders with constituencies who would receive word of what we had experienced during our time in China. The delegation was headed by Bruce MacLaury, the President of the Brookings Institution in Washington. As the plane landed, I remember thinking that I was walking into a culture that I had no understanding of other than the fact that they had been hostile to the United States all my life. This was a true cross-cultural experience, which would test my intercultural understanding. We were more than welcomed and provided with great hospitality. Not only were we fed well but we met with Chinese political and military leaders, visited schools, hospitals, factories, and even a divorce court to understand how the Chinese society was operating. While the entire three weeks had been carefully staged by the Chinese, we were still exposed to a society we had never seen before.

I made several trips back in the 1970s, 80s, and 90s to facilitate conferences and try once again, now in China, to start a high school exchange program for AFS. I encountered the same objections that I had in Moscow during the same years. While I failed at the time to get them to start a high school program, I did get them to compromise by sending high school teachers to live with American families and participate in American high schools. The idea of teacher-student interaction and experiential learning was just beginning to seep into the most advanced Chinese schools as part of Deng Xiaoping's *Opening Up* program of the 1990s and a teacher exchange was intriguing to the Chinese.

At one point in the late 1980s, after Deng Xiaoping had become chairman of the Chinese Communist Party and had initiated a loosening up of the society, I remember having discussions regarding Deng's change strategy versus Gorbachev's. At that time 'Gorbachev believed that to create change he needed *perestroika* or restructuring of the government and the destruction of the Soviet Communist Party first, and then it would be easier to change the economy. Deng Xiaoping, on the other hand, never gave up control of the Communist Party but was open to allowing entrepreneurs great experimentation throughout China. He also encouraged a system of economic competition among local provincial governors that produced the building boom that is today modern China.

We now know which approach was more successful. Deng Xiaoping retained the political capacity to make economic decisions. Unfortunately, Gorbachev destroyed the political decision-making capacity and gave the economy to a small group of powerful oligarchs, some of whom began to challenge the government and his authority. This led to his ouster and eventually to Putin's crackdown on those entrepreneurs who violated this implicit agreement, which was that they could run their businesses and become fabulously wealthy, but they could not be involved in politics.

Perhaps the most unique opportunity I had to learn about China's opening was in 2009 when I worked with John and Doris Naisbit to do an analysis of government decision-making in Chengdu, the capital of Sichuan province in the Western part of China. Chengdu had been one of the more advanced local government systems since the opening of China and the Chinese asked John and his wife Doris to write a book about it. There's not enough space for me to describe what we found in terms of local government functioning, but I may say that it was unique, very open, and a fascinating new experiment in local government administration.

REFLECTION

I consider it an enormous privilege to have seen the world unfold from unpaved African villages of the 1960s to the Chinese skyscrapers of the 2010s. Likewise in Russia, limited economic development has made great strides in the development of Moscow, St. Petersburg, and other regional capitals. It's hard now to go to any country in the world and not find the impact of modern development. Having traveled to over 100 countries (including all of Latin America in the 1970s), I feel like I have seen the world as an interculturalist and benefited enormously from the training and development I received during my time as a graduate student at the Graduate School of Public and International Affairs in Pittsburgh. The opportunity to work and learn from the pioneering professors in the field was foundational. Many of the concepts they taught, such as the relationship between societies that are group-oriented versus individually-oriented have been a bedrock for me in understanding the countries I have visited over the years. This has enabled me to make a differentiation between individual loosely-oriented Australia, New Zealand, and Scandinavia and those countries that were more group-oriented like Japan, Africa, the Middle East and most of the rest of the world.

Reflecting on 60 years of travel, management, teaching, study, lecturing, and research throughout the world, I realize that I have led a globalist life which has been highly unusual. I am now retired in a small community in Southern New Hampshire. At the same time, I continue to work a few days a month for Merck KGaA in Germany via Zoom. Before COVID-19 I commuted to Germany every three weeks for five years. I continue to have meetings with senior people in the Merck family and company leadership and continue to be involved in the complexities of operations throughout the world.

Developing a global mindset, which is something I have written about over the years, is an important and critical perspective for everyone, not just interculturalists. The ability to have curiosity and empathy for people who are different is a great gift and enriches one's life. Living now in a small state in the northeastern part of the United States, I am familiar with people who have never been out of the state let alone abroad. They have the comfort of places they know but are missing all the customs and cultures of people throughout the world with different ways of looking at themselves, the world, and society. Hopefully, more people will be able to develop a global mindset in the generations ahead that will allow the world to live together in some modicum of peace and security.

Summing Up

It turns out I have been an interculturalist all my life—without really calling myself that. But I have shared the vision and purpose of interculturalists to help people become more global in their curiosity, more fascinated by the new cultures and perspectives they witness and more empathic and compassionate about the people and world around them who share different perceptions and beliefs. The process of intercultural understanding of others requires our own ability to accept our reality as one in a million. The path to intercultural understanding begins with cultural self-awareness before we can appreciate other rich perspectives. I have spent my whole life trying to help people—from teenagers, to business leaders, to top government officials—understand and appreciate our global similarities and differences. I truly believe that this is the key to our ability to overcome the many barriers that lie before us as a collaborative, successful and peaceful world.

Stephen H. Rhinesmith has no conflicts of interest to declare that are relevant to the content of this chapter.

REFERENCE

Rhinesmith, S. H. (1996). *A manager's guide to globalization: Six skills for success in a changing world*. New York: McGraw-Hill. 2nd.

CHAPTER 10

The Art of Intercultural Communication: Seeing With New Eyes

Fanchon J. Silberstein

In 1962, I thought Cambodia might be in Africa. In 1963, only slightly prepared to live in *Southeast Asia*, I stood outside a small airport in Phnom Penh while my husband looked for the embassy car that had been scheduled to meet us. Alone, I was in the middle of fields, rice paddies as I was told, wearing the gray wool suit I'd changed into to leave Chicago after our December wedding on a snowy day. Among the paddies of Cambodia, I was an odd and sweating visitor, now closely observed by several women, appropriately dressed for work in loose black clothing, who now hunkered close to me like a friendly flock of birds. They were the welcome to my new Cambodian home, teaching me to be curious about so much I didn't understand.

I was like a teabag dunked into hot water absorbing everything—the sensation of extreme humidity, green landscape, pink bougainvillea, saffron robed monks walking silently in early mornings with their begging bowls, smells of rice and fish oil, lines of working elephants, and mixes of sounds that were not yet language. Even when I studied Khmer and practiced simple sentences at a stilted ladies' tea party in my living room, I

F. J. Silberstein (✉)
Washington, DC, USA

© The Author(s), under exclusive license to Springer Nature
Switzerland AG 2025
S. M. Fowler, D. C. Yalowitz (eds.), *Creating the Intercultural Field*,
https://doi.org/10.1007/978-3-032-01370-5_10

scarcely understood that I was in a different culture among people who did not have the same interior map of the world that I did.

Then What Happened?

After one year in Cambodia, I lived in Vietnam, in Laos, in Thailand and later in Pakistan and Brazil as the wife of an American Foreign Service Officer. At the same time, I was fortunate to have an independent career. In all the countries we lived, I studied their languages but without the subtle awareness of cultural differences that filled my later career with questions about the complexity of our existence. I am offering here some of my story—not a chronology or an autobiography—but a story of comings and goings that led to adventures set among confrontations with myself as a perpetual stranger.

I savored living among peoples in many parts of the world, but with that savor came confusion and avoidance infused with an embarrassingly persistent desire for the familiar. At the start of what became an unlikely career in building training programs for the field of Intercultural Communication, I had not yet seen its barest outlines. Becoming an interculturalist was an ill-defined process for me, very different from following a predetermined career path.

Beginnings

As I write this, I am an older woman who was born in Chicago, and, enjoyed long holidays in northern Michigan with my mother's extended family. I graduated from the University of Michigan where I felt the world open when art history brought stories from cave paintings to modernism. I later taught in elementary schools in Arizona and California, and in 1962, with little notice, I said goodbye to my sixth grade class in Watts so that I could live with my very new husband who was finishing a Foreign Service assignment in Cambodia where the story that began this chapter unfolded.

Early and Later

I had been trained by the American Poverty Program and after that by the U.S. Information Service to teach English using the audio-lingual method. In Los Angeles, I taught children from Mexico. In Phnom Penh, I taught Cambodian government employees and students preparing for college in the United States. In Thailand I taught children in a Mon village, and in Pakistan a local teacher and I established an English program for a diverse group of students at the International School in Islamabad. (I also taught one literature class to 9th graders, some of whom had already read more widely than I.)

In 1970, my husband and I moved to Washington, DC where I completed a master's degree in special education at the George Washington University and worked for a school system in Northern Virginia. The program at GW was far from the standard ways universities in the U.S. were preparing teachers for classroom work. The critical difference was its emphasis on children's perceptions and the high value it placed on community action in building responsive educational programs. This was my first foray into conscious interculturalism, an awareness that not all of us see the world the same way. We learned to breathe and ask questions to learn about others' interests, concerns and conflicts. Teachers showed immense creativity in their instruction and despite a heavy classroom load, some were willing partners in adjusting their teaching to support challenging students.

The aim of the GW program was less to work with disabilities than to build programs that jointly supported the needs of teachers, children and their communities. Part of our learning involved a close look at "percepts"—our very individual perceptions or ways of seeing just about everything. Rather than "diagnosing" from a pre-existing playbook, we learned to interview school-aged children themselves. We studied systems theory to inquire into how schools and communities lead and what then follows. We read psychology from the field's beginnings to the present. We also read modern sociology and other writings growing out of a country engaged in an unpopular war in Vietnam. We wrote many short papers inspired by our readings and also by our work in the schools where we were assigned positions as resource teachers. We drew upon Fritz Redl's writing on The Life Space Interview whose value is in giving the child a voice to speak on his/her own behalf, an approach that I carried over in my training with adults as well.

The University monitored our work and provided support, regularly returning us to our classroom to talk over troublesome events and small successes that sometimes involved only one student who backed off from destructive behavior because one of us had given up blaming in favor of insight into what drove that child. I woke up to the power of dialogue that enhanced my later docent work at the Hirshhorn and led eventually to "Art as Intercultural Dialogue" for the University of Pennsylvania.

Brasil. In 1974, the State Department sent my husband to Rio de Janiero for a four-year assignment during which I was fortunate to have a Brazilian friend introduce me to the director of the newly established National Center for Special Education (CENESP). Using material from my GW program, I worked for several organizations, designing and delivering teacher-training workshops and ran an intervention program for special needs children at a school staffed by American nuns

I also accepted a position as a counselor for the Fulbright Commission where I met Brazilian students aspiring to study in the United States. And through the Federal University, I helped organize a convention of educators who came to Rio from different states throughout Brazil's vast country. I was struck by the range of needs they presented. Prosperous districts in the south were refining their curricula while educators in the north worried that flooded roads could prevent students from even getting to their schools.

I became fascinated with Macumba or Condomblé, a spiritual practice, synchronized with Catholicism. On Monday evenings we visited "templos" that invited outsiders to observe or even participate in rituals that involved trances or being counseled by Mothers of the Saints. Every Tuesday morning, at a cemetery gate near the school where I worked, I saw the remains of Monday's ritual offerings—manioc meal, candles and chickens. One of the American nuns at the school had been raised in Brazil and became my guide into these rituals that I learned to see as a rich abiding practice that held communities together.

For all the fascination that this and other traditions in faraway countries held for me, I am dismayed that I was unaware of the extent to which I filtered my experience through the unconscious views of an American girl who grew up in the Midwest. I might have done better work at the time had I been more conscious of looking out from within my own model of the world.

At the same time, varied cultures did offer a pageant of sound and color, food and dress, music and dance, and friendship. I felt affection and mistrust, fear and pleasure, humor and outrage, confusion and slight glimmers of understanding. Context later became a very salient word for me. Just WHERE is all this happening? What is the backdrop? What is the cultural context in which a wedding ritual took place? A casual dinner party? A performance in Rawalpindi by a vocalist where everyone sat on the floor and platters of "paan", (betel nut) were passed? How does the audience relate to the performer?

Back to the United States. After four years in Rio my husband and I returned to the U.S., first to Syracuse University where I took classes in special education and psychology, and then back to Washington, DC where, at the State Department's Foreign Service Institute, (FSI) I became Director of the Overseas Briefing Center (OBC), an office charged with preparing employees and families from the foreign affairs community to relocate and live abroad. For the first time, I worked and studied with people who provided programs centered on cultural awareness.

The OBC's mission was to prepare employees and their families to represent the United States in embassies and consulates throughout the world. The Center offered classes on American Studies that included understanding the election process, separation of church and state, economics, journalism and underpinnings of American culture in history and the arts. Speakers came from universities and other institutions where they were leaders in their fields. Classes also provided practical information on using needed services through the State Department's offices on transportation, packing, budgets, education for children and health care. The Center also offered career planning for spouses and explained bilateral agreements with other countries. On weekends, for families with children, the Center ran day-long experiential classes to help with adjustment during moving and settling abroad. And it offered evening classes for those returning home after tours abroad. We also provided support to other courses at FSI with lectures on protocol and patterns of human adjustment to change.

For the most part, training in intercultural communication took place in other schools at the Foreign Service Institute. However, the OBC did offer a popular and challenging session—a simulation that involved a parent dealing with a school system where the headmaster used corporal punishment to discipline children. The session was run by a skilled actor who engaged in a conversation with a volunteer from the class. The volunteer was an American mother who had other views on properly disciplining children. The debriefing at the end, when the actor does not step out of his assumed role, brought a sobering realization that certain cultural attitudes may be deeply embedded in practices that could not be argued away.

For me, personally, my work at the OBC was stimulating and often exciting. I met remarkable people who taught me to see what I never had. At monthly meetings of the Interagency Roundtable I met others working in the intercultural field, and I joined The Society for Intercultural Education, Training and Research (SIETAR), I also became a member of the board of directors for the National MultiCultural Institute (NMCI) under Elizabeth Salett, helping to advise an organization that ran an annual conference on diversity and establish training for a number of local institutions.

In 1985 I entered the docent program at the Smithsonian Institution's Hirshhorn Museum and Sculpture Garden where, for 30 years, I led tours and participated in training other docents. I was immersed, for the first time, in the world of contemporary art as a reflection of our many interests and concerns including the environment, politics, concepts of beauty, social ills, thrills of flight, and how we see history. It tells its stories in inventive and sometimes abstract ways. Once again, I had multiple lessons in intercultural communication that included confusion, bias, *ah hah* moments, thrills of discovery, and much more.

WHEN ART SPEAKS—LISTEN

Art As Intercultural Communication

In the 1980's Sandy Fowler and I began offering Training of Trainers workshops, drawing on Sandy's extensive experience in training design and my delving into andragogy or adult learning. Later we introduced our workshop, "Art as Intercultural Communication" through the Summer Institute for Intercultural Communication (SIIC).

Workshop participants at SIIC described objects from many cultures to focus attention and bring all of us closer to seeing together. We abandoned received knowledge and previously held opinions in an attempt to stay in the present. Of course, opinions and past learnings were still there but were left unspoken at a moment of focusing on visual information right in front of us. The result was a newness, a fresh look, and an understanding that another's vision or perception could enhance our own. Later we welcomed personal stories and opinions that were either evoked by works of art at the time we were looking together or remembered from earlier experience with the same or similar images. We looked for meaning through questions. Participants saw the flexibility of the arts to fit into many aspects of communication across subject areas and in many work settings. I had read about Project Zero, a Harvard based education program focused on learning through the arts. It continues to be an inspiration.

Art As Intercultural Dialogue

The vitality of the arts in training programs combined with my years at the Hirshhorn opened me to ways that art reveals spiritual beliefs, views of science, considerations of beauty, reactions to social upheaval, history, family life, landscape, time and many explorations of mystery. Artists offer their stories through film, music, painting, sculpture and all other forms of art. For me, art continues to be the world's cultural messenger.

In intercultural training, I found a constant—always in the form of a question—*what do we see?* It inspired me to write *Art inSight* that led to an invitation to co-teach "Art as Intercultural Dialogue" at the University of Pennsylvania, a class about looking closely at many forms of art, with students responding to one another's observations in the moment—avoiding back stories or reporting what they had already learned before they shared the experience of looking together. They listened closely to one another. Past learning was to become useful, but in the classroom, they created a community of explorers sharing wide and sometimes unexpected, travels. They found they got to know one another better than they expected.

The students read physicist and writer David Bohm's cogent little book *On Dialogue* and consistently referred to his teachings. They also read *Art inSight: Understanding Art and Why It Matters* (2020) about art's role in inviting our reflections on the seen and unseen in all of life.

Throughout 14 weeks of engaging directly with art from antiquity to the modern age and across continents, the students delved into belief systems and visited built spaces meant for communal worship or contemplation: a cathedral, a synagogue, a Japanese teahouse, a Hindu temple. They watched film clips, among them—"My Dinner with André" and "Tar"—to identify true dialogue and non-dialogue. In listening closely to one another, they discovered profound communications in many forms of art. They wrote papers on dialogues they experienced outside the classroom and evaluated the difference between a true dialogue and one that was not. The class was supported by the Stavros Niarchos Foundation, Paideia, whose mission is to encourage "informed, engaged, and effective community members... to lead fulfilling and integrated personal, professional, and civic lives." The Greek word *paideia* is a complex concept better understood by the foundation's mission statement above.

For me, the class and its focus on Paideia's mission to integrate the personal, professional and civic brought together much of what had concerned me in intercultural training. I was not doing research but working with people in many professions to help design programs suitable for their own settings. The opportunity to contribute to this book, that combines the autobiographies of several of the finest thinkers in intercultural communication, came just after I finished the Penn class and has made me aware, more than I was, of how this glowing field of thought and action came into being and the gift it has been to me.

Dialogue—or as David Bohm posits, "true dialogue" is special. It requires respect and close listening to another human being. It is the opposite of knowing before asking or inserting one's own experience into that of another's before listening to what the other has to say. The class at Penn, inspired by art, brought students together through their looking, listening, paraphrasing, asking and asking again. Painting, sculpture, color, line, size, and subject taught many lessons: what did a particular artist want to say and how did each tell a story. What IS the story? What story do *you* bring?

In the classroom, I was most uplifted when participants located insights within themselves and brought the rest of us into their stories and spoke about new realizations. The students came from varied backgrounds and brought many talents: music, sculpture, photography, philosophy, writing. They considered the values inherent in true dialogue: reflection, a search for shared understandings, a respect for multiple points of view. They became aware of imposing past meanings on present situations, avoided dogma and sought to stay in the present. They recognized opinions and assumptions. They got to know one another through their dialogues. They found humor and poignance among them.

The Original Skype: What the Human Form Can Tell Us

The software Skype advertises itself as enabling the world's conversations. It eventually became a verb—to "skype" was to start a conversation. The first chapter of *Art inSight* offers glimpses of the human form as it was sculpted, painted, and collaged over millennia to give visual speech to the values of people everywhere.

From prehistory to now, there is evidence that ways of depicting the human form is a great communicator of life as it was lived or imagined. What was important, scary, beyond comprehension, celebrated or meant to tell a story?

African kings, Egyptian pharaohs, Greek goddesses and athletes, Christian saints, iconic Buddhas, and regular people tell us about themselves through their bodies, their costumes, their postures, their size, and where they are in deserts, temples, huts, in nature, enclosed in structures, or exposed on mountain tops. Each communicates something of its time and space. Figures are likely made from available materials: wood, marble, clay mud, plastic. And we find these figures in locations that give us more of their purpose—in sacred spaces to inspire awe, on buildings to comment on street life, in murals to dignify workers, on walls anywhere to amuse us with jokes about everyday life.

In *Art in Sight*, I write about the rock star Elvis Presley as he was sculpted by artist Robert Arneson in 1978. Playfully, Arneson borrowed a classical form and gave us Elvis in the form of a gilded Roman general. As contemporary viewers, we have a chance to roll our eyes over his choice or to consider the message embodied in the glitter of gold, the placing of a performer on a raised pedestal, and a rock star looking out over our heads without meeting our gaze. Arneson chose his materials and the placement of his work with care. Now it's up to us to ask about each decision.

Art offers many clues to cultural values. We can quietly interview those distant others.

Intercultural Communication Writ Large

In a work of art, whether a human being appears or not, it is usually implied. For me, contemporary art exposed another aspect of intercultural communication that hit like the proverbial ton of bricks. It is culture's proxy in unexpected forms, often confusing and blank, impenetrable or maddening. But many of those forms opened thought through asking what our senses take in: sleek bronze, broken glass, splashy paint, neon blue that read the word green, smelly wax, jagged lines, a chair on the wall, a sink without a faucet made by artist, Robert Gober.

What would I feel if I needed water from a sink without a faucet; what's the point of a recognizable household appliance such as a sink that doesn't function and won't give me what I need. I can't wash my hands or get a drink of water. Well, this is not a "real" sink, and it isn't in a kitchen or bathroom. It's in a museum where there is a story in this thing. What did Robert Gober want to say through a dysfunctional sink, one that he took a lot of trouble to make?

In the contemporary art world, when something looks familiar but doesn't behave in predictable ways, we might ask:

What's missing?

The thing that would make this work, the faucet.

What is it supposed to do?

Give water.

So here I am with a sink-like thing that doesn't do that. How does that make me feel?

Frustrated. Confused. Manipulated.

Might we be getting closer to something the artist may have felt?
May he also be expressing confusion and anger?
We can't know exactly what an artist is thinking or feeling. But we are now bringing ourselves into the picture, into the object, and perhaps getting closer to the artist's intention. That is one reason that art is such a potent means for building understanding. We never know exactly what another person is feeling, but maybe we can get closer to a shared emotional truth. There is a chance we may come out of this dialogue with insight into ourselves and draw closer to understanding another person.

Describing visual material opens conversations that may lead to true dialogues among us. This is not a predictable form of learning. It requires patience, imagination, and respect. When meetings among us are satisfying, it is often because we listen to the perceptions of others and pay attention to our own points of view before searching for shared meaning. Looking and describing a work of art focuses on our senses and the ways we relate to the world. We can recognize those and also our emotional responses or feelings about something before examining what it means.

Next -what does it say to us? And then, respectfully—what was the artist up to? What inspired the making of this thing. What does the artist want to say? What's the story behind this?

Recognizing what we sense (see, hear) and noticing our emotional responses, (happy, sad, confused, curious) remind us that we are part of the picture. We have looked into ourselves. After that, when we inquire into the artist's intention, we are more prepared to find it AND to respect a meaning others outside ourselves may find.

It is intimidating to be in novel situations where what we confront is confusing and where, at times, something appears to be looking back at us with its own confusion or bewilderment. This is what happened in Phnom Penh when I arrived, standing alone, oddly dressed where a foreigner was not often seen.

One part of adjusting to strangeness is in figuring out how to live where we are. Another is the satisfaction of seeing more deeply—understanding complexity that defies any one explanation. That is one of the great benefits of a career in the intercultural field: recognizing discomfort and confusion as part of living. The direct experience of looking together at a work of art and reflecting on what others see is a journey into a puzzling place. It can help us begin to fathom how others live. For the curious, the search for understanding can begin and continue.

My Gratitude to the Arts

In 2005 I discovered Japanese artist Hiraki Sawa. In his video, "Dwelling" he invades his bare London apartment with airplanes moving randomly through kitchen and bathroom. He makes his living space wobble, uncertain, and even threatening. Our homes are meant to be safe, a comfort. His apartment was to have been a retreat from an unfamiliar city, a new language, and the demands of life far away from his home in Japan. In addition to the unsettling movement of the planes, we notice the apartment has nothing personal among its installed appliances.

How often have I felt unsteady in a new home before hanging a picture or unpacking a toothbrush—and felt reduced to a childlike dependence on someone else to translate a language, find a food market, show me how to take a bus and reassure me that I have access to friendly advice. Hiraki Sawa's work is highly personal, as much art is. It tells one story that links to our own and makes us aware of sensory and emotional parts of ourselves we share with others. In his video, we find the value of metaphor, another way of telling a story, this one about uprooting and discomfort, going deeply into his private experience and offering a vivid image to

invite the rest of us to sense his world. Therein lies an invitation to participate in his emotional response and develop empathy for his experience.

To live far away in another land is to be thrust into a demanding experience that makes us aware of the unavoidable process to learn to live with
confidence in ourselves and trust in others. My arrival in Phnom Penh
amused me only later when I tried to see myself as those Cambodian
women saw me.

Who We Are and What We Do

Early intercultural training, when it intended to prepare people to live in
other cultures, was often based on observable behaviors (how close to
stand, how to greet and say thank you, how to dress correctly). It is useful
to behave appropriately in all settings. But there is more because these
external expressions of propriety, politeness and correctness are often
linked to customs and related values. Thanks to the scholarship of histori-
ans, communications experts, anthropologists, educators, and thinkers in
a number of academic fields, many of whom have contributed to this
book, I woke to the richness of looking into cultural patterns that include
spiritual beliefs, life's priorities, attitudes toward time and nature, the
importance of family and more. I continue to be the learner of lessons I
try to teach.

NOW

Writing this essay makes me ask myself, who was I before and who am I
now? Who was I before the intercultural field took hold of me? I am not
the young naive I was, but then none of us are as we've aged. And all
occupations and professions change us. I am biased in favor of how the
intercultural field has changed my life. I did not start out choosing it;
rather it chose me as I was living every day.

Communicating across cultures is part of nearly all occupations.
Teachers who are expressly in classrooms to teach Intercultural
Communication are in rarefied positions because they are typically among
people who are in the room with them to learn what that is. But I cannot
think of an occupation or a profession that does not encourage us to be
curious about the lives of others and their ways of making sense of the
world. The great gift of studying interculturalism is its urgings to observe,
inquire, and respect people's behavior as the foreground of a background

we cannot find without listening or giving attention to visual cues including posture, dress, eye contact and much more.

I am concluding this essay as a new U.S. president is inaugurated and while fires are raging in Los Angeles where I have close family. I wake each morning in a comfortable bed with breakfast ahead and the pleasure of a good cup of coffee. I have friends near who are loving and supportive. This paradox of my personal comfort along with my fears for actual people in perilous situations is present. At other times, I need stories and images to take me into the lives of those I may never meet.

I work in a field that invites me to peer outside myself and into diversity in its many forms, to move beyond my limited vision and, perhaps, to behave more appropriately. When the arts became the bases for my classes and training, I came upon a treasure. Marcel Proust wrote, "through art alone are we able to emerge from ourselves to know what another person sees of a universe."

Including the arts invites the viewer to share the feelings and perceptions of another person. The art of Hiraki Sawa and Robert Arenson carry us into their sensations and experiences of the times and places in which they lived. Analyses of culture deepen when combined with the expression in art that matters to its makers. It provides a window into the awareness and intelligence of that distant other. Artists are our partners in this journey if we invite them in.

Occupations and professions change us. I am biased in favor of how deeply the intercultural field has changed my life. If I had to make up a new name for the work, I might call it "The Joy of Noticing."

Fanchon Silberstein has no conflicts of interest to declare that are relevant to the content of this chapter.

REFERENCES

Bohm, D. (1990). *On dialogue*. Routledge.

Proust, M. (1981). *Remembrance of things past* (C. K. Scott, M. Moncrieff, & T. Kilmartin, Trans.) Chatto & Windus.

Redl, F. (1966). *When we deal with children. The Free Press.*, 35–67.

Sawa, H. (2002). *Dwelling.* You Tube. (Ruben Carrera, Jan 25, 2018).

Silberstein, F. (2020). *Art inSight: Understanding art and why it matters.* Intellect Press and The University of Chicago Press.

CHAPTER 11

Significant Emotional Events Lead to an Intercultural Team

Donna M. Stringer

Nearly everything that has happened to me has happened by surprise. All the important things have happened by surprise. And whatever has been happening usually has already happened before I have had time to expect it. (Wendell Berry, 2001, p. 322)

I was finalizing last minute details for a cross-cultural communication training in Mexico with a Costa Rican colleague. ME: Miguel, I will meet you at baggage claim at 8:15. HIM: My dearest Donna, I am looking forward to seeing you and working together again. Please travel safely. ME: I am bringing the materials with me so you don't need to bring anything. HIM: My lovely colleague, I appreciate how easy you make it for us to work together. I look forward to a hug tomorrow.

When we met the next day, I asked him what he noticed about our email exchange and we laughed at how task-oriented and direct I was and how relationship-oriented and indirect he was. We used this exchange as an example in our training. We had worked together for years and understood our different styles; if we had just begun our relationship, this communication style difference could have negatively impacted our growing trust and ability to work together.

D. M. Stringer (✉)
Seattle, WA, USA

S. M. Fowler, D. C. Yalowitz (eds.), *Creating the Intercultural Field*,
https://doi.org/10.1007/978-3-032-01370-5_11

207

How It All Started for Both of Us

Donna's Story	Andy's Story

As a 4-year-old I was cautioned not to walk on the railroad tracks behind our house because "your shoe could get stuck, and you might get run over". My immediate reaction was to go out and try to get my shoe stuck which, of course, it didn't. Therein began my lifelong endeavor to challenge authority and think for myself. Another significant, but unconscious influence from my childhood was my parents' example of inclusion. We were a family of six, but I don't ever remember a household of 6: we always had others in our home. Family, friends, strangers who need a meal or a place to sleep, or an ear to listen and a heart to accept. I learned to always make room for others, and it underscored my values and my success in virtually every chapter of my life.

Andy's story is gleaned from unpublished interviews conducted by Kathleen O'Connor and Russ Brubaker before Andy died, and from the hundreds of conversations we had during our 40-year relationship. With apologies to his memory for any inaccuracies.

Andy's childhood in segregated North Carolina was far from solitary. Despite being an only child, he was enveloped by the vibrant embrace of a close-knit community. With educators as parents—a mother who shared her knowledge as a teacher and a father who commanded respect as a principal—Andy's upbringing was shaped by the values of love, discipline, and the undeniable significance of communal ties. Every child in the neighborhood belonged not just to their own family but to the collective, an interwoven tapestry of support that nurtured them all.

(continued)

(continued)

Donna's Story	Andy's Story
"You don't need to get married and have children like every other woman in your family, you know. You are smart. You should go to college and have a career": this from an "old maid" teacher when I was younger than a teenager. Really?! I am smart? I have options? This was my first Significant Emotional Experience (SEE)[1]—the thought that I was smart. It shook me to my core—although the idea didn't take hold immediately. In my early 20's I was the mother of three young sons. We moved to Sacramento where I began working as a secretary for Sacramento State University (then College) in the Educational Opportunity Program, otherwise known as educational assistance for low-income students, mostly people of color. I had not seen or known a person of color until I was 17 years old—which is difficult to believe in today's world. So, working with Black and Brown people energized me in a way I did not fully understand. What I did know was that I resonated with the "causes": the energy of social justice, the Vietnam War protests, the marches with Brown Berets and Black Panthers. Quite regularly, my new friends would point out my ignorance about white privilege and how their life realities differed from mine. Some days I was excited; others I was simply shell-shocked. But every day I felt alive and energized, engaged, and involved.	Andy's childhood summers were also engulfed with community: they were spent with his mother's family in Ohio while his father spent the summer in graduate school, completing his master's in educational administration. Andy learned to value hard work and education from his father's model; he learned unconditional love from his extended community. It was his senior year, 1960, and the student sit-ins in Greensboro, North Carolina took place. Four African American college freshmen walked into the F. W. Woolworth store and quietly sat down at the lunch counter. They were refused service, but they stayed until closing time. Over several months, dozens of students were arrested but continued the sit-ins. Sales dropped by a third and six months from the very first sit-in, the four freshmen were served at Woolworth's lunch counter. Andy did not participate in the sit-ins; rather he was an observer from the second day through the end of the sit-ins. One night as he and a friend were leaving for home several white men followed them; one pulled a gun and shot at them but missed. This was a Significant Emotional Event, of course, and resulted in Andy reflecting, seriously, on both the risks and the rewards of working for social justice. This led to his persistence in telling people, throughout his life, that they needed to consider what they would be willing to die for. His answer to that question was "social justice".

(continued)

(continued)

Donna's Story	Andy's Story
In my late 20s, having supported my husband through college, I was working on my own degree at night while working during the day to support our family. As I approached completion of my BA and was applying for Ph.D. programs my husband told me that "if I had known you would like education so much, I never would have let you go." Something snapped! I decided it was time to go solo—well not exactly "solo"—I did have three sons, whose lives were central to my decisions. My second SEE, although uncomfortable, was learning to be single with no partner in life decisions or responsibilities.	The sit-in was Andy's first contact with the civil rights movement that would become his life's passion. After this, he joined CORE (Congress of Racial Equality) and became the co-chair in Winston-Salem. It was clear as he did this work that he was destined to be a leader. After high school Andy was admitted as a pre-med student, to Lincoln University, founded in 1854 and the nation's first degree-granting Historically Black University located in Pennsylvania. Lincoln was also an all-male school that recruited internationally, which was Andy's first opportunity to engage in meaningful ways with men from very different backgrounds than his own, including many from African countries.
As a graduate student in Social and Developmental Psychology at UC Davis, I faced the challenge of juggling studies with the responsibilities of being a single parent. I envisioned a future as a teacher, researcher, and writer, eager to make my mark in the field.	After graduation, Andy returned to North Carolina to work on cancer research at the Bowman Gray School of Medicine at Wake Forest University while waiting for admission to medical school. This work (determined to be in the national interest), plus a close family friend who sat on the local draft board, got him a military deferral as the Vietnam War began to heat up and young men were being drafted.
As fate would have it, an incredible opportunity presented itself to me, intertwining my professional journey with my academic pursuits. Davis, California, the place I lived and studied, extended a job offer to me, marking my first step into the professional world. It was an exhilarating prospect, allowing me to dive into my studies while also supporting my family.	Andy's Civil Rights activity with CORE increased in the summer of 1963. A key event in the Civil Rights movement with the Poor People's March on Washington organized by Bayard Rustin, the Congress for Racial Equality (CORE) and other civil rights groups. Andy attended this event and remembered sitting in a tree where he had direct vision of the platform. He had driven all night to get to Washington, D.C. at 7 a.m. He had no idea the number of people who would be there so was deeply touched by viewing the lines of buses and cars as far as he could see. Hundreds of thousands of people heard Martin Luther King's "I *Have a Dream*" speech on the Capital Mall and millions watched on TV. This was a pivotal event in the Civil Rights movement and American history—and a Significant Emotional Event in Andy's life.

(*continued*)

(continued)

Donna's Story	Andy's Story
Taking on the role of the inaugural Program Director for the UC Davis Women's Resources & Research Center (WRRC), I discovered an increased passion for social change. I sensed that effecting transformative shifts might be within reach by working "inside" systems. With each passing day, my commitment to creating a better future for women, and to including women of color and lesbians in our work, grew stronger. Several years in this position saw the WRRC, and my commitment to social justice, grow exponentially. I helped develop services exploring gender equity, stood firm in demanding that the University include the words "lesbian" and "racially diverse" in the definition of the Center, held the first-ever "Men's Conference" exploring male identity issues, started a statewide network of gender equity programs, a statewide sexual assault service funded with state funds as part of a sexual assault settlement, and helped develop domestic violence awareness with the first national conference on battered women. The success I experienced in this role was really SEE number 3: I began to see myself as a capable leader and role model—and I enjoyed being in the public eye.	This exhilarating event, however, was followed by the bombing of the Ebenezer Baptist Church in Birmingham, Alabama where Denise McNair (11), Addie Mae Collins (14), Carole Robertson (14), and Cynthia Wesley (14) were killed while preparing for Sunday school. CORE became more active, and Andy's leadership became more public. In 1964, as part of the Voter Registration push, Martin Luther King came to Winston-Salem, N.C. During this visit, Andy met MLK and shook his hand. This was yet another important event in shifting Andy into non-violent civil rights. He began to think he did not want to be a doctor, helping individual patients—he wanted to be an activist who could help shift attitudes, policies and practices that could affect lives of thousands and create culture change. Shortly after returning from Washington, D.C., on November 5, 1963, Andy received a draft letter for the Vietnam War. He believed that his CORE activities were too public, leading to a loss of his "national interest" deferment. After basic training, Andy was sent to Fort Lewis, in Tacoma, Washington where he was assigned to hospital duty because of his pre-med training and cancer research experience. Andy served there for 2 years and was offered an opportunity to go to Officers' Training but declined, unwilling to commit additional years to the military.

(continued)

(continued)

Donna's Story	Andy's Story
After successfully completing my Ph.D. coursework, I accepted the position of first-ever Human Resources and Affirmative Action Director at Montana State University in picturesque Bozeman, Montana. This opportunity not only provided me with the ideal environment to complete my dissertation but also served as a steppingstone toward securing an esteemed academic faculty position. But women's issues called me to community social change. While working at the University, I also spent virtually all my spare hours helping to establish a statewide Battered Women's Network and a community sexual assault center. My dissertation sat on the back of my desk, and I drifted further from the academy. I was only in Bozeman for three-plus years, but the impact of that time was monumental. I published my first book, *Battered Women* (Sage Publications, 1979), and created lifelong personal and professional friendships.	It was during his work in the military hospital that he met his first wife, whose father was the editor of the Bainbridge Island (Washington) newspaper and featured in the book *Snow Falling on Cedars* for being the first journalist in the area to write a scathing editorial against the evacuation of the Japanese to the WWII internment camps. Andy was fascinated by his father-in-law's role in journalism and the power of having a voice for the underdog. After leaving the military Andy returned to North Carolina to work at North Carolina Advancement School, a residential technology school. Andy taught math & biology in the 10th to the 12th grades. Students were 95% Black; teachers were 95% White. Black students were failing. Some of the white students cared about racial issues and asked teachers to do something to change these numbers. Andy and a colleague agreed to work with students in a way that would facilitate their engagement in education. They moved to a new school in Philadelphia where they developed the idea of using cameras. Each student was given a disposable camera and was told to shoot pictures that would tell their story. They needed to supplement the photography with a written story. Students got very excited about this process and the success ratio began to shift. This planted a seed in Andy's thinking about how using creative and/or artistic avenues can engage people in expanded thinking about their world.

(*continued*)

(continued)

Donna's Story	Andy's Story
A significant emotional event occurred in Bozeman when I "took on" a local judge. A young son of a police officer was accused of rape and pleaded guilty. The case hit the news when the judge said to the accused, from the bench, that "next time you think about doing something like this, go home and take a cold shower and read a good book." I spearheaded a letter to the judge expressing that the community was aghast at his statement. As we collected signatures, virtually every attorney and social worker in town refused to sign because they had seen others' careers ended by this judge if they disagreed with him. Unexpectedly, the judge published a letter apologizing to the community and he and I became cautious allies. The President of the University later told me, very indirectly (I pushed but he could never really say it directly) that if the judge had not turned the corner, I would have been terminated for my actions which, while not related to my job, could have embarrassed the university. This was another instance of my challenging the power structure and "winning"—learning how to use my own power for social change. It also helped me identify "what I was willing to die (or lose a job) for."	Teachers loved the project because they could see how student achievement improved, but the administration said the kids were too vociferous and should not have been so candid about their experiences of racism and discrimination. Consequently, the department was "reorganized "and did not include Andy and his colleague—or some of the most creative elements of the project. Both Andy and his colleague resigned from the school, which was a SEE for Andy in several ways: he reflected on the success of creative education and on the power of leaders to either support or stop success. He also recognized the power of communication and how it can lead to either success or failure. It was at this pivotal time in his life that he completely abandoned his medical goals and moved fully into social change work. Andy's journey took an unexpected turn when he received an invitation to apply to Columbia Journalism School. Columbia was starting a new program aimed at recruiting minorities for journalism and putting them on a fast track through a 3-month, fast-paced training program. He applied and was accepted, changing his life from science and education to a new field of journalism. Drawn to the allure of storytelling and the power of both the visual and written word, he embarked on this new adventure, immersing himself in the bustling streets of Philadelphia. His experiences as a journalist deepened his understanding of the world, its complexities, and the transformative role that media could play. Driven by an insatiable curiosity, he sought to craft narratives that would inform, inspire, and challenge societal norms.

(*continued*)

(continued)

Donna's Story	Andy's Story
A friend in Seattle asked me to apply for a job and I declined, saying I didn't want to move or take another job until I had completed my dissertation. However, on Memorial Day weekend, I went camping with friends and it snowed on the first day—hard! I do not like snow, so I informed my camping mates that I would be in the truck waiting until they were ready to go. Sitting alone for the remainder of the day, I peeked at the Seattle job description, and it simply called my name. To be able to work on policies impacting women and sexual minorities was a dream job. When I returned home the next day, I applied for the job as Director of the Seattle Office for Women's Rights. Three months later I moved to Seattle where I completed my dissertation while holding down the job as a City Department Head. I was not in this position for long before realizing that I was, unconsciously perhaps, making a shift from identifying myself as an academic to an identity as a social justice professional. Shifting a life-long dream required considerable self-examination and not a little grieving. This Significant Emotional Experience helped me understand that opportunities often require shifts in life aspirations, so being flexible can be a useful characteristic. One of my first projects in this new job was to conduct a study of sexual harassment in the city workforce—the first such study in the country. Andy Reynolds, a recently retired TV journalist and a member of my advisory board, helped me prepare to release the results publicly, beginning a partnership of 40+ years based on love, common values, and a passion for social change. More about that later.	With a wealth of experiences under his belt, Andy's path led him to KING 5, a prominent television station in Seattle that was reputed to be a training ground for network television. His new aspiration was to work for one of the networks as an international correspondent. At KING TV, he honed his skills as a broadcaster, captivating audiences with his insightful reporting and unwavering dedication to truth. Two of his more interesting assignments included covering the Ted Bundy trial in Miami, Florida and his coverage of the Mt. St. Helens volcanic eruption in 1980. He consistently spent time creating "specials" about new immigrant populations, redlining in Seattle, and campaigns affecting specific communities. He turned down two network jobs, at which point he had to ask himself why he would decline the very opportunity he had wanted. The answer was simple: he did not want to leave Seattle. Experiencing racism that denied him entry to the management level of television, Andy finally left TV and became the Marketing Director of a local technical institute, returning to education. As a result of this experience, Andy became vigilant about the lack of people of color in the television and other public-facing industries—frequently pointing it out in public forums. The entrepreneurial spirit within him yearned for more, however, propelling him to launch his own marketing business. This bold leap allowed him freedom to find clients who gave him license to develop compelling, creative messages. A call from a local Black leader and Director of the Seattle Parks and Recreation Department resulted in an offer of a job as marketing and Public Relations Director for the organization. Andy could not tell this man no—he closed his business and was, for the first time in his life, a public sector employee.

(*continued*)

(continued)

Donna's Story	Andy's Story
The Mayor of Seattle sent me to Boston to attend a summer program on public administration at Harvard University on the condition that I promise to return to Seattle. He joked that he feared I would fall in love with Boston—which I did, of course. This experience gave me additional information, helped me develop additional management skills and, most importantly, solidified my decision that I was unlikely to ever return to academia full-time. It also gave me a "close up and personal" look at how working on women's issues was connected to working on issues of importance for other demographic populations. Focusing solely on women's issues was no longer enough for me. Returning from Boston, I was given one more fateful opportunity: to be Deputy Director of the Washington State Department of Licensing—important because it gave me the chance to oversee a multi-million-dollar budget, a staff of hundreds, and the requirement to manage publicly elected officials who did not report to me. This experience became important as I later worked in consulting roles for large organizations and could relate to the challenges my clients faced. This was my second public political appointment which was to be one of my greatest Significant Emotional Experiences. After just under four years, the political leadership in the state shifted, resulting in my being replaced by another political appointee. I was just fired! By now, Andy Reynolds had become my life partner. Andy and my best friend both insisted I had not been fired—just replaced by a political appointee of the "other" party. But I had not quit, and I was unemployed, which felt like being fired. This significant emotional experience gave me yet another opportunity to pivot my professional identity.	Andy had shifted his career focus from medicine to medical research to education to journalism, became a marketing entrepreneur, and now he was entering the world of public service. Once he left television, he was free to be involved with community organizations in a way that he could not do as a "neutral" journalist. A City Council member appointed him to the Seattle Women's Commission where Donna Stringer had just become the Executive Director. This was a volunteer position, and he entered just as Donna was preparing to release data from research on the sexual harassment experiences of the City of Seattle employees. He was able to put his journalism skills and contact to use immediately by coaching Donna as she prepared for a press conference to release the findings.

(*continued*)

(continued)

Donna's Story	Andy's Story

In a brief attempt at returning to academe, I experienced the power of listening to one's body. I had three separate appointments for interviews at the University of Washington. Each time, I arrived directly across the street from the interview location and literally could not move. My body simply would not cross the street—the thought of engaging in what I had experienced as misogynistic academic politics was viscerally debilitating. I cancelled each appointment and after the third time, accepted that my life in academe was over and that I needed to think about something else. Here I was, once again, at a junction in my life, needing to decide whether to seek a "job", or to do something else. I had never considered myself an entrepreneur. I enjoyed the security and status of career appointments. After a lifetime of financial challenges and identity struggles, starting a business felt very risky. I had learned to enjoy both risk-taking and the joy of life from my father, who loved life and it's challenges. He also went bankrupt three times— starting over each time as if he had never "failed". I was 40 years old, and I wanted to be available to my sons, both financially and emotionally, as they launched their adult lives. I took inventory of all the risky "wins" I had experienced and decided that starting a business would be a new adventure from which I would have time to recover if it didn't succeed. With no small trepidation, the consulting firm Executive Diversity Services was born.

THE MERGER

Perhaps the most important Significant Emotional Event for both me and Andy was meeting each other. Beginning in 1981, we merged our personal and professional lives and goals. Only weeks after meeting, Andy became my coach in preparing to deliver the results of a city-wide sexual harassment study to a less-than-supportive media audience. An important piece of our history is that Andy left TV the day before I arrived in Seattle, so I had never seen him as a news reporter, nor did I know who he was in the context of Seattle politics.

It was not love at first sight: misperception occurred on both sides. Andy perceived me as arrogant—an impression I have struggled with my entire life as an introvert who is slow to engage on a personal level. And I thought Andy was gay. I had asked the City Council to appoint a gay male of color to my advisory board and Andy was always with his best friend who was openly gay—so I assumed they were partners. As we prepared for the press conference, Andy's perception of me changed, and after the press conference, he asked if I would be interested in doing something with him socially and I said yes, if it was okay with his partner. He clarified that he was not gay so we made a date for dinner.

Our first dinner together involved long discussions of the values we shared for social justice. Shortly after that dinner, we became committed life partners. One of our first decisions was not to marry until our gay and lesbian friends could do so—a simple but important way to demonstrate our value of equity. This began a 40-year journey of identifying even subtle ways in which social structures discriminated against populations and working to change those structures.

The first five years of our life together, we had separate work lives with Andy in his marketing business and working for the Seattle Parks and Recreation Department, and me as the Executive Director of the City Office for Women's Rights and the Deputy Director of the State Department of Licensing. When my political appointment ended in 1986, I decided to start a consulting and training business with my friend Linda Taylor. Because I was known for my work in sexual harassment, LGBTQ and women's issues, I decided to focus on those three areas while simultaneously developing my expertise and increasing my reputation in the broader area of racial and gender diversity. Seattle was known as a "predominantly white" city, both demographically and culturally, and this was a significant time for development of public services that were inclusive of diversity. Both Andy and I had been in public-facing roles and had positive reputations as social justice advocates, so starting this business was a "natural".

It was 1986. Two major events occurred within the first half of the year. I started Executive Diversity Services, Inc., in January with the under-standing that Linda would join me in the summer. I had never seen myself as an entrepreneur but here I was. It was not long before I had attained a very large contract to conduct diversity training for a transportation com-pany. We grew like topsy by the summer and shortly after incorporating, Linda invited Andy to quit his job and join our business because we des-perately needed another partner. I walked into our office one morning and Linda announced that Andy would be joining us as a third partner. I had not been a part of that decision, but once it was made, Andy and I had to identify how to manage our personal and professional partnerships in a way that would maintain the commitments to both our relationship and our business.

Together we launched a business to provide consulting and training services to organizations with a focus on structural and behavioral changes to increase the inclusion of diverse employee and client populations. This was in 1986—the height of the AIDs crisis and early in the new wave of concern about civil rights. Believing in life-long learning and my need to be cautious and authentic in how I advocated for demographic groups to which I do not belong, I worked to create a business team that could chal-lenge my accuracy as I developed training curricula for corporate and public-sector clients. Over a two-year period, the business expanded to include a team of four owners, a diverse training team of several dozen, and an advisory group of representatives from African American, multiple Latinx groups, Indigenous, multiple Asian populations, disabled people and the LGBTQ community.

The second major event was when Linda and I attended our first classes at the Summer Institute for Intercultural Communication (SIIC) in the summer of 1986, shortly after incorporating our business. To say this was life-changing would be an understatement of monumental proportions. My first classes on Intercultural issues were from Dean Barnlund, Jack Condon, Milton Bennett, Michael Paige, and Janet Bennett—imagine the impact these giants had on me! Driving home from Portland to Seattle after almost three weeks of intense learning, Linda and I were literally in tears. Those classes had changed our perspective on how to create training curricula that started with culture and then moved to bias, and how to create a developmental approach that was safe for learning. I was shaken to my core.

EXECUTIVE DIVERSITY SERVICES

Two important insights formed the groundwork for the work of Executive Diversity Services for the next 40 years under my leadership: first, it was important to understand that training people about diversity, inclusion and engagement was meaningless if the organization's policies, procedures, and culture remained unchanged. And secondly, creating curricula that was developmental, (beginning with intercultural understanding), and environments that were safe for participants was our key to success.

I set out to learn everything I could about culture and biases, and how these two things interact. It was 1986 and I bought every book on intercultural research and training on the market. This was early in the field and Intercultural Press was still in the publishing business, but the number of books was so small that I could, literally, own every book on the topic of interculturalism. This changed rapidly until the early 1990s when publications outran my ability to buy/read everything. Imagine being so early in the development of a field that you could own and read every book available—and then watching the field grow so rapidly that it was impossible to keep up with the publishing world. It also did not escape my notice that many of the theories, and significant research had been central concepts in my education in social & developmental psychology. Dinner conversations at our home became focused on a multitude of cultural issues and how they mattered to creating an inclusive world. We became obsessed with understanding culture and how such understanding could lead to more equitable organizations and communities.

Even as the field expanded, there were certain things as a consultant that I found disconcerting: primarily, the lack of readily available training materials about some key topics. Specifically, I was taken aback that there were not more materials for the teaching of cultural value systems. This led to working with my colleague Patricia Cassiday to publish three books of intercultural training materials in values, communication styles, and international relocation. Not unlike other events in my professional life, publishing these books was not planned on my part. Patricia was a Ph.D. student at Seattle University. She walked into my office one day and said she wanted an internship with me. My response was that I didn't take internships—managing a newly organized and rapidly growing business was all I could handle. She asked if there were any areas of curriculum that I needed help with, and "Values" immediately came out of my mouth. Before she left my office, she convinced me that she could help me without taking much of my time. Her "help" resulted in publishing our first book and she later convinced me to tackle two more books on intercultural topics.[2]

Like many others, (i.e., Dianne Hofner Saphiere with Cultural Detective) I was able to develop some outstanding training materials (e.g., Diversafari—a board game for exploring culture) but was never able to successfully market them. I had to finally admit that I loved developing new things but once they were developed, I had no interest (or skill) in marketing them. A hallmark of our consulting and training was providing practical tools based on theory and research. Combining academic and applied fields in ways that left clients with actions that worked.

THE SUMMER INSTITUTE FOR INTERCULTURAL COMMUNICATION (SIIC)

In the meantime, Linda and I continued attending classes at SIIC and in three years Andy and I became faculty members, teaching Foundation courses beginning in 1989. I continued co-teaching with giants like Michael Paige and Anita Rowe until the last summer the Institute was held in 2019. In support of my value of lifelong learning, I also attended classes each year as well. Andy and I would teach for two weeks and attend a class in the third week. The richness of this environment and the openness of faculty to share information and resources with each other and with students was extraordinary.

The impact of SIIC expanded the field in several ways. The Masters in Intercultural Relationships (MAIR) was a partnership between the Intercultural Communication Institute (ICI) and Pacific University in California. Students in the MAIR program attended classes at SIIC in the summer as part of their degree requirements and during the winter months, classes were held specifically for those in the MAIR program. I taught principles and models of the intercultural field for several cohorts of this program.

From 2013 to 2017 Andy and I were part of a smaller group of faculties conducting a Winter Institute of Intercultural Communication (WIIC) held for shorter times in cities around the US as a way of making intercultural communication available to people who could not afford either the time or money to attend sessions in Portland, Oregon. It was an effort to create greater inclusion and accessibility to the intercultural field. Further expansion included the Qatar Institute of Intercultural Communication (QIIC) where a small group of 4–6 faculty members traveled to Doha, Qatar to conduct three-day courses on intercultural issues. I was a faculty member in each of these institutes, conducting sessions on intercultural conflict, intercultural values and intercultural mediation. These sessions were envisioned and made possible by a Qatari woman who had been at SIIC—one small, but important, example of how the field was spread because of SIIC.

THE SOCIETY FOR INTERCULTURAL EDUCATION, TRAINING, AND RESEARCH (SIETAR)

We continued to collaborate with other business owners, to mentor younger trainers, and to be active in the intercultural field. It was the late 1980s when we became active participants in the Society for Intercultural Educators, Trainers, and Researchers, making presentations at annual U.S. conferences and attending the SIETAR Europa conference.

Andy became President of SIETAR USA from 2009 through 2010. His goal during his presidency was to institutionalize structures for the organization that had relied so heavily on Peggy Pusch who had started SIETAR USA and shepherded it through a decade of growth. While he was not as successful as he would have liked, the idea of becoming independent of Peggy's leadership did take hold and the organization moved toward one with board and committee leadership that honored Peggy while spreading intercultural networks. One of the things that he considered a success was working with Sandy Fowler to develop the Margaret D. Pusch Founders Award, given to someone in SIETAR USA who had contributed both to the field and to the organization. I was Andy's silent partner in this work, consistently helping him think through both his strategic vision and his tactical actions.

I agreed to co-chair the SIETAR USA conference in 2014 in Portland, Oregon with Lillian Tsai. We did several things that were "firsts" for the conference: we organized a time for "elders" to meet and discuss the growth of the field and their role in it; we had a nationally recognized speaker who was not an interculturalist but who spoke about the importance of structural change as important to effective intercultural organizations in a global context; and we had a speaker discuss the importance of including LBGTQ communities for effective intercultural organizations. Andy was my unofficial partner in this work—helping me think through how expanding the reach of conference speakers could facilitate the growth of intercultural thinking. It bears sharing that part of our commitment to SIETAR USA was demonstrated when Andy was taken to the emergency room with a post-surgery infection the day before this conference started and he insisted that I leave him to carry out my responsibilities for this conference.

SURPRISES

In 2019—the height of the pandemic and the latter stages of Andy's battle with cancer, Sandy Fowler, then President of SIETAR USA, requested a zoom meeting with us—together. We scheduled that meeting and then Andy and I began our speculation about what Sandy wanted—she had been a bit secretive in her request. We speculated a dozen things—wondering if she was going to ask Donna to be a board member or ask Andy to reflect on his days as president. Not even once did we identify the real reason for the call: the board wanted to surprise us as the first team to be awarded the Margaret D. Pusch Founders Award for contributions to the field. We were totally surprised! And honored! And humbled.

A surprising benefit of being interculturalists is how it enhanced our creativity. Andy was a lifelong photographer, and he began seeing things in the world to photograph that he had never seen before. I have been a lifelong quilter and painter and my projects have become more diverse as my view of the world has expanded. The content of our reading broadened; the museums we were interested in visiting enlarged. The nature of our weekly dinners and parties expanded. In short, everything in our lives became more creative as we became interculturalists, not just diversity consultants. One minor example of this is that we had many dinner parties. Andy loved to cook, and we both loved great conversations with interesting people. As the intercultural field became central to our lives, our home became a mini-salon several nights every week. We persisted in inviting a diversity of dinner guests to each meal, which made the conversations even more engaging.

What It Meant
to Be Interculturalist Entrepreneurs

Andy frequently said he was an angry Black man. He was quick to see racism in both large and small ways. But I dare say that most people who worked or socialized with him never saw that anger because, as an interculturalist, he understood and practiced ways to help people see injustice in ways that left them feeling challenged but not judged. Dozens of people have told me that Andy asked questions that made them think without ever making them feel judged. One of his favorite questions was "how do you know that?" which often caused people to stop and consider their positions.

Over the course of our years as entrepreneurs, we were able to work with organizations as small as 7 people and as large as 150,000+. We were able to work in over 40 countries and make lifelong friendships on five continents. I became an ardent interculturalist in the field of Diversity, Inclusion and Engagement (and all the other words used over the years!) because I saw first-hand how understanding culture could be a way to understand differences and to disarm the conflicts that DEI could ignite. We consistently noted that when people understood how their own culture affected their perceptions, and behaviors toward others (and vice versa!), they were then able to consider how powerful the diversity of friends, colleagues and clients could be. Interculturalism became the doorway to understanding diversity and bias with curiosity and without defensiveness.

Looking back at this career path, it seems to be laden with Significant Emotional Experiences. I had planned to be an academician, not a leader, an interculturalist, or an entrepreneur. But the consistent themes in my life include the willingness to pivot to something unknown when an opportunity presents itself, while also staying true to the values of social justice, inclusion, equity and a meaningful and productive love-filled life. In short, becoming an interculturalist changed everything: my career, my relationships, and how I used my time and treasure. And, I would assert that U.S. culture does not encourage such pivoting. We begin asking children "what do you want to be when you grow up?" very early in their lives—and once such decisions are made, we do everything to encourage a linear life, which does not encourage risk taking or adventure. My career story could be titled "nothing planned but everything gained."

Andy's career path was also laden with SEEs—he was nothing at the end of his life like what he thought he would be at the beginning (or even middle) of his life. He began as a pre-med student, shifted to education, became a journalist, and easily moved into DEI and cross cultural roles. When he was diagnosed with a non-treatable cancer, he consistently said "I am clear-eyed about dying. I have lived a very good life, and I am not afraid to die." I could not imagine a better way to end a career—or a life!

Donna M. Stringer has no conflicts of interest to declare that are relevant to the content of this chapter.

NOTES

1. This a term coined by Morris Massey as one of the three ways that values can be changed, and it helped form the core of my consultation, training, and personal life.
2. Stringer, Donna M. and Patricia A. Cassiday. (2003) 52 Activitiers for Exploring Values Differences. Yarmouth, ME: Intercultural Press. Stringer, Donna M. and Patricia A. Cassiday (2009) 52 Activities for Improving Cross-Cultural Communication. Boston, MA: Nicholas Brealey Publishing. Stringer, Donna M. and Patricia A. Cassiday (2015) 52 Activities for Successful International Relocation. Boston, MA: Nicholas Brealey Publishing.

REFERENCE

Berry, W. (2001). *Jayber Crow*. Counterpoint LLC.

CHAPTER 12

My Experiential Approach to Interculturalism

Sivasailam Thiagarajan (Thiagi)

I set about figuring out why people think I am an interculturalist. I came up with several skill sets, bits of knowledge, attitudes, beliefs, and experiences, and a funny accent that people associate with me being an interculturalist. How did I acquire these aptitudes and attitudes? I read a lot and listened to several interculturalists. I participated in courses and workshops. But most importantly, I experienced several encounters in life and obsessively ruminated about them. Living and thinking were my major learning techniques. I have a passion for brooding over my experiences. (Incidentally, this behavior pattern has nothing to do with my culture.)

In this chapter I narrate a series of life experiences and the lessons I learned from each of them. I will try to do this in a roughly chronological order, but I must forewarn the readers about my grasshopper mind.

A DEATH IN MY FAMILY

One of the earliest episodes that I recall was the death of my mother when I was six years old.

S. Thiagarajan (Thiagi) (✉)
The Thiagi Group, Bloomington, IN, USA
e-mail: thiagi@thiagi.com

© The Author(s), under exclusive license to Springer Nature
Switzerland AG 2025
S. M. Fowler, D. C. Yalowitz (eds.), *Creating the
Intercultural Field*,
https://doi.org/10.1007/978-3-032-01370-5_12

My big brother Maniannan was combing his hair when I woke up in the morning. This was surprising because it was not daylight outside; the electric lamp was on. More surprising was the strange look on Maniannan's face.

"Are you going somewhere?', I asked.

"Yes, Father wants me to go to Usman Road uncle and some other relatives."

"Why?"

"Because he wants me to take a letter to them."

"What letter?"

"This one."

I looked at the letter written in Father's tight handwriting. I recognized some words, but the others were too big for me. I asked Maniannan, "What does it say?"

Maniannan read the letter.

After a long illness, my wife Valliammal attained the gracious feet of Lord Muruga at 4:30 this morning. Her cremation will take place at 11:30 at the Mambalam mayanam.

I did not understand what the letter said. I asked Maniannan, "What does it mean?"

"It means Mother is dead." Maniannan said.

Maybe "Mother's dead" meant she was in greater pain.

I slowly went to the sick room where Mother lay in bed the last few months. Several grownups were in the room. They all had a serious look and were whispering to each other.

I understood the reason for their whispers. They did not want to wake Mother up.

I sidled over closer to Mother and gently touched her face.

"Mother, are you awake?'

She did not answer. I asked the next question in a louder voice.

"Mother, what does *dead* mean?

She did not answer.

I would ask Granny. She knew all the answers.

I went to the back room. Granny was in a corner, crying silently. Tears were running down her cheeks.

Several women around Granny were also crying. When my aunt saw me, she started wailing.

"My Sister, why did you die so young? Who is going to take care of your little ones?"

This served as a signal for the other women to start crying. I heard the words but could not understand what they meant. One woman complained about God's cruelty. Another woman talked about how Mother took care of her when her husband lost his job. My aunt talked about the time she and Mother were little girls.

I became scared by all the crying women. I went back to find Father to ask my question.

The men in the sick room all looked sad. Some of them were crying silently. But not Father. He never cried or smiled. He had his usual frown on his face when I saw him.

Mother was still sleeping. Our cook placed incense sticks in the corners of the room. Maybe they are going to celebrate because Mother was not sick anymore.

I asked the cook, "What does *dead* mean?" He did not answer. So, I changed my question.

"What is Mother going to do?"

The cook thought for a minute and said, "She is going on a trip."

"Are we going with her?"

"No".

"Will she be gone for a long time?"

"Yes".

Some men brought in a mat of green coconut fronds. They tied two stout bamboo poles to the sides. My cousin's grandfather, the oldest man in our family, went to Mother's bed and put some holy ash on her forehead. A few women put flowers in Mother's hair. My aunt removed Mother's gold wedding chain and replaced it with a yellow string. All through these activities, my mother continued to sleep.

At 11 o'clock Father and Uncle lifted Mother from the bed and laid her on the coconut mat. After placing a garland around her neck, they carried Mother to the street.

Mr. Natarajan, a nice clerk in Father's office placed me behind the handlebar of his bicycle. Then he went inside the house and carried back my little brother Chidambaram and put him on the saddle.

Mr. Natarajan pushed his bike, and we followed the others in a procession behind Mother. Maniannan walked with Father, carrying a small clay pot with glowing embers.

Sometimes people came out of their houses to watch the procession. Some women reverently patted themselves on their cheeks.

Soon I saw the railway line. Instead of going to the station, the procession moved away from the city. We came to a halt near a small temple. Five huts stood behind the temple. The huts looked strange because they had roofs and floors but no walls. On the floor of one of the huts, a lot of firewood was piled up neatly.

The men who were carrying Mother climbed up a few steps and placed the mat on top of the firewood pile.

My cousin's grandfather said something to Mother. I did not think she heard him.

Mr. Natarajan put the bicycle on its stand. He straightened up Chidambaram and covered his eyes. The men poured something on the firewood. It smelled like ghee.

And then the scary thing happened.

Father put a sliver of firewood inside the clay pot. When he took it out, I saw a flame. Father touched the firewood pile with the burning stick and the whole pile lit up.

I let out an anguished wail and closed my eyes.

When I opened my eyes, the fire was burning brightly. I tried to figure out what was happening. I asked Natarajan, "When the fire goes out, will Mother be better?"

Mr. Natarajan looked perplexed. "When the fire goes out," he said finally, "We will collect your mother's ashes and sprinkle them in the holy river."

When we returned home, everything was quiet. Most men went to work, and the women disappeared from our house.

I went to the sick room. Somebody had removed Mother's bed and had wiped the floor with medicine.

I sat down in a corner, trying to figure things out. I was thinking about what happened during the day when Granny came to the room. She sat by me and gently laid my head on her lap. I looked at Granny's sad, kind, and wise face.

"Granny, where did Mother go?"

"She has gone to God."

"Will I ever see her again?"

"Yes, Thiagi, but not in the way she looked before."

I was glad about that. Mother looked very skinny and sad the last few days.

"What will she look like when I see her? Will she look old?"

"No, she will be born a baby. It all depends on God's will. She could be a baby ant or a baby elephant. She could be a baby boy or a baby bird."

"Granny, why does God do these things?"

Granny looked at me and said, "Do you remember how to play *Hide and Seek*? God is playing a graceful game. He is a wonderful game master. His game never comes to an end. He keeps making new living babies out of dead people."

"Granny, I want to die so I can speak to Mother."

"You cannot do that."

"Why not?"

"Because they are the rules of God's game. The game must go on. You must explain the rules of the game to your little brother. We all must be nice to ants and birds and elephants because all living creatures are our relatives. Remember, God's game never ends."

Granny patted my cheeks.

I went looking for Chidambaram to explain the rules of God's never-ending game. Then we will look for ants and kittens.

The lesson I learned from the intense experience of my mother's death was that all living things are members of my family. This lesson helps me to treat all sentient creatures—and all types of people—as my siblings.

THE GIRL WHO ATE SOAP

We lived in a busy area of Madras, a large city. Our neighborhood had Muslim and Andhra households. Being a shy person, I seldom interacted with people from other cultures—except when I exchanged my tiffin with an English girl.

During the Summer vacation, we took the train from Tirunelveli to Vikramapuram. Tirunelveli is the biggest city in the district. Vikramapuram was a mill town, with a textile mill managed by a group of English people. Hundreds of local people, including one of my uncles, worked in the mill.

The train was crowded. Seats in the first- and second-class compartments were sold out. We never travelled in these higher classes, which cost more and had reserved seats.

We arrived at the railway station way ahead of time. Father went to the back corner and sat near a window. Many passengers embarked. After about 10 minutes, an English lady came to our compartment with a girl in tow. The girl looked about my age. The lady looked around, trying to find space.

My father put some of our luggage under the seat and stood up. He looked at the lady and said, "Please sit down, madam".

He left to sit in the front of the compartment.

The lady said "Thanks" and sat at the window seat. The girl sat next to her, and I sat at the edge of the seat.

The lady said something to the girl. I did not understand English, but I guessed she said something like, "Don't let him touch you" or "Don't talk to him".

The train started to move. Since it was near lunch time, most passengers pulled out their food packets and began to eat.

The English lady pulled out a piece of yellow soap. She took a knife and cut a piece and gave it to the girl. She cut another piece and, much to my surprise, began eating it. The girl also ate the soap but in small nibbles.

The compartment was hot and humid. The lady looked ready to take a nap. She closed her eyes and leaned against the seat corner.

I opened my tiffin box. It was a round aluminum box packed with five idlies (rice and dhal dumplings), covered with hot chili powder. The girl held out the piece of soap she was nibbling. She looked slyly at the sleeping lady. She said in a whisper, "Cheese". She broke a piece of the soap and gave it to me and said, "Eat".

I showed her the idlies. I showed the chili powder on top of each idli and said, "Gun powder." She laughed at my joke. Before I could warn her, she grabbed one of the idlies and stuffed it, with the hot gun powder in her mouth. Her face became red and her eyes started tearing.

I began nibbling the piece of cheese. It tasted like a salty piece of soap.

The girl chewed and swallowed the spicy idli. I gulped down chunks of the cheese, without chewing it.

She looked at me struggling with the cheese and asked, "You like?" I said "No".

It was my turn. I pointed to the idli and asked, "You like?"

"Yes" she said and reached for another.

Here are the lessons I learned from the cheese-and-idli exchange:

- *Children have no cultural constraints.*
- *It is a universal principle that children team up against grown-ups.*
- *Exchanging food is an effective mode of cross-cultural communication.*
- *People like you if you like the food they like.*

"You Talk Funny!"

When I was in the elementary school, I tried to behave like the others. I particularly remember the time I ventured to sound like my classmates.

I became suspicious when Premchand showed me a banana and asked me, "What do you call this?"

"Banana," I said, in Tamil.

He listened carefully to me.

Premchand was the sixth person who wanted me to identify a banana that day. To find out what my friends were up to, I watched Premchand. He returned to the corner of the classroom where Krishnamurty was talking with others. Premchand held up the banana, pointed in my direction, and said something in a low voice. His listeners burst out laughing.

Later that evening, I asked Sankar what banana joke made them laugh so much. Somewhat reluctantly, Sankar blurted out, "You talk funny, Thiagarajan. Nobody says 'banana' the way you do. Krishnamurty says you are not really a Tamil person. Your voice is different, you speak too fast, and you use strange words. Sometimes it doesn't sound like Tamil at all!"

It was true I spoke a southern dialect, but that was not as if I spoke Hindi. It was true that the rapidity of the southern Tamil was different from the lazy drawl of the Madras Tamil. Everyone in my family pronounced some Tamil words differently.

Krishnamurty's campaign made me extremely self-conscious of the way I spoke. I worried everyone laughed at my speech patterns. If I did not change the way I spoke, Krishnamurty was going to make all my friends suspect that I was not a Tamil.

I devised a plan to change the way I spoke: Keep my mouth closed and my ears open until I had mastered the Madras Tamil. I paid special attention to the way my classmates spoke. I tried to remember the words they used. I listened to the way my friends greeted each other. I eavesdropped on conversations in the railway station.

That evening, as I rode the train for 15 minutes from the school to my house, I kept mumbling an imaginary conversation between me and Sankar. I exaggerated what I considered to be the way Madras people spoke. Strangers in the crowded train looked strangely at me as I mumbled the words. Embarrassed, I continued the conversation inside my head without moving my lips or making a sound.

Next day, I accosted Sankar and blurted out, "So what do you think of my new Madras speech?"

Sankar looked blankly at me.

"Uh, I don't notice any change in the way you speak, Thiagarajan!"

Obviously, I needed to make more changes.

I could not figure out what made my Tamil different. Maybe I was talking too fast. I slowed down my speech. Maybe my voice was too shrill. I made it deeper. Maybe it was too soft. I raised my volume. These changes made my voice sound different to me—but not to the others.

I kept using my Madras Tamil throughout the school year. When we went to Tirunelveli for the annual vacation, I was excited to show off my new voice. No sooner did I get off the train in Tirunelveli than I started blabbering to my cousin Ramalingam. I explained excitedly my plans to play cricket and to swim in the river.

Ramalingam interrupted me.

"You talk funny, Thiagarajan. Your voice is different, you speak slow, and you use strange words. It doesn't sound like Tamil at all!"

This is what I learned from my inability to change my speech patterns:

- *People speak different dialects of the same language.*
- *People who speak the same dialect feel a kinship.*
- *Dialects differ in different ways such as pronunciation, pace, words, combinations, and intonation.*
- *It is difficult to become aware of your speech patterns and to differentiate between different sounds.*

MY FAVORITE TEACHER

In the elementary school, my classmates and I were all afraid of our teachers—except for my third-grade teacher.

My mother was a teacher. My father was a teacher.

Both our parents discouraged us from following in their footsteps. They did not want us to become teachers. They wanted us to become engineers or doctors.I probably would have fulfilled my parents' wishes except for the disruption of my role model, my third-grade teacher.

When I was promoted from the second grade to the third grade, I was assigned to the A section. My father was happy because the teacher who taught the class, Mr. Seshadri, was a strict disciplinarian. He rigidly followed the lessons in our textbook. He made us read each lesson silently. Then he had us take turns to read the lessons aloud. Later, he had us copy the lesson in our notebooks. By this time, we had memorized the lesson. Mr. Seshadri did not add anything to the content in our textbook.

Because the Third Grade A section was overcrowded, Mr. Seshadri had 10 of us transferred to C Section. I was one of the students who was transferred. Later, I found out how lucky I was.

Mr. Narayanaswamy, the teacher for C Section taught his class differently from the other teachers, He did not know the term, but he taught us in an integrated fashion by combining different subject matters. The students did not know whether a class period was devoted to language, mathematics, or geography. We seldom opened any of our textbooks. Instead, we went through different learning activities designed by our teacher. These activities felt like games. They required cooperative learning among the students.

For example, Mr. Narayanaswamy had created 20 envelopes, each with an arithmetic problem (like 7×3 or $5-4 +2$) written on the face of the envelope. He wrote the answer to each problem on a slip of paper. He inserted the answers randomly inside the problem envelopes. He organized the students in teams of five, had them pull out the answers, and place the correct answer inside the appropriate problem envelope. We raced against the other teams to complete the task.

My team won some games and lost some. We enjoyed working with friends, matching the problems with the correct answers. At the end of each round, we exchanged the envelopes with another team.

We played Envelope games repeatedly to explore different subjects. For example, Mr. Narayanaswamy gave us envelopes with names of different countries and names of their capitals on the answer slips.

During one round of the *Countries and Capitals* game, we figured out Toronto as the capital of Canada by a process of elimination. Later that evening, when I looked at the map of North America, I found Ottawa marked with a star to indicate it was the capital. I was confused because we were always told that teachers are never wrong. I thought Mr. Narayanaswamy had intentionally misled us to emphasize the name of the capital.

Before the class the next day, I talked to Mr. Narayanaswamy. I showed him the map of Canada in the book with Ottawa as the capital. I thought my teacher will come up with a suitable explanation or make up an excuse to save face and maintain the infallibility of teachers.

But Mr. Narayanaswamy did not defend his mistake. He simply said, "You are right, Thiagarajan. I made a mistake. Thanks for catching it."

Later, when I grew up and made training my career, I borrowed Mr. Narayanaswamy's style and techniques. For example, I use many variations of his Envelope game with suitable variations in my management training.

One approach I use with great pride is to thank my student participants for pointing out my mistakes and coming up with improvements to what I do.
I learned several lessons from my favorite teacher:

- *It is not necessary for me to do what other members of my professional culture do.*
- *Making mistakes does not make me lose face.*
- *Accepting my mistakes and thanking people who gave me corrective feedback is a desirable behavior.*
- *I transmit my personal and cultural values through my behavior.*

STUDENT TO TEACHER TO STUDENT

My schooling proceeded uneventfully. I continued to live and learn until I passed my high school final examination. I joined Maras Loyola College for a Bachelor of Science Degree. I majored in mathematics, physics, and chemistry.

Like most parents in India, my father wanted me to get an Engineering degree. Both my older brother and my younger brother had obtained Engineering degrees. But my college education was not impressive enough for the competitive selection process in Engineering.

With my B. Sc. Degree, I became a high school Science teacher. I enjoyed my job, and much to my father's dissatisfaction, I decided to make a career out of it.

The teaching job provided ample amounts of spare time. Most teachers spent their extra time providing tutoring services to their students for a price. But I did not do that.

Early in my teaching days, I was attracted by an article in Readers' Digest with the inviting title, *Learn Twice as Much in Half the Time*. The article was about the technique of programmed instruction.

Through several books from the United States Information Library, I taught myself how to develop programmed instructional materials. I produced a module on *The Chemistry of Chlorine* as a part of my Fifth Form science curriculum. Instead of lecturing to my students and demonstrating Chemistry experiments, I let my students work independently through the programmed instruction manual. Most students enjoyed the small steps of this material, the use of frequent questions, and immediate feedback.

I wrote an article about the process I used and the results my students achieved. I sent it to the Ministry of Education's *Center for Research* in New Delhi. I did not hear anything about this article until four months later, when I received a note congratulating me about my work and inviting me to attend a workshop to be conducted by an American expert, Dr. Ellson, in Madras. I attended the day-long workshop and learned several new things and relearned old things. After the workshop, Dr. Ellson chatted with me about programmed instruction. Somewhat impertinently, I pointed out the example of a second-language teaching program that he talked about was not an original piece of development but a replication of an earlier work. Without thinking, I blurted out that Dr. Ellson will find a description of the original work on page 169 of Taber, Glaser, and Schaffer's *Anthology of Programmed Instruction*. I was not trying to show off, but I used to have photographic memory those days.

I told my father about my conversation with the workshop leader. My father thought I was discourteous and hoped that the expert would forget my comments that corrected his statement. But Dr. Ellson did not forget them. A week later, I received a cable from Bloomington, Indiana that concisely said, "I checked your citation. You are right and I am wrong. Would you like to be my research assistant?' Through a series of cables that cost a lot of money, I found out the assistantship would pay me a salary of $80 a month. I sold my wife's jewelry and ended up on a flight to the U. S. A. with my wife and my 2-month-old son, Rajah.

In addition to working as a research assistant, Dr. Ellson suggested that I enroll for a Master's degree in Education. Since I did not have to pay the tuition (because of my assistantship), I immediately signed up to become a graduate student.

Here's what I learned by cycling through being a student, a teacher, and again a student:

- *I can learn anything I want by studying relevant books.*
- *Learning is an interesting and immersive activity.*
- *Teaching teenage learners keeps me young.*
- *If you share your knowledge without showing off or criticizing, you do not offend real scholars.*

MID-SEMESTER EXAMINATION

I may be stereotyping, but people in India take their examinations very seriously. Every year, when the public examination results are published in the newspapers, several failed students commit suicide.

I know the types of examinations (usually with several essay questions) conducted in India, but I had only vague ideas about examinations in the United States. I conjectured they usually presented several multiple-choice items. I knew that I was supposed to bring a couple of No. 2 pencils and completely fill in the bubbles on the answer sheets.

When Professor Levie announced that we will have the mid-semester examination next week, I was scared. The course was on instructional message design. The examination will cover the first half of the course on designing training materials for attitude change. I was worried about being tested with hundreds of multiple-choice items that required regurgitation of facts. In such a situation, I was doomed to fail.

On the examination day, when I got the question paper and a blue notebook, all my anxieties turned out to be unwarranted. There was no collection of multiple-choice questions. Instead, there was a single essay-type question. And it was an all-encompassing question that asked me to write everything I knew about the topic—in a creative fashion:

How would you apply the attitude-change principles to achieve an affective objective in a course you are designing?

I became excited about the question. I recalled 17 different principles that Professor Levie taught us. I made a list of these principles. I subdivided some of the principles to end up with 20 items. Then I took each of the principles and wrote a short paragraph to illustrate how it could be applied in training design. Finally, I took the topic of brushing your teeth regularly and described how the principles can be used in various combinations to achieve the affective goal of caring for the teeth. I had to ask for an extra notebook to complete my answer.

During the next class period, Professor Levie returned our answer notebooks. But first he drew a table on the blackboard to display the distribution of scores. They ranged from 7 to 12 points divided into three approximately equal groups. There were 25 students in the class and one of them was left out from the table. Professor Levie explained that this student's answer was an outlier with 19 points. It was 7 points above the next higher score.

Professor Levie returned the notebooks. Unlike in India, nobody showed their scores to the others.

With trepidation, I opened my first notebook. I had received 19 points. I was the outlier. Professor Levie had written "Good job!" under the 19.

Here are the lessons I learned from my examination panic attack:

- *Do not ruminate about the explicit and hidden rules followed by the members of other cultures.*
- *Play by a set of rules that make sense with respect to the goal you are trying to accomplish.*
- *Do your best and enjoy what you do.*

DISSOCIATIVE IDENTITY DISORDER

During the first semester at Indiana University, I took a required course on instructional development. With classmates from all around the world. At the end of the semester, a Nigerian cohort gave me a book that he had received from a U. S. American friend. The book was called *An Introduction to the American Culture*, written by an author whose name I don't remember.

I read the book with great interest. I learned key cultural variables (such as *punctuality, focus on results, respect for achievement, individualism, teamwork, and gender equality*). I also learned how typical U. S. citizens rated on these variables. Most importantly, the book introduced me to interculturalism and how people from different nations, races, genders, and age groups differed in their behavior patterns. The introductory chapter in this book explained cultural variables with metaphors that were beyond my awareness: *icebergs, bowls of salad, and wall murals*. I eventually caught on the idea that groups of people shared common mindsets. This idea appeared to be startling—and self-evident.

I plodded through several books on interculturalism and struggled to differentiate between multiculturalism and interculturalism, between race and ethnicity, and between nationality and regionality. To better figure out the nuances, I made myself a game. I wrote on pieces of paper different culture-related characteristics (such as *assertive, hard-working, fatalistic, pushy, future-oriented, truthful, cooperative, competitive, corrupt, and modest*). I shuffled these pieces of paper and selected the words that best represented specific people in my class. The results of my card-sorting exercise were confusing: *The differences within a "cultural" group were frequently greater than the differences among the groups.*

I conducted another word-sorting activity by asking a group of my friends to select pieces of paper that best described my behavior patterns and characteristics. The results of this peer evaluation were also confusing and frightening: I seemed to be suffering from multiple personality syndrome. Different people saw me in different aspects. To clarify the situation, I pored through a copy of the diagnostic manual *DSM-3* from the Psychology Department library and recognized that I was suffering from DID (Dissociative Identity Disorder) characterized by several distinct personality states.

This is what I learned from my confusing introduction to interculturalism:

- *I am both the white soldier and Gunga Din.*
- *I go through life totally confused about who I am and what are my cultural values.*
- *The only thing I am sure about is what my grandmother taught me: I am a sibling to all other human beings.*

Reconciling Opposing Approaches

I received my doctorate in 3 years. Indiana University did not offer courses on the subject of interculturalism. Nor were there job opportunities in that exotic field so, my doctorate was in instructional development.

My dissertation analyzed Instructional Systems Development (ISD). This is a systematic—almost mechanical—approach for developing training materials and methods. To implement this approach, the practitioner began with several analyses: *needs analysis* to confirm the existence of a performance problem and to identify various gaps in skills, knowledge, and attitudes; *learner analysis* to determine the entry level of typical students; *concept analysis* to discover critical features of relevant abstractions, *task analysis* of the steps for achieving different levels of the training objectives; *systems analysis* of factors that influenced learning; and *dissemination analysis* related to the implementation of the training program.

All these analyses contributed to specifying unambiguous instructional objectives that were specific, measurable, and timely.

After my doctorate, I did not have to wait for a job. I had an immediate offer to lead the instructional development efforts at one of the research centers affiliated with the School of Education. The project was to develop training materials to help classroom teachers to effectively "mainstream" learning-challenged children (such as *low IQ* and *emotionally disturbed* students) who currently are often segregated into special classrooms. The intent of this project involved aspects of interculturalism. With great enthusiasm, I undertook different analyses and began to build teacher-training modules. I was convinced that my instructional products would help the teachers to achieve the training goals. Unfortunately, I was also convinced that the learners would be bored. They would not enjoy the learning process nor enthuse about the results.

At the beginning of the project, I hired an illustrator named Leela as a part of my development team. Leela told me that her mother had selected an Indian name for her and wanted to know what it meant. I had no problem remembering that *leela* meant *divine play*. I recalled my grandmother reading stories from a *purana* book called *The Legend of Divine Play*. On further exploring the word, I figured out that it stood for frivolous play without any specific objective. God created *leelas* to entice people to enjoy playing and achieving unspecified outcomes. Intrigued by the concept of *leelas*, I decided to experiment with a playful approach (that I called Play-Based Instruction or PBI) for my training development challenges.

This is how I used PBI to explore mainstreaming of learning-challenged children:

My game required the training participants to solve a crossword puzzle with random words unrelated to mainstreaming. I created two sets of clues to the same puzzle: the easy set and the difficult set.

For example, here is the easy clue for a 3-letter answer:
This pet says, "Meow".
Here is the difficult clue for the same answer:
A feline mammal.
(The correct answer to both these clues is "cat".)
Here's another pair of examples for a 7-letter word:
Easy: *Favorite U. S. fast food that has a meat patty between two halves of a bun.*
Difficult: *A resident of the second largest city in Germany.*
(The correct answer to both these clues is "hamburger".)

The next step in the PBI approach was to come up with an activity that incorporated the two sets of crossword clues.

I organized the participants into groups of six. The group members worked secretly and independently. Unknown to them, five group members received the easy clues and the sixth person, the difficult clues. After a suitable pause, I announced the correct answers and immediately explained how two sets of clues were used to playfully drive home the point that people frequently confuse task difficulty with personal incompetence. During a debriefing discussion, I asked people for real-life examples of this confusion.

I was happy with the training package I had created earlier by using the ISD approach. I was also happy about the training game designed with the PBI approach. These two approaches were entirely different from each other. The ISD is a systematic, step-by-step approach. It is logical and consistent. It encourages and rewards self-directed study. It could be boring to the isolated learner. It focuses on cognitive learning. In contrast, PBI provides freedom and creativity to the designer. It is a free-flowing approach that encourages learning through experience. It rewards cooperative team learning.

Given these drastically different approaches, I was faced with these dilemmas: *Which approach should I use to develop training materials and methods? Which approach is likely to produce learning that is instructionally effective and motivationally engaging?*

I wanted immediate answers to these questions so I could continue dealing with my training challenges with confidence.

While floundering around this impasse, I learned a technique for reconciling dilemmas from my Swiss friend Samuel van den Bergh. (Sam had learned this technique from his English mentor Charles Hampden-Turner.)

Here's my take on the reconciliation technique: I would *not* begin with the question "Which is better: ISD or PBI?" A more useful trigger would be "How could I combine ISD and PBI to yield the best results?" I do not treat ISD and PBI as the opposite poles of a linear continuum and settling for the midpoint as the preferred approach. Instead, I combine the advantages of ISD (such as *logical, self-guided, and cognitive-focused*) and of PBI (such as *motivating, cooperative, and emotion-focused*) to make the developer and the learner more effective and engaged. I came up with such a reconciled approach and used it for informing and inspiring the design of training packages during the past two decades. I am still tweaking this approach to improve its effectiveness.

Sam's (and Hampden-Turner's) techniques for reconciling dilemmas has become a powerful tool for dealing with different aspects of interculturalism such as direct and indirect communication, monochronic and polychronic time management, subjective and objective logic, individualistic and collectivist workstyle, low and high context, tolerance of ambiguity and of rigidity, and respect for elders and skepticism of their competency.

This is what I learned from my continuing attempts at reconciling dilemmas, beginning with my search for the best way to design training:

- *Cultural differences are sets of contrary values and beliefs.*
- *Dealing with interculturalism is not A or B; it is always A and B.*
- *Do not obsess over the middle ground between two approaches. Instead, reconcile them to create a third approach that is superior to the original two.*

AROUND THE WORLD IN MANY GAMES

Barnga, Liberia

During 1979 1981, I directed an education project funded by United States Agency for International Development (USAID) in Liberia. After about a year, the project was disrupted by a military coup that overturned the government. During a couple of months of limbo, my Liberian staff of writers and illustrators worked in a small town called Barnga, waiting for instructions from the Ministry of Education. To keep the project personnel occupied, we palyed card games. I photocopied the rules of *Eucher*, a popular card game from Indiana. All my Liberian colleagues had great fun playing this game—except different people interpreted the rules of the game in different ways. In spite of the resulting chaos and arguments, the participants made up their own rules and had great fun. This made me wonder if we could simulate cultural clashes by creating a game with different sets of rules for different groups (without the players being aware of these differences.)

This was the origin of one of my long-lasting simulation games (named after the Liberian town) that is plagiarized and played all around the world.

In *Barnga*, the participants learn to play a simple card game in small groups. They don't realize is that the rules of the game are slightly different for each group. After a few practice rounds, the participants play the game without talking. Sometime later, the winners at each table move to the next table. Conflicts arise as the players begin the tournament round. They experience a miniature culture shock, which is magnified by the rule that they can only communicate through gestures or pictures. The final debriefing discussion emphasizes the importance of checking one's assumptions even when people apparently play by the same rules.

From Hobart to Perth in Australia

Marie Jasnski, from Adelade, Australia, attended one of my *Play-Based Instruction* workshops in San Francisco. After returning to Australia, she wrote a proposal to the government's Tertiary and Further Education (TAFE) department for funding to spread PBI throughout Australia. The proposal was accepted.

I traveled with Marie to conduct workshops in different Australian cities, beginning with Hobart in Tasmania, through Sydney, Melbourne, Canberra, Adelaide, and ending in Perth in Western Australia. The workshops were well received, especially by technical trainers working with young adults.

One of the popular games that Marie and I demonstrated in our workshops was called *Naked Monsters.* This game taught the trainer-players how to select suitable examples and non-examples to teach a concept to the learners. It consisted of 50 cards, each with a different picture of an alien creature. In one of the concept-teaching games, for example, the participants were organized in groups of 10. A random player (called the

Teacher) was given the definition of a class of alien creatures (such as *Cotsies who have a bulb nose and six arms.*) By showing different pictures of aliens to the other players, the Teacher tries to help them figure out the critical features of the concept. The first player to correctly define the concept wins the current round of play. The game continues until each player gets a chance to play the role of the Teacher. The player with the highest total score at the end of the last round wins the game.

Portland, Oregon

I was invited by Janet and Milton Bennett to teach a week-long course on games, simulations, and role-plays for intercultural communication. (Someone told me that I was invited to be a faculty member just because I had a Ph.D.) I enjoyed teaching the course and I learned lot from my students, most of whom were knowledgeable in intercultural communication. In addition, I learned from my conversations with my fellow faculty members.

My students learned eagerly and designed their own intercultural communication games. My course was a popular one and I repeated it several summers. Every year, many of my colleagues and students invited me to conduct the *Play-Based Instruction* course in their institutions.

One of the favorite games that I (and several other colleagues) played was called *Barnga*. (Spoiler alert: In the description below, I expose the secret element of this game. If you plan to participate in the game sometime in the future, stop reading until the end of the next paragraph.)

The *Barnga* game is introduced as an exercise to explore how to play card games. The participants are organized into play groups of four. They are given the printed rules of a card game and asked to read it silently. After a few minutes, the rule sheets were taken away from the participants and they were asked to play practice rounds of game, to help each other learn the game. After a few rounds, the participants are asked to keep score. Aft some more rounds, the two highest scoring partners at each table are moved to next and asked to continue playing the game silently. Very soon, confusion prevails, and fights break out among the players. This is because unknown to the players, the rule sheets at each table are different. At the end of the aborted game, during the debriefing discussion, we highlight how frequently we assume that people from different cultures play by different rules.

Zurich, Switzerland

Samuel van den Bergh was a participant in a Portland summer course. He did not like the aggressive behavior of some of the U.S. participants in the competitive games I conducted. But he liked the idea of using training games to explore different aspects of interculturalism.

Sam organized a shortened version of Portland courses in Zurich. I was one of the people he invited to repeat the Portland session. My course became a popular one, even though it competed with other courses taught by experts in different aspects of interculturalism. Many people enrolled in the game-design course.

Sam repeated the sessions for several years in Zurich. He and I also conducted *Play-Based Instruction* courses for corporate trainers (such as those from SwissAir).

One of our favorite games in the Switzerland course was a team building activity called *Give and Take*. I encouraged Sam to conduct it because he did it effectively and fluently. In this game, each member of a team secretly made a list of help they wanted from the other members. They also made a list of help they were eager to provide to the other team members. Later, all participants predicted what their teammates are eager to offer them. Eventually, they discussed their preferences and predictions to agree on mutual collaboration.

Jena, Germany

Alexander Schiller is a scientist, coach, facilitator, and trainer who attended the Zurich workshop organized by Samuel van den Bergh. He currently trains and coaches scientists on advanced management and communication skills. He also conducts workshops that train trainers on *Play-Based Instruction* from Jena, Germany. I "co-facilitate" Alex's workshops through brief guest appearances through the Internet.

One of Alex's favorite training activities is the *Memory Test*. The participants listen as Alex reads a list of 15 words such as *dream, sleep, night, mattress, nap, giraffe, and blanket*. The participants do not take notes or talk to each other. Ten seconds after the list is read, the participants are asked to write down the words they recall. Alex uses this recall test to illustrate important principles of human memory. Most people remember the first word from the list (demonstrating the *primacy effect*), the last word from the list (demonstrating the *recency effect*), the surprising word (demonstrating the *novelty effect)*, and the word that was read more than once (demonstrating the *repetition effect*). The participants are surprised by the *false-memory effect* because several people recall the word "bed" even though it was not a part of Alex's list. This is because human memory tends to close logical gaps in what they recall. During the debriefing discussion, the participants discuss how they could use of these principles to make their presentations more memorable.

Guandong, China

I conducted a training game workshop in Atlanta. After the workshop, Mark Mayan, a participant from China, asked me for clarification of details in my workshop manual. It took me some time to explain and it took Mark some time to understand my explanations. At the end of our conversation, he claimed to have figured out my clarifications and left the room happy.

A month later, I had an email note from Mark saying that he has organized a *Play-Based Instuction* workshop in Guandong, China for 20 participants. He would collect registration fees and pay me all the money he collected. I suggested that he should keep half of the money for his work.

The workshop went well. Some of the participants understood English (and some better than Mark) and an interpreter helped the others with simultaneous translation of my presentations. Before the workshop, a few of the participants warned me that Chinese trainees were too serious for play and games. But I went ahead with several games, mostly exploring technical training topics related to smart phones. The participants enjoyed the activities and came up with ingenious adaptations of the game structures to their own topics.

After this workshop, Mark organized three other sessions in Shanghai and one in Beijing during the rest of the year. I subsisted on soup and dumplings and had an enjoyable time with the enthusiastic participants. Mark also had me conduct game-based training workshops in instructional development and human performance technology.

INTERCULTURAL PROFESSIONAL ASSOCIATIONS: A HOME
FOR HANDS-ON TRAINING

NASAGA, I have been a long-time member of the North American Simulation and Gaming Association (NASAGA). I served on the Executive Board and edited *Simages,* the monthly newsletter for 10 years. As the President NASAGA, I organized its annual conference four different times.

I have made several presentations at the NASAGA conferences. My first presentation was at Gaithersburg, MD in 1969. As a newcomer, I submitted three different proposals, hoping that at least one of them will be accepted. All three of them were accepted and I became a regular NASAGA presenter during the subsequent years.

I made my NASAGA presentations in different locations including Los Angeles, CA; Washington, DC: Rochester, NY: Vancouver, Canada; Ann Arbor, MI: Bloomington, IN; Montreal, Canada; and Louisville, KY. All my presentations featured hands-on training activities. I followed up the games, simulations, and roleplays that I conducted with extensive debriefing discussions. I also demonstrated how to retain the structure of different training activities and change the training content and objectives.

ISAGA: Several times I was invited to make keynote presentations and preconference workshops at the annual conference of the *International Society of Simulation and Gaming.* I did this in Edinburgh, Scotland; Munich, Germany; and Dornbirn, Austria. The sessions (especially the training game workshops) were well received. It was refreshing to observe how people from different European cultures enjoyed designing and participating in training games, dealing with sales, technical, and management topics.

Here are the lessons I learned in spreading Play-Based Instruction to different parts of the world.

- *We are all* homo ludens. *People from all cultures enjoy playing games.*
- *People from all age groups learn from playing games.*
- *Players get immersed in games. They don't fret about cross-cultural clashes. They just play the game.*

TODAY AND TOMORROW

As I slide into my Golden Years, my intercultural insights follow me. I continue to be amazed and amused by the similarities—and the differences—among the people I grew up with in a bustling Tamil metropolis and I am currently growing up within a calm Hoosier college town. I continue teaching interculturalism to others and learning from them.

I am an interculturalist after all.

CHAPTER 13

Mission Statement on Our Coffee Mugs: Promoting Peace Through Intercultural Understanding

Michael F. Tucker

In his best-selling book, *The Lexus and the Olive Tree*, Tomas Friedman (1999) observed during his world travels that no two countries that both had a McDonalds had fought a war against each other since they got their respective McDonalds. He called this "The Golden Arches Theory of Conflict Prevention." This made great sense to me because countries that have reached the level of global trade and middle-class economics necessary to have a McDonald's would rather trade with each other (and the global community) than make war. Building on this concept, but switching to an intercultural career, my mission has always been to promote peace through intercultural understanding. The idea being that if people could reach deep understanding of each other across cultures, they would be more inclined to peaceful interactions than hate and conflict. By deep understanding, I mean having an interest in other people and why they believe as they do and what drives them to actions and lifestyles so different than one's own.

M. F. Tucker (✉)
Tucker International, LLC, Boulder, CO, USA
e-mail: michael@tuckerintl.com; https://www.tuckerintl.com

S. M. Fowler, D. C. Yalowitz (eds.), *Creating the Intercultural Field*,
https://doi.org/10.1007/978-3-032-01370-5_13

This idea, "promoting peace through intercultural understanding," is evident through my life and work.

However, I didn't start out this way....

EARLY INFLUENCES

The Coal Miner and the Teacher

My father was a coal miner, producing coking coal for the carbon required in making steel for the World War Two ships built by the Kaiser Steel Company. He was also a baseball player and drummer in a swing band. My mother was an elementary school teacher, getting her university degree after many years of teaching and continuing education. My older sister was always awarded better grades in school than me, which set pretty high expectations. I grew up in a small mining town and county in Eastern Utah. Some people say they come from a "one stoplight town." We had no stoplights. Although a mostly Mormon community, we had many cultures and languages including immigrants and African Americans seeking work in the coal mines. We didn't pay much attention to these cultural differences and had not heard the words "diversity or inclusion." We were friends and teammates in high school and junior college football, track, basketball, and baseball. It was natural for us to have fun and compete together, not to think about our differences.

My parents made it clear to me that I was not to go into the coal mines, but to get as much education as possible, and then take that education into whatever career it led to. A new high school was built for us, and I became President of the first Senior Class and an Honor Student, so I thought maybe I would follow the dream of my parents. However, my passion was elsewhere at that point.

The Athlete

At our new High School, I earned All State Honors in football, and I was the State Champion in sprints and relays. This led to an athletic scholarship in college, where I competed for two years.

Going further in my athletic journey was not to be, as my interests changed. I married Loretta Sunter, who became my partner in life and business. We entered the University of Utah in 1962, where I was later awarded undergraduate and graduate degrees, including a Ph.D. in Industrial Psychology and Labor Relations.

Creativity Research

As an undergraduate at the University of Utah, I was invited into the Psychology Department and was then recruited by Dr. Calvin Taylor's Creativity Research Laboratory. We were studying creativity among NASA scientists, engineers, and international project managers, as well as pharmaceutical scientists.

We were joined at the Lab by Albert R. Wight, who would become a close friend and colleague. Because of our work on creativity, we were awarded one of the first research contracts by the American Peace Corps to identify the characteristics of creative Volunteers (unfortunately, research was soon removed from the Peace Corps mission). Our research was based on the idea that more creative people would be more able to learn foreign cultures and languages and be more effective in development projects, person-to-person relationships, and promoting peace.

One of our team members was Kan Yagi, a Japanese American. He and his family had endured life in an internment camp during the war (I think it was the Topaz site in Utah). His stories really affected me, comparing my happy early life to his. He went on to earn a Ph.D. at the University of Utah.

Another of my colleagues at Utah was a Jewish fellow, Uri Gluskinos. I learned much from him about the Jewish experience in Utah and the world. At his urging, I read *The Source* by James A. Michener (1965). This was perhaps the first of a lifetime of intercultural reading, studying, researching, and training.

The Job Corps

During my graduate studies, I was hired, along with Al Wight, by the Thiokol Chemical Corporation to work at their Urban Job Corps Center in Clearfield, Utah. This was an Advanced Corpsmen Institute, with multiethnic enrollees from all over the United States. The Institute included a twelve-week Human Relations Laboratory Training Program in preparation for employment as para-professional aids in counseling, teaching, and recreation. My job was to conduct research in order to measure outcomes of the training, which led to my Doctoral Dissertation (Tucker, 1969).

THE AMERICAN PEACE CORPS

Iran, 1966–1967

Because of our earlier research with the Peace Corps, Al Wight negotiated a pre-departure training program on Iran. This was contracted to Thiokol and was to be conducted at the Job Corp Center in Utah. It was decided that I should travel to Iran to conduct needs assessments and design the program. I knew very little about Iran, but I was very excited to have the opportunity to test myself and see for myself some of what I had read and wondered about at an early age by reading (among other sources) from my mother's library and the National Geographic Magazine. I still look forward to receiving each issue, as well as its History Magazine (Fig. 13.1).

At the age of 23, I went to Washington, D.C. for a Peace Corps briefing and to get a visa from the Iranian Embassy. I traveled to Tehran on an around-the-world trip on Pan American World Airways. I stopped in as many countries as I could along the way, exploring and learning. Then,

Fig. 13.1   Women in Abaya dresses

beginning in Tehran, I traveled around Iran in a jeep with a current Volunteer. I collected stories and experiences from Volunteers and Iranians for training design and content. Was I fearful during this hot and dusty trip? Of course I was, especially at rest stops when local men stared at us strangers and when we stayed at an old hotel with the bedroom windows open and I could hear people talking outside on the roof. However, I guess my curiosity and confidence carried me through.

Culture Shock
This was my first face-to-face experience with deep culture shock. Although I had friends, teammates and colleagues of different ethnic backgrounds, Iranian culture was a world away from my life in Utah. Sounds, smells, women's faces covered by the Yashmak and the Chador dress following obediently behind their husbands, the camel market, Islamic minarets, calls to prayer five times a day broadcast over loudspeakers, were all totally new to me and difficult to deal with. At our first rest stop, I learned very personally why Iranians consider the left hand to be unclean and only shake and eat with their right hand. This was a transformative moment in my life, making me determined to understand and to adapt to cultures so different from one another.

The training program in Utah was organized with trainers that included Peace Corps volunteers returned from Iran (RPCVs) and a group of Iranians to teach the languages of Iran and serve as cultural resource people. It was conducted following my design and the Instrumented, Experiential Method that Al Wight had learned from Robert Blake at the University of Texas and the National Training Laboratories. This method is fundamentally different and opposed to the trainer-centered, lecture approach. It is trainee-centered, active, not passive, participatory, not authoritarian, and problem-oriented, not information transmission/rote learning. An example is the Critical Incidents Exercise, based on stories I had learned from Volunteers and Iranians.

Living and learning at the Center together, the volunteers in training, Iranians and Job Corpsmen, all got along well and had the added benefit of learning from each other.

This was the first time that I had been directly involved in an intercultural training program, although I had done the field research in Iran and the design for the program. It was an uncomfortable role for me because I was not a trainer. I was an I/O (Industrial/Organizational) Psychologist doing research and design. However, learning how to implement the experiential training method from Al Wight was an important milestone in my development.

Puerto Rico and Central America, 1968–1969

Following the successful implementation of our intercultural training methodology for Iran, I was recruited by Mr. Jim Frits to join his team at the Peace Corps training center in Puerto Rico. I was very reluctant to approach this exciting opportunity with Loretta, who had recently delivered our third daughter. When I explained it to her, she said "Yes, absolutely, when do we leave?"

I traveled to the training center in Puerto Rico for a Latin America training conference. The training center was located in the rain forest above Dos Bocas and Arecibo. There were two sites at the Center, Camp Crosier and Camp Radley, both named after Volunteers who had died while in service. I then traveled to Costa Rica to do field work and create a design for my first assignment, which was to lead the Costa Rica Nine training program at Camp Radley. I linked up with active Volunteers Ralph Bates and Jim Cuzsensa traveling around the country to observe and interview Costa Ricans and Volunteers, getting stories to create Critical Incidents and other training exercises.

Family Relocation

I returned to Utah, preparing for our first major relocation to Puerto Rico. Loretta and I and our three young daughters—Jodi, Lori and Lisa (Lisa being 6-weeks old) drove across the country. We departed from Miami to San Juan, and then headed for the Peace Corps Training Center. We settled into a house at Camp Crosier and prepared for life in a much wetter environment than that of Utah. In addition to mosquito nets, we had to use electric blankets to keep our beds dry and lights in our closets to keep our clothes dry.

Jim Frits and I recruited a staff of Returned Peace Corps Volunteers and Costa Ricans to deliver the three-month training program at Camp Radley. I brought in Steve Rhinesmith to help train my staff (Jim Doxsey, Francisco Hernandes, Mike and Cindy Bresnen). Steve had caught my attention with a paper about how to prepare diverse trainers for their roles. Steve was to become a life-long friend, and important colleague. I also brought in Al Wight to help with staff training and to continue with our participative, instrumental training methodology.

Loretta worked to support the training and at the Administration Center at Camp Crosier. Our daughters traveled down the mountain in a 'Gua-Gua' van for school in Arecibo. The Costa Rica Nine Volunteers were a mix of young men and women who were genuinely committed to the Peace Corps mission set out by John Kennedy and Sargent Schriver to bring peace through interpersonal relationships and development. We were about the same age of the Volunteers, and we had been totally caught up in Kennedy and Schriver's mission— we really believed that we could "change the world." But there were also trainees there who were escaping military draft and possible duty in Vietnam. They were a challenge, but soon most bought into the participative and engaging training activities.

Writing in the Rain Forest

I had finished my Ph.D. work at the University of Utah, and I boxed up and brought my research documents with me to Puerto Rico in order to write my dissertation. Loretta and I dedicated about one week to get this done. I sat in my little office near the river in the rain forest and typed the 177-page document on my Corona typewriter. At night, while I tended our daughters, Loretta typed the manuscript on the training center Wang computer. When we returned to Utah, Thiokol graciously provided their Wang to print out the document. Imagine our shock when the document was printed in Spanish! Loretta feverishly re-typed the manuscript in English while I held off the university librarian and my doctoral committee. We did get it done on time and I was awarded the degree.

Following completion of the Costa Rica Nine program, I traveled throughout Central American with the Center Director, Jim Frits. We recruited new training staff and conducted needs assessments in Panama, Nicaragua, Honduras, and Guatemala. Now as Director of Experiential Training at the Center, I assisted in applying our training methodology to the programs for these countries.

Loretta and I and our daughters really enjoyed living in Puerto Rico. The warmth and friendliness of the people, learning to dance the Merengue, making daiquiris from our own banana trees and the wonderful beaches afforded a nice balance to the training work.

Costa Rica and Haiti

We had many exciting experiences in Central America and the Caribbean, including tarpon fishing on a remote river between Cost Rica and Nicaragua. We hooked some big tarpons—Loretta boated one. She still has the scar from the fishing line. It was about as big as she was— we gave it to the local folks. We also traveled to Haiti for an unforgettable visit. A long story, but briefly, we were met at the airport and informally hosted by

Mr. Aubelin Jolicoeur, a Haitian journalist and columnist. We were surprised and a bit concerned to appear in his morning columns. We stayed
in the Hotel Oloffson, made famous in Graham Greene's book "The
Comedians.". We were hosted for dinner by the Manager of the
Barbancourt distillery, during which the road was closed, and we could
hear gunshots below us (apparently fired by Baby Doc's Tonton Macoute
secret police). The extreme poverty was very difficult to see, alongside
fascinating culture, arts and the well-to-do.

The Estes Park Center for Research and Education (CRE, 1970–1978)

Following our time in Puerto Rico, we relocated to Colorado to join CRE
and continue my association with Al Wight. CRE was a non-profit organization founded by businessmen in Estes Park and Colorado State
University. It was a major Peace Corps training contractor, because of the
Center Director, Pauline Birky (later, Birky-Kreutzer). Working with Dr.
Maurice Albertson at CSU in 1961, they performed field research and
wrote a Congressional Feasibility Study of the Point Four Youth Corps,
which became the Peace Corps. According to Dr. Albertson in his forward
to her book, *Peace Corps Pioneer* (Birky-Kreutzer, 2003), "She was truly
the pioneer and mother of the Peace Corps."

CRE was interested in my approach to experiential training in Puerto
Rico and how it could be better implemented into their Peace Corps training programs. My role on the CRE team was therefore to serve as a coach
to their training staff. Mrs. Birky was particularly interested in how to
strengthen the evaluation of their vtraining programs, so I took on the
additional role of working with her to design and implement evaluation
measures.

Afghanistan, 1971

Among many other Peace Corps training projects, CRE created the first
in-country training program in Kabul, Afghanistan. I traveled around the
world again, this time to support the program and its Director, Kris
Engstrom. I traveled around the country with Kris, visiting Volunteers
and Afghan agencies who we worked for.

I found the Islamic culture there similar to that in Iran, but different in
the way of the individual strength of the people, especially those living in
the Hindu Kush mountains. Compared to the Afghanistan of today under

Fig. 13.2 Bamiyan Buddhas

the Taliban, I found it to be fairly open, with some women not wearing dress coverings and following professional careers. Afghan friends took me around to become acquainted with the country and culture.

It affected me deeply when the Taliban first took over the country. The second time was worse, because the ambitious and talented Afghan women were denied the education, aspirations and freedoms that they had enjoyed (Fig. 13.2).

I was able to visit Bamiyan, a beautiful valley in the Hindu Kush mountains. It is the site of ancient Buddha carvings into the mountainside. I climbed all over and into the giant Buddha. These were tragically blown up by the Taliban when they took over the country the first time.

OECD Africa, 1975

CRE was awarded a contract with the Organization of Economic Cooperation and Development (OECD) to consult with and evaluate a funded project in Upper Volta (now Burkina Faso). Mr. Collins Reynolds, who was then CRE Director, and I traveled to Paris for an OECD briefing and then on to Ouagadougou, the capital. This project was designed to combat desertification which is the process by which fertile land becomes dessert, in sub-Saharan Africa. My job was to instill an evaluation process into the project to assess project outcomes and justify OECD investment.

Out on the streets in Ouagadougou, I found myself the only white guy in crowds of black people. This was a very strange and uncomfortable feeling, and I began to understand a little how a black person must feel in white American communities—being stared at, standing out as different, not sure who to trust or talk to. Mr. Reynolds was an African American, as well as my friend and colleague at CRE, Freeman Pollard. Following my experience in Africa, I became more aware of how they felt in situations where they sensed they were in the minority. We had many discussions about this as we worked and travelled together.

Brazil, 1972–1973

I was invited to the Peace Corps in Washington, D. C. for a briefing on training Volunteers for Brazil, and then traveled to Salvador, Bahia, for a training conference. I won a contract for CRE over the current company, the Westinghouse Learning Organization, for in-country training of Volunteers. I moved to a beach home in Recife where my family soon joined me. Located in the North-East, Recife was the closest Brazilian port to Africa, and a major entry for the slave trade.

Working with my team, I set up intercultural and Portuguese language training programs in Recife, Mato Grosso, Salvador, Belo Horizonte, Fortaleza, and Natal, hiring over 100 Brazilian staff, RCPV's, and training some 300 Volunteers. Each program involved coordinating with CRE Estes Park, our Administrative Headquarters in Belo Horizonte, Peace Corps Brazil, and Peace Corps Washington (all without today's digital communication technology). My team recruited and hired training staff, leased training facilities, conducted needs assessments, coordinated with Brazilian host agencies, and designed and delivered the programs. I again brought Al Wight in to help with the programs, this time to run the program for Minas Gerais state out of Belo Horizonte.

NUCLEO

An important contribution that we made in our training programs was to change the way Portuguese language and Brazilian cross-cultural training was done. These two areas had been pretty much separate, with different trainers, schedules, and materials. Working with Guara Rodrigues Dorsey and Maria Chapira, our language coordinators, we created a way to integrate the two, which we called the NUCLEO (the letters do not stand for anything, the name represents our concept of a nucleus for combining culture and language training). An example was to focus on cross-cultural aspects of the extended Brazilian family while introducing the Portuguese words and phrases that characterizes family life. This formed the basis for our later approach to integrated culture and language training for expatriates of multi-national corporations.

As in Puerto Rico, our family enjoyed living in Brazil. We found the Brazilian beach life a nice change from the rain forest. The Brazilian people, food, deep and rich culture, unique belief systems, and learning to dance the Samba, were memorable for all of our lives. One of the many highlights of our time in Recife was seeing the great soccer player, Pele, play against our local team.

Adventures in the Amazon
On our way back for a trip to the United States, Loretta and I traveled up the Amazon from Belem to Manaus on the ship *Rosa da Fonseca*. Returning from Manaus, we had unforgettable experiences. Again and again, we were not able to directly connect from Manaus to Miami, so we boarded a DC 3 to Leticia, Columbia. Soon after take-off, the plane engine began to smoke, so we returned to the Manaus airport. Leaving again, we were surprised to land in the Amazon jungle on a small runway. Workers came out rolling fuel barrels to fill our tanks. We landed in Leticia, to learn that a connection to Bogota/Miami was no longer in service. Since we had no Columbian passports, a guard sat with us while we tried to figure out what to do next. Loretta made a connection with a pilot who was taking a cargo load to Bogota. She talked him into taking us along in his DC 6 cargo plane. Landing in Bogota, the pilot insisted that we go home with him as guests. We stayed several days with him and his family, enjoying the Columbian culture. Our pilot/host turned out to be a senior air force officer, so he arranged a flight for us from Bogota to Miami. The story ends some months later in Denver when a box of beautiful ruanas that we had admired (wraps or ponchos) was sent to us by our pilot/host.

Seminal Research Project: Measuring Cross-Cultural Adjustment, 1973

Following the first year of our training contract in Brazil, we followed up on the Volunteer who had been trained and were in for a surprise. Some of those who we thought were the best trainees were not doing so well and others who were not thought of so much during training were doing well. We wondered what might have been missing in our training, so we set out to discover a solid research-based definition and description of intercultural adjustment but could not find one. We approached the Peace Corps about this and were awarded a field research project to study this issue.

We assembled over twenty people to engage in the CRE intercultural research - CRE intercultural consultants, Brazilian colleagues, Peace Corps Brazil staff, and faculty/consultants from the University of Florida and the University of Miami. We developed a model to measure cognitive, affective, and behavioral aspects of cross-cultural adjustment.

The results of our study formed not only the basis for revised Peace Corps Training, but also for my later research and application with the US Navy and global corporate expatriates. The six factors that have emerged are as follows (Fig. 13.3):

Origins of SIETAR

Closing out some eight years of life and work with the Peace Corps, we relocated to Colorado to resume my career with CRE and Al Wight. While we were in Brazil, CRE, under the direction of Al Wight, was awarded a contract to develop *Peace Corps Cross Cultural Training Guidelines* (Wight & Hammons, 1970). The idea of SIETAR emerged in a

Acceptance	of the host culture.
Knowledge	of both current and historical information.
Affect	is a positive mood state.
Lifestyle	when engaging with locals on and off the job.
Interaction	with locals on and off the job.
Communication	both verbally and non-verbally.

Fig. 13.3   Six factors of adjustment

cross-cultural training conference in Estes Park, sponsored by the Peace Corps. The purpose of the conference was to seek input for development and writing of the four-volume Guidelines. Invited were a number of people considered to be doing the most significant work in the intercultural field.

According to Al Wight "Steve Rhinesmith suggested that the group form some sort of intercultural society. They settled on naming it the Society for Intercultural Training and Research, SITAR (the Indian musical instrument), because they liked the acronym. (This of course was later changed to SIETAR to accommodate members in education.)

I especially liked the concept of having an international society where researchers could communicate with trainers, since I was both. Intercultural research could inform trainers with their findings and recommendations, and trainers could in turn inform researchers with tryouts and feedback from participants in their programs.

IAIR

Unfortunately, this is no longer the case, since researchers, under the leadership of Dan Landis, split off to form the International Academy of Intercultural Research—IAIR—and the International SIETAR was later ended. The *International Journal of Intercultural Research* (IJIR) was created to publish our research. I was an original member of IAIR, became a Fellow, and am still a member of the Membership Committee. I also joined SIETAR USA, delivered Advanced Workshops at SIETAR conferences, was the Chair of the Ethics Committee when we created the Living Code of Ethical Behavior, and organized and delivered a day-long Senior Summit session with Sandy Fowler at a SIETAR conference.

However, I was not in attendance at the first conference because I was in Puerto Rico, but I was in attendance for the second one in Estes Park in the Spring of 1971. I was able to contribute my training and research experiences in Iran, Afghanistan, Puerto Rico, Central America, and Brazil. A steering committee was formed, and Al Wight was named the Executive Director, assisted by Irene Pinkau, International Secretariat for Volunteer Services. SIETAR was thus initially organized as an international organization, first housed by CRE in Estes Park.

Al Wight was moving on to other opportunities and it was decided that CRE was not an appropriate long-term home for SIETAR. Al and Steve Rhinesmith approached the University of Pittsburgh, which had an Intercultural Communication Project funded by the United States

Department of State. They agreed to sponsor SIETAR, and the State Department project newsletter "Communique" became the SIETAR Newsletter. David Hoopes, Director of the Project, then took over the responsibility for SIETAR from Al. An official SIETAR organizing conference was held in Washington, D.C. in 1974.

The Overseas Diplomacy Program of the US Navy (1973–1978)

CRE was awarded a major contract with the US Navy to support its Overseas Diplomacy Program for personnel and families. A good description of the origins of this program was written by Anne O'Keefe (2019). Briefly, it was created under the direction of Chief of Naval Operations, Adam Elmo Zumwalt, and the leadership of Commander Richard McGonigal, who had been a Chaplain in Vietnam. Navy Chaplains provided Intercultural Relations Training for in-country marines and Navy personnel. This training resulted in measurable success, which led to the Intercultural Relations Program, then the Overseas Diplomacy Program, and finally the Overseas Duty Support Program.

The Program was operated out of the Naval Amphibious Base in Coronado, California, and the Pentagon in Washington. Working with Navy Human Resource Management Centers and Detachments that included those in Puerto Rico, Italy, Spain, Iceland, and Great Britain, we were tasked over some six years to design and develop intercultural training programs for overseas duty personnel and families as well as for shipboard personnel.

At this point in my intercultural journey, it became clear that my contributions were to apply my passion for research in measuring and predicting intercultural adjustment and then applying results. My part of the Navy project was therefore to conduct large scale field research in order to develop a screening and selection process for overseas assignment candidates.

The Navy Overseas Assignment Inventory (NOAI)

Beginning with the Cross-Cultural Interaction Inventory of Yellen and Mumford (1975), I began to develop a multi-scale assessment/prediction instrument. Working with I/O Psychology faculty members of Colorado State University, we identified and sorted through a large number of potential items and settled on a 78-item set, which we called the Navy Overseas Assignment Inventory (NOAI).

We administered the NOAI to 3010 Navy men and women prior to their international postings. Then, based on my earlier work with the Peace Corps, we applied our six-factor model to measure intercultural adjustment and serve as a predictive target for the NOAI.

We followed this group for about a year into their international assignments. We were able to locate 1627 of them in 60 countries. We administered the six-factor instrument to them and ran statistical analyses to establish multi-item scale reliabilities, norms and NOAI-to-six factor predictive validities (Tucker et al., 1978.

The results were significant enough to introduce our "first of a kind" product to the Navy and to the intercultural world. Sandy Fowler, who had become our client on the project and worked with me to institutionalize the NOAI, was the first to suggest that I continue with this work and offer it beyond the Navy.

The OAI (Overseas Assignment Inventory)

We edited and re-designed the NOAI and then called it the OAI. We expanded our research to conduct a study with the OAI and our six-factor intercultural adaptation model for the Canadian International Development Agency (Hawes & Kealey, 1979). We also conducted a study of Youth for Understanding international exchange students.

Tucker and Associates (1979–1982)

I left CRE and set out with Loretta to found an organization with the goal of providing our assessment and training products and services to multinational companies. They were not yet called "global companies." This was difficult, because these companies considered our work as *soft* and not applicable to their *hard* business practices. We did succeed with one senior executive, Mr. Richard Jackson, head of International Human Resources at Reynolds Aluminum in Richmond, Virginia. Reynolds at that time had a large aluminum operation in Puerto Ordaz, Venezuela (now Ciudad Bolivar). They had many expatriate employees and families living and working there, but were experiencing a significant turnover, costing a lot of money to replace. We entered into a contract with Reynolds to apply our assessment, selection, and training services to candidates for assignment to Venezuela. I traveled to Puerto Ordaz several times with Mr. Jackson to perform needs assessments and design our program.

We assembled a multi-national staff and began delivering our six-day, residential program (including Venezuelan Spanish) to groups of candidates and their families who traveled to our campus at the Colorado Women's College in Denver.

Training in Bangor, Wales

We were excited when Mr. Jackson informed us that Reynolds had recruited a group of European employees and their families for assignment to Venezuela and wanted us to deliver our program on Venezuela to them at a site in Bangor, Wales. Our team traveled there to deliver the program. At our completion ceremony and party, we enjoyed the wonderful singing voices of the Welsh men, women, and children. Following the conclusion of the program, Loretta and I traveled to St. Andrews, Scotland, to play golf at the Old Course, which is the "home of golf."

Reynolds was pleased with the results of our program over time to the extent that Mr. Jackson was quoted as saying that "the early return rate from Venezuela had pretty much dropped to zero, saving enough money to pay for our program."

Moran, Stahl & Boyer, Inc. (MS&B—1983)

During a marketing trip to visit multi-national companies in New York City, I met Brian Moran, Chairman of MS&B. It was a consulting company specializing in managing large group relocations. Brian and his partners were interested in creating an International Division, and Loretta and I were interested in linking up with a larger organization. After much negotiation, we joined MS&B and set out to found MS&B International. We were adamant that we would remain in Boulder, Colorado, although the other partners were located in New York City. We merged Tucker & Associates into MS&B and acquired CRE, which had been purchased by SYSTRAN Corporation of Chicago. We moved into the Lotus Building, a striking Asian-looking structure in Boulder which would become our HQ and training campus.

We grew rapidly, so that by the mid 1980's we had about 30 full-time employees, language instructors, university professors, and a large number of resource people, who were foreign-born Americans representing their own countries in our programs. At one point, we enjoyed 8 of the top 10 Fortune 500 companies as clients.

Assessments and Coaching with the OAI

We were very protective with our OAI, knowing that our predictive research would be used not only for feedback and coaching, but also for selecting candidates for international assignments. It was not incorporated into our training designs but was applied by client International Human Resource (IHR) people for their own employees and families. They participated in a face-to-face, three-day training and certification program and were only certified by me. One of the strongest innovations we made was to add the Behavioral Interview technique to verify OAI scale results with relevant life and work stories.

Our OAI was applied following candidate completion of our IMA® International Mobility Assessment to ensure that they were at a time in their lives where they could take on an international assignment.

INTEC JAPAN

We were approached by Gadelius, a Swedish-based company that had been operating for many years in Japan. Their president, Mr. Goran Holmqvist, had created a Service Support Division which included a business school for their employees. They added an English language component to their curriculum by acquiring the "Stanford English Institute" founded by Mr. Itoh. (No relation to Stanford University.) Mr. Holmqvist traveled to Boulder to discuss how his school might incorporate our intercultural training into their new division. Loretta and I then traveled to Japan to meet with Mr. Itoh, to develop relationships, and discuss the concept further.

Mr. Itoh took us around his old neighborhood in Tokyo, showing us where he and his family lived before the war. They had escaped to the countryside during the worst of the bombing.

We entered into a business relationship to offer our programs to Japanese companies and to support our MS&B International clients in Japan. The new organization was called the Intercultural Training and Education Center (INTEC). We went on to Australia to work with our partners, Karen Huchendorf and Martin Sims, before visiting New Zealand, and then the long flight home.

Acquisition (1990)
MS&B was acquired by Merrill Lynch Relocation Management, which was soon acquired by Prudential Relocation Management. Our International Division therefore became a part of Prudential. We remained in Boulder and continued to grow our business. It soon turned out, however, that our participative, intercultural consulting culture was very different from their more hierarchical, real estate-based relocation culture. We had thought that our association with Prudential would bring access to a large number of potential clients, but their clients were in a different area of these companies than ours. Our corporate clients were focused on global mobility and leadership and theirs focused on domestic relocation. I had a hard time managing our business in Boulder while trying to fit in and report to Prudential in New York.

A Hard Time
Loretta soon left the company, and I later departed under very negative conditions. This was one of the lowest points in our intercultural careers, leaving all that we had built over the years. Friends, family, and physical activity kept me going during this bad time. Encouraging talks with friends and colleagues were very helpful, especially Steve Rhinesmith, who for a short time had been President of MS&B.

After a short time, I experienced a feeling of clarity and calmness as if a great burden had been lifted. However, it had never been *more true,* than "when one door closes, another one opens." Hence, another chapter in our lives was about to begin.

Tucker International, LLC (1994)

With the help and support of our three daughters (who became employees), we picked ourselves up and started over again. With our OAI as a base, we founded Tucker International in 1994, which is still going today. Loretta and I visited client companies that we were close to and some new ones that were referred to us. We will never forget the first call we got from a long-term client: "Mike, do you have the OAI?" "Yes" "Good, we want to order four of them." We soon moved back into the Lotus Building, which Prudential had left!

Utilizing a similar approach to our work at MS&B International, we recruited a multicultural team of managers and consultants. These included Master Trainers who had personal experience and were experts on the assignment countries, business culture consultants, history professors, assignment country national resource people, youth trainers and certified OAI coaches.

We changed our approach with the OAI, however, so that in addition to training and certifying client IHR people, we designed a feedback and coaching module into our programs as well as delivering candidate sessions with our own consultants.

We always believed in on-site situation and needs-assessments in order to custom design our programs. We were able to do this with client/partners for major projects all over the world. A highlight for me was to conduct situation and needs-assessment for a large mining company in Peru and then leading a management retreat/seminar at Punta Sal. I co-trained the seminar with our consultant, Dr. John Adkins. We developed a way to integrate low-impact, experiential team building activities into our training so that participants could "try out" and practice what we were teaching. (This approach was based in part on the higher impact activities of the Center for Creative Leadership.)

NASA (1996)

I was recruited by NASA to join the faculty for their International Project Management Program (IPM). They wanted a research-based assessment and development instrument and process as part of the week-long program, so my OAI fit the bill. We created a non expat version of the OAI to measure intercultural competencies necessary for working with people from other countries. Participation in the pilot and other original IPM programs were only for NASA scientists, engineers, and program managers from the NASA facilities across the US and HQ. It was later expanded to international partners including the Japanese Space Agency and the European Space Agency.

We delivered the pilot program at the historic Chamberlin Hotel, on the grounds of Fort Monroe in Virginia (the only moated fort in the US). This area is known as Point Comfort, and because of its history, was very appropriate for my intercultural module. It was where the first enslaved African Americans landed in Virginia, where Harriet Tubman treated sick and wounded soldiers as well as nursed, housed, and assisted black refugees who were fleeing slavery, and where Jefferson Davis was held after the Civil War.

My IPM module began with participants completing the OAI beforehand. I delivered their OAI Profiles and Feedback Guides during the program and had them develop actions for overcoming "areas for development" and recognizing strengths in performing as multicultural team members.

I continued as the IPM Senior Faculty Member for some 18 years, as the program moved from Virginia to the Kennedy Space Center in Florida. Once we had developed the Global Leader TAP® Tucker Assessment Profile (GLTAP), described later in this chapter, it replaced the OAI. I created and delivered an intercultural simulation in order to experience key intercultural concepts: It was really enjoyable to engage with these space engineers and scientists to see them having fun and learning to be effective multicultural team leaders. Once again, I learned that we interculturalists bring a very valuable, different message and perspective to even the most highly educated performers in their fields.

Over the years, there were over 1000 participants in my program. During this time, I wrote a chapter for a book on managing space projects (Chesley et al., 2008).

The TAP® Tucker Assessment Profile, and the Survey of Expatriate Training and Development (SETD)sm

After working with the OAI for many years, we decided to take advantage of our large corporate database and conduct another major research project. We created an entirely new instrument and named it the Tucker Assessment Profile (TAP).

We created an instrument to measure our six-factor model of intercultural adjustment, which we call the Survey of Expatriate Training and Development (SETD). We were to use this instrument to validate the TAP (Tucker et al., 2004). Below is our full model (Fig. 13.4).

As technology evolved, we created an on-line platform for our instruments. We call it *ExpaTracks* which is used by our consultants and clients to access our instruments and reports. Our TAP Feedback and Coaching sessions moved from in-person to Zoom or teleconference formats.

Global Leader TAP® Tucker Assessment Profile (GLTAP) and the Survey of Global Business Experience (GBE)®

We were approached by Right Management, a consulting company, to work with them on the crisis in global leadership. We noted the

PRIOR TO ASSIGNMENT
Expectations
World View
• *Open-mindedness*
• *Respect for Other Beliefs*
• *Tolerance for Different Conditions*
Behavioral Approach to Situations
• *Flexibility*
• *Patience*
• *Sense of Humor*
• *Initiative*
• *Risk Taking*
Social Interpersonal Style
• *Trust in People*
• *Interpersonal Interest*
• *Social Adaptability*
Locus of Control
Spouse Communication

DURING ASSIGNMENT
Cognitive
• *Knowledge and interest in the country of assignment*
Behavioral
• *Acceptance of the local people and culture*
• *Lifestyle adjustment to the country of assignment*
• *Effective intercultural communication across cultures*
• *Interaction with local people and their culture*
Affective
• *Affect or positive feelings of well-being*

Fig. 13.4 Predictive model of intercultural adjustment

overwhelming evidence that global organizations were in need of leaders who have the ability to move easily between different cultures, and that interculturally competent leaders are the greatest need and key to success. We decided to conduct a study to determine the *markers* of global leadership success and the intercultural competencies that could be used to assess and develop this success.

We recruited some 1867 global leaders for the study, representing 13 nationalities and 134 industries. For the markers of success, we created the Survey of Global Leadership (GBE). Based on our work with the TAP, we created the Global Leader Tucker Assessment Profile (GLTAP). Together with Right Management, we published a White Paper (Right Management, Leadership Insights, 2011), and then a technical article (Tucker et al., 2014) (Fig. 13.5).

In order to operationalize these results, we created the Horizontal/ Vertical (HV) Model of Global Leadership Development. (Tucker & Tucker-Eccher, 2017). The GLTAP measures the intercultural competencies in need of development. We then turned to the work of Kegan and

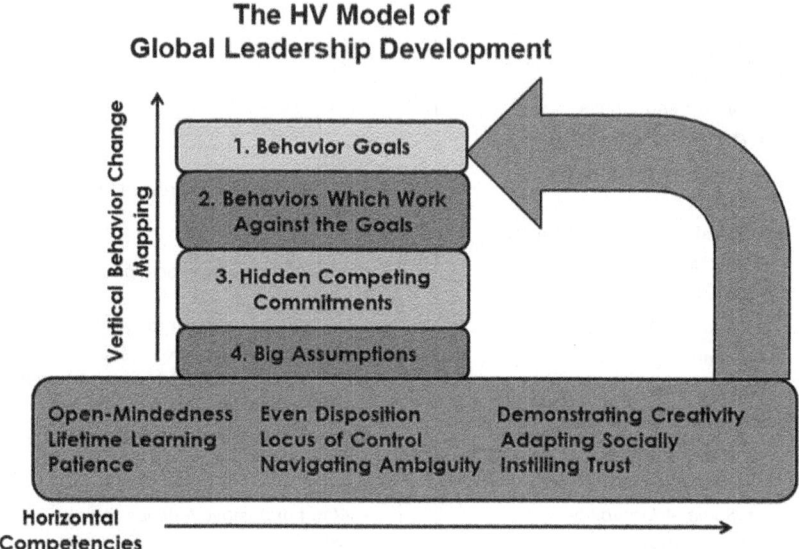

Fig. 13.5 HV Model of Intercultural Leadership Development

Lahey at Harvard to combine the GLTAP with Behavioral Change Mapping. (Kegan & Lahey, 2009). This is a very powerful way to "overcome an immunity to change" in developing the needed competencies and achieving the "Level 5" mental complexity of the transforming mind. For example, if someone falls below the GLTAP norm on Instilling Trust, a set of behavioral goals can be created for overcoming this by examining false assumptions standing in the way of goal achievement, hidden commitments, and behaviors that work against the goals.

We continue to apply this approach both to incumbent and aspiring global leaders in order to incorporate intercultural competencies into what it means to be a leader.

Conclusion

Have my efforts resulted in peace through intercultural understanding? On a macro-scale, certainly not, with hatred and wars continuing around the world. But, looking back on each of the many thousands of individuals we have touched (and many of whom we have heard from) I think most of them adapted peacefully to working and living with people much different from them. It is said that major change begins with individuals and small steps, so there is hope that my mission and the incredible work of all interculturalists will someday lead to a more peaceful world.

POSTSCRIPT

Looking back over my life story, I don't think Loretta and I ever had a grand plan. We took advantage of the opportunities afforded us and made some opportunities of our own (e.g. founding three companies). We believed more and more in what we could do despite the unknown. We were often told that we reminded people of the movie *Joe Versus the Volcano* in which Tom Hanks and Meg Ryan are told by Abe Vigoda to "just jump" into the Volcano to save the island instead of first going through an elaborate ceremony.

With respect to learning and transformation, during my early years I was very uncomfortable speaking to large audiences. However, this became one of the most enjoyable and rewarding activities in my career, as I engaged more and more with audiences and was supported by stunning power-point presentations created by Jodi Tucker Young. Although I have been able to measure and teach intercultural aspects of trust, I have learned that I trust too much, assuming that others are as trustworthy as I am and then being disappointed when they are not. A cornerstone of my story has been my role in the intercultural field, from early cross-cultural training to intercultural assessment, coaching and training. All of this had been grounded in my training as an I/O Psychologist with a passion for research.

REFERENCES

Birky-Kreutzer, Pauline (2003). *Peace Corps Pioneer*. Thomson-Shore.
Center for Research and Education. (1972). Center for Research and Education/Action Contract PC-72-42043. *Improving Cross-Cultural Training and Measurement of Cross-Cultural Learning*.
Chesley, J., Larson, W., McQuade, M., & Menrad, R. (2008). *Managing Projects Across Cultures*. Applied Project Management for Space Systems. Chapter 20, pp. 619–647. McGraw Learning Solutions.
Friedman, T. (1999). *The Lexus and the Olive Tree*. Farrar Straus Giroux.

Hawes, F., & Kealey, D. J. (1979). *Canadians in Development: An Empirical Study of Adaptation and Effectiveness on Overseas Assignment*. Canadian International Development Agency.

Kegan, R., & Lahey, L. (2009). *Immunity to Change. How to Overcome It and Unlock Potential in Yourself, and Your Organization*. Harvard Business School Press.

Michener, J. A. (1965). *The Source*. Random House.

O'Keefe A. (2019). *Launching the Navy Family Support Program: A Heartfelt Blend of History and Memoir*. The Overseas Duty Support Program. Chapter 10, pp. 258–275. Amazon Kindle Direct Publishing (KDP).

Right Management. (2011). Why Global Leaders Succeed and Fail. *Insights from CEOs and Human Resources Professionals*.

Tucker, M. F. (1969). *An Experimental Investigation of Human Relations Laboratory Training Among Disadvantaged Job Corpsmen*. Ph.D Dissertation, Department of Psychogy, University of Utah.

Tucker, M. F., & Tucker-Eccher, L. (2017). *Horizontal and Vertical: Meeting the Global Talent Challenge*. Author House.

Tucker, M. F., Benson, P. G., & Blanchard, F. (1978). *The Measurement and Prediction of Overseas Adjustment in the US Navy*. Center for Research and Education. US Navy Bureau of Personnel Contract #N00600–73-D-070.

Tucker, M. F., Bonial, R., & Lahti, K. (2004). The Definition, Measurement and Prediction of Intercultural Adjustment and Job Performance Among Corporate Expatriates. *International Journal of Intercultural Relations*.

Tucker, M. F., Bonial, R., Vanhove, A., & Kedharnath, U. (2014). 3:127— Leading across Cultures in the Human Age: An Empirical Investigation of Intercultural Competency Among Global Leaders. SpringerPlus—A SpringerOpen Journal: http://ww.springerplus.com/content/3/1/127

Wight, A. R., & Hammons, M. A. (1970). *Guidelines for Peace Corps Cross Cultural Training, Part II Specific Methods and Techniques*. Office of Training Support Peace Corps. Contract No. PC-25-1710.

Yellen, T. M. I., & Mumford, S. J. (1975). *The Cross-Cultural Interaction Inventory: Development of Overseas Criterion Measures and Items That Differentiate between Successful and Unsuccessful Adjusterss* US Navy Personnel Research and Development Center, San Diego.

CHAPTER 14

Conclusion

Daniel C. Yalowitz and Sandra M. Fowler

Out beyond ideas of wrongdoing and rightdoing.
There is a field. I'll meet you there.
When the soul lies down in that grass,
The world is too full to talk about.
Ideas, language, even the phrase "each other".
Doesn't make any sense.
—*Jallaluddin Rumi (1995)*

COMING 'ROUND FULL CIRCLE … BEGINNINGS, BUT NO ENDINGS

Interculturalists set out to build their careers, perhaps creating new jobs while doing so. Without knowing, they formed a new field of action, study, and research. Now, seventy or so years later and with the passing of many of the early interculturalists, this small group of pioneers has created

D. C. Yalowitz
Greenfield, MA, USA
e-mail: danielcyalowitz@gmail.com

S. M. Fowler (✉)
Carlsbad, CA, USA

© The Author(s), under exclusive license to Springer Nature   273
Switzerland AG 2025
S. M. Fowler, D. C. Yalowitz (eds.), *Creating the Intercultural Field*,
https://doi.org/10.1007/978-3-032-01370-5_14

a book dedicated to serving interculturalism and hopefully its survival for upcoming generations.

This *field*—the field of intercultural communication—didn't exist as recently as 70 years ago. These individuals didn't realize that they were building something as new and large as it came to be. There were no maps or blueprints to help them with logistics, mission, or vision. They met and worked—sometimes in a coordinated, planned manner—but mostly through a series of un-orchestrated, even uncalibrated events. All this came from what began as an exploration of how cultures and those within and across them can communicate and cooperate effectively.

A book, like a photograph, is simply a snapshot of a person or a group of people during a moment in time. These are the stories of the people who were the implementers of the intercultural field in their own words. From each author's inception point, what we read is a compressed set of memories and reflections that conjure up images depicting situations and scenarios demonstrating how the lives of these individuals evolved through a series of decisions, transitions, risks taken, and opportunities engaged.

In each writer's narrative we see that they achieve some degree of peace within themselves knowing that they are not in control over all the comings, goings, and doings that together construct their lives and careers. The rhythms of their work and their roles sometimes holds a sense of continuity that allows for spaciousness, planning, and growth. At other moments, things come to a full-stop without predictability or prior awareness.

Life experience and observations of self and others were great teachers for our intercultural pioneers, and they were able to use these to their advantage in building non-linear professional trajectories.

How Does One Summarize a Life? How About Twelve?

A conclusion—this conclusion—is not an ending, not a closure, and certainly not a summary. The lives of these individuals as well as the intercultural field itself continue to evolve. Variations on so many of the themes described within each chapter will continue to occur.

Our goal in this concluding chapter is to point to critical learnings that have come to life through the sharings offered in previous pages. This is our attempt to illuminate moments in these narratives that hold common ground. These moments are interconnected, much like Ken Kesey's "Hundredth Monkey" phenomenon (1981) of the 1960's, a phenomenon in which a new idea spreads rapidly by unexplained means from one group to all related groups once a critical number of members of the first group exhibit new behavior or acknowledge a new idea.

The beauty of these long and fascinating lives has been preserved through the words of the authors themselves when we asked them to describe their powerful and vulnerable lives and lessons learned in a very limited yet liminal space. This formed a sense of compressed time and place—not necessarily the way they (or we) live from moment to moment. Our strongest request was for *reflection upon their transformational experiences*, more than just descriptions of the experiences themselves. *Therein lies the learning;* we asked them for a *debriefing* of their lives. In retrospect, many of them came to see that life is all about making sense of things.

The synergies across many of the relationships are important: our authors worked with, learned from, and shared freely with one another. As with each individual life, the shared relationships make the whole of the field greater than the sum of its parts. One example of this is Mike Tucker first meeting Steve Rhinesmith in 1968 when he hired Steve to help prepare his Peace Corps training staff in Puerto Rico. That relationship has lasted a lifetime, during which Mike claims Steve has been a "guiding light" during the highs and lows of Mike's own career.

Any effort to summarize another's life is also a way of restricting it. Rather than trying to crunch their life's learnings in such a limited space, our authors took the lead in trying to expound and expand on their growth moments (as Donna Stringer characterizes her SEEs—Significant Emotional Events) to learn about how best to sensitize themselves to learning or how teachable moments impact others.

Why and How We Form Conclusions and What They Mean

While each author created their own journey, there are several commonalities that are integral to the journey and arc of this book. Let's begin this journey here.

Interculturalists are—and must be—risk-takers. In any new field or endeavor, the path is not clear, not even opened. These individuals asked an impressive questions, followed them up, and went beyond the proverbial box to find their answers and make their own analyses and interpretations. For example, Thiagi left his home country. Cliff Clarke learned how to live as a cultural nomad. In many ways they have all been risk-takers.

Interculturalists make their own unique assumptions. They have their own idiosyncratic ways of following up and cross-checking what they think they know or have learned. They mostly seemed to hold a *let's learn as we go* mentality. While there is ample evidence in these pages regarding meticulous fact-checking and precise sourcing of data and accurate statistical analyses, many authors used their intuition and sense of timing and were able to make leaps and bounds when synergizing their knowledge and wisdom. Mike Tucker and Alvino Fantini are good examples of the care the early interculturalists took to collect data and use data-based information to inform and develop their practices.

Interculturalists are a unique integration of the "lone wolf syndrome" and collective collaborations. When you build something new, you must hold a vision of what you are seeking. In many of these pages, our authors describe a "go it on my own" framing. They had to proceed, often without a trusted colleague to lean on. There are many examples contained in these pages of our contributors striking out on their own by trying a new job or a new role, entering a new working relationship, or following up on the recommendation of someone whom they respected. Steve Rhinesmith taking over the role of President and Chief Operating Officer of Holland America Cruise Lines is a fine example of moving beyond one's comfort zone. He wrote, "the only thing I knew about the cruise business was that the pointy end of the ship should be going first!" It seems the entirety of Robert Hayles' professional career was one of moving beyond his comfort zone.

Along a continuum from solo to shared, the interculturalist pioneers also became skilled collaborators. They excelled in networking, bridge-building, knowing how to scale up projects, and how best to share their personal visions to build a collective endeavor. In fact, it is their ability to travel smoothly between their individual sensibilities and larger, collective commitments that makes their knowledge and action-plans so vital: they have often pivoted at a moment's notice. Many have built businesses, consultancies, and services on their own, layering others in at strategic moments to enhance the momentum of their endeavors.

Multiple intelligences are not uncommon among interculturalists. Among others here, Alvino Fantini points this out with regard to spoken and written language. Fanchon Silberstein graces us with languages of the arts; Thiagi sees the world through his playful-games lenses, Nancy Adler is a skilled artist in several mediums, while Carlos Cortes writes and enacts autobiographical theatre-arts pieces. There are many *languages* contained in these stories, all seeking opportunities to make thoughts and feelings known to others. Beyond the *ABCs* of any written or spoken language, these pioneers learned and practiced how to develop and master multiple pathways to reach and teach the human mind and psyche. According to Gardner's *Theory of Multiple Intelligences* (Gardner, H., *Frames of Mind*, 1983), many of us draw from one or more of the nine elements of MIT (Multiple Intelligences Theory). This is certainly the case with the majority of our intercultural pioneers.

The zoom lens. What helps interculturalists succeed in their visions and endeavors is the use of a metaphorical zoom-lens. Although none of our authors is trained as a photographer, most of them have demonstrated adeptness at being able to use a flexible zoom lens to find a key question, approach, or practice as needed when working with individuals, groups, or organizations. They offer numerous examples in their essays regarding the fluidity of their movements between building individual partnerships to working systemically to produce new programs and services, and then to an even greater macro level when they assessed the impact of their innovations. There is an ease and a grace in the ways they flow between the micro and the macro.

Curiosity leads to action. It seems obvious, but still worth saying: those who become interculturalists don't sit still and are not restrained by portals that are potentially blocked. One of their most abiding qualities is that of ubiquitous curiosity. This keeps them at fuller attention. These are not individuals who are easily intimidated by something major needing to be done: world travel, quickly tracking down donors and grants for five or six figures for much-needed funding, finding the perfect colleague in a pinch, making a formerly unmakeable deadline. Each writer has queued up at least one story or scenario invoking their unrestrained curiosity. While building a methodological under-pinning for their work, our intercultural pioneers are women and men of action. One adage among others seems to pull this together: *if it is to be, it is up to me.* So true—but if one of our pioneers initiated something solo, surely they were soon to engage like-minded colleagues from other and similar domains. Collaboration helped enhance their visions and consolidate their novel ideas.

Transition and change are the norm among interculturalists. Change is one of the few guarantees and universals in life. In addition to action, motion, and striving, these intercultural pioneers came to grips with the necessity and importance of change. It's not only about understanding the inevitability of change, but the extent of grace with which change is acknowledged in their lives, their careers, and their families. Developing the grace to accept change in their own lives helped them to assist others to move toward the same realization. Jack Condon wrote that "we wanted to continue to live abroad and that for our children, maybe the only thing we could offer beyond our love, would be the gift of learning another language at the age when children learn a language effortlessly. Often it is only years later that a child recognizes it as a gift."

While no one person is totally unflappable, we have evidence from within their stories that the interculturalists within these pages found support from all their transitions. They ask discerning questions, think a lot, get the help they need, problem-solve, reflect, evaluate, and move forward. Transitions are stepping-stones and opportunities rather than stumbling blocks for status. Embedded within this approach to one of life's universals is a sort of stoicism and resiliency—both are needed to bounce back from the challenges of the moment.

Using Metaphor, Rubber Bands, and Beyond

We all have our ways of framing our lives such that others can *see* what we are trying to describe and define. This has the net effect of expanding one's field of vision and moving beyond the immediate. Metaphors, similes, aphorisms—even a well-placed cliche—can be eye-opening, in that they can change the frame of reference from what is expected to what is unanticipated.

One thing that evolved from all the life narratives found here is that all these intercultural pioneers have found a way to articulate their work in the world. An intercultural perspective enables them to see our world in terms of patterns, relationships, and metaphors. In other words, they are at their best when envisioning not only what one sees, but what one cannot see. In Antoine de Saint Exupery's (1943, p. 70) iconic book, *The Little Prince,* the fox says to the little prince,

> *It is only with the heart that one can see rightly;*
> *what is essential is invisible to the eye.*

I live with the idea that friendship—one's self-selected interpersonal relationships—is like a rubber band (Yalowitz, 2021): each pairing builds its own boundaries, rules, and preferences. Everything between friends is contained within this rubber band. The band is flexible; it bends, twists, contorts, expands, and shrinks—and all is safely contained within. And yet, at any given point or moment in time, it can snap, and what was once known and held may devolve and dissolve. Throughout their lives, many of these interculturalists have added great value to their working relationships by understanding and working with the plethora of nuances that enable them to generate deeper connections by capitalizing on their intercultural sensitivity and awareness.

Likewise, the lives and work built by our pioneers of the intercultural field have been predicated on bringing their passionate way of seeing and doing things. Just as culture remains invisible to many people, one cannot rightly *see* at any given moment what interculturalists are doing. They are busy *doing* it. We give all manner of aphorisms, similes, and metaphors to our work: my "pet project", one's "first rodeo", and so on. We each have our unique ways of expressing who we are and what we do in the world by using other framing and wording, and our intercultural pioneers do as well. Inspired by art from all over the world, Fanchon Silberstein created workshops and classes where participants gained insight into their own and other cultures by looking closely and engaging in dialogues with one another. In their own way, each of our contributors have literally *opened the lens* in order that others could gain entrance into their thinking and their activities and apply them to their own lives and needs.

These narratives clearly contain a chronology of accomplishments of their writers. In that regard, they stand by themselves. Our authors, who are considered by many as giants in the field of intercultural communication, underscore that attribution, as do many thousands of people around the globe who participated in their workshops, read their books, and in some cases have become friends. On another level, though, these life stories are beyond literal. They are representative and symbolic of creating change on the micro (individual), meso (group), and macro (systemic/institutional) levels, even to the point of occasionally upending the status quo.

We can attach words to the work they've done, and we do—often using superlatives to describe not only the *what* but the *how, how well,* and *why.* Added to the pragmatic realities of the endeavors they created, we have other terms that offer greater depth and dimension, cliched as they may be. Concepts like "breaking the ice," "building bridges," "networking," and more offer us a glimpse into the magnitude of change they have created over time. It is not enough to simply let the stories stand as they are. This is necessary, yes—but not sufficient. Beyond *seeing* what they have done and established, are we ready to *envision* the impact and influence of these human beings?

BRIDGE BUILDING IN A NEW FIELD: IDENTIFICATION OF NEED AND INTEGRATION

Planning and building something novel never comes only from one side or one person. Always, there are tendrils that exist from the *other side*, perhaps latent and merely waiting to be activated. If it takes a village to raise a child when that child is born into the world, then the village needs to already exist.

Networking and Synthesis

Edward T. Hall was responsible for establishing the first buildings in the intercultural village giving refuge to the earliest pioneers in the intercultural field. The intercultural pioneers have many things in common, but one of the clearest was the keen sense of opportunity and possibility. Pitching new ideas, translating theories and methods, engaging others who were previously strangers—all are essential to building a new professional field. Because of their aptitude with sensing potential, their heightened curiosity, their skills articulating critical questions, and their ability to synthesize and synergize ideas and relationships, extraordinary careers and experiences were generated over a period of seventy-plus years.

The early interculturalists were eager to test and apply what they knew into practical solutions for pressing issues and problems. With their entrepreneurial spirits high, many invited other colleagues to join them; others searched for and found like-minded if highly different personalities to join them. Few rode solo for very long. Building trusting relationships was a high priority. In the end, doing so proved critical for their sustained growth and success.

Networking is not a new term invented over these past few decades. Going back to the formation of the golden age of television, TV networks were compilations of smaller stations connected together. Today, we understand networks as groups of people who exchange information, contacts, and experience for professional or social purposes. The dozen people whose lives are briefly portrayed in this book knew intuitively the value of networking to reach greater numbers of potential clients and colleagues, thus extending the possibilities of donors and fundraising, and having others vouch for the efficacy of their ideas. To that end, professional groups such as SIETAR International (and nowadays, SIETAR USA and the many SIETARs around the globe), the Interagency Roundtable in Washington, DC, and the International Academy of Intercultural Research (IAIR), were all formed as natural gathering places for sharing research, ideas, techniques, and needs.

Donna Stringer and Andy Reynolds brought their two livelihoods together to make one larger project and a successful business. Some of our other authors met one another through proximity or a common passion and joined forces to create a synergy. In their Art as Intercultural Communication workshops, Fanchon Silberstein and Sandy Fowler introduced methods for adding lively content to others' training programs. In a way, each endeavor evinced by one or more of our writers came about because they were nimble, flexible, and open to collaboration. Cliff Clarke's focus was on building intercultural relationships within an organization of 60 full-time professionals working on multidisciplinary teams to engage hundreds of client organizations developing intercultural skills in teams that strengthened and changed their corporate cultures while facilitating productive working relationships in such a way that yielded measurable results in organizational performance.

Hegel's Dialectic (thesis→antithesis→synthesis) can be applied to many of the projects carried forward by these intercultural pioneers. Even something as simple as a name (or branding) change for one of their consulting services is often a product of this process. Rarely in the nascent field of intercultural communication did an idea move forward as first articulated without any significant changes. The use of Hegel's approach as a vetting process involves all four aspects of bridge-building: (1) identification of need, (2) integration of ideas, (3) networking of those ideas, and (4) synthesizing those ideas into practical realities. One example of this was George Renwick, David Hoopes, and Cliff Clarke fighting for years to break through the status-quo defense they encountered from NAFSA and corporations against their early attempts to interculturalize their training and consulting programs. It took three years in the late sixties to open the minds of the highest-level NAFSA administrators to both the future and the needs of the present.

It takes time, patience, vulnerability, resilience, and creativity to enable an initial idea to become real. Even when one or more of these were in short supply, our authors were flexible enough to reconstruct some aspect of an envisioned idea that it would inspire new hope and new energy if only subtly changed. Not all their original ideas landed. The very nature of being a pioneer means that some trails will lead to meaningful places while others do not. But original ideas sometimes die hard, and it remains for either the initiator or a secondary person to revisit and revise a former brainstorm to come up with precisely what is needed to try it out in a first iteration. It was critical for these pioneers to remain centered and as unruffled as possible to keep something floating along. That has been the life-process and evolution of most of our authors' professional activities and experiences.

Through Adversity to Wisdom

In a word, it would be easy to describe the authors in this book as holding one thing in common: they are *passionate*. They believe in themselves, their vision(s), and their ability to implement something new. They have all expressed that they are not averse to risk. One of the things passion brings with it is the understanding that when one is given a lemon, the least they can do with it is to make lemonade—if not something far grander. For example, when and where is the best time and place to break out a new simulation, given the potential risks and nuances involved? Thiagi, Sandy Fowler, and Mike Tucker, among others, struggled with this, and often had to redesign plans and decide whether or when to employ one of their experiential training activities.

Even when things don't work out well, there is the potential to learn by reflecting, deconstructing, and evaluating why something didn't work, thus acquiring new understanding. Self-doubt is a natural component of the human condition, yet these pioneers did not allow questions of competence or confidence to block their forward movement. They made personal and professional judgments that the risk was worthwhile and compatible within their respective life-views, no matter the consequence. They were *prepared* to fail, or for the possibility that their initial concept might be a swing-and-miss. We see in their adventures a willingness to attract and endure adversity simply by putting something new "out there".

Positions of leadership require that one wade into and through adversity. Whether through the loss or transition of personnel, budget readjustment, public or client response to program development and design, or efforts to channel energy into a synergized working relationship, introducing novelty does require one to acknowledge and reckon with negativity, from the subtle to the virulent. Their stories speak of an inner strength and resilience that allowed them to think and act out loud, even if the initial response/reaction was not positive. There was no sense of quitting or abandoning an idea. In this way, we can state that personal and professional experiences with *adversity* enabled these intercultural pioneers greater latitude and comfort in exploring and heightening awareness of *diversity*.

It takes a lot of self-knowing as well as the skill-sets that involve social and emotional intelligence. Daniel Goleman's work in these areas (1995, 2006, 2009) points to the critical sense of self-knowing and awareness along with an understanding of how to read others. This is especially poignant when it comes to discerning the subtleties of intercultural communication. In effecting change on systemic and institutional levels as our intercultural pioneers have done, they faced challenges of how to be authentic and read one's companions and colleagues in times of heat and change.

Many of our intercultural pioneers developed their wisdom as their careers evolved. Perhaps all the challenges, the many transitions, and the demands of many competing constituencies helped them accumulate the knowledge, insights, and ability to use their learnings to support their work and this growing field. In most professions, wisdom is a gift of time, patience, and growing into oneself. How does anyone start with wisdom that only accumulates over years of carefully carved and discerned life experience? All our intercultural pioneers wrote about how and what they learned through mistakes, trial-and-error, the gifts of their mentors, sometimes even sheer luck, good timing, and good fortune. But, far more important than *accumulating* wisdom, they began *using* that wisdom as soon as they could find appropriate ways of engaging others.

Humility is one of the most difficult and honorable skills and values to learn and master. I noticed that some of our authors struggled with this as they put their lives into words. Humility is a way of being that goes far beyond one's professional roles and capacities. Humility is fraught with the challenges of its arch-enemy—the ego. When speaking of one's achievements, it is better to allow experience to speak rather than one's sense of self-satisfaction. This is a continuing growth point for all of us, including many of these intercultural pioneers.

With humility comes the understanding and acceptance that one's professional trajectory is not always straightforward. Several of the contributing authors of this book have shared moments, or stories, through which self-doubt, questioning, pause-points, vulnerability, and rethinking assisted them to find resolutions to complicated and challenging situations. I applaud all of this! Acknowledgement of one's vulnerabilities is paramount in overcoming them, in that they now become conscious reckoning points for their owners. There are always opportunities to practice if one leads with humility and not with pride.

WHAT DOES THE FUTURE HOLD?

The life stories in this collection deal largely with the past, yet there are hints of what the future holds for interculturalists. As we write, the value and usefulness of interculturalism is being questioned and in some cases being rejected as too *woke*—but the world still needs us. Corporations will continue to need the practical applications of intercultural training. Both public and private organizations will continue to recognize the value that intercultural professionals bring to their operations. But interculturalists will need to be more skillful and open-minded in the ways we introduce the value of our skills and perspectives to potential clients and the world writ large.

Marketing our knowledge and skills is not new to interculturalists. In the beginning we had to learn to frame and sell our worth to the private sector using productivity data when dealing with mergers and joint ventures. Retention and effectiveness were our selling points in the public sector. And the nonprofit world has learned from us how better to manage cultural differences that were causing difficulties. In the beginning we had to explain to clients about culture shock. This has since become a household phrase. Even more than before, the focus needs to be on facts, data, and empirical evidence as interculturalists carve out their careers in the second quadrant of the twenty-first century and beyond.

Going forward, technology will continue to make rapid advances and change the ways interculturalists interact with their clients. Some of the new technologies (such as AI) are mind-bending. Technology as a field is progressing even more quickly than intercultural thinking and practice. Those in the intercultural field will survive and thrive only if they can become more nimble in their understanding and application of ongoing and novel technological innovations.

And, perhaps most importantly, communication between cultures is not going away. Nations will continue to negotiate with other nations. Multinational corporations need to understand how to manage culturally diverse workforces. Individuals need information and training to live and work effectively in cultures other than the one (or two) on their passports. What do interculturalists bring to these situations? What interculturalists bring into the world is two things: hope and vision. That hope—*our* hope—is that the world can be a better place. We know that our work will never be done, no matter what governments say and do. Our vision is to continue to serve people and institutions around the world in ways that catalyze bridge-building and connections across cultures, within and across our differences, as well as continuing to identify and focus on what is common to our shared humanity.

SUMMING UP

The world would become a kinder and gentler place if we could invoke the learnings coming from these contributing pioneers in the field of intercultural communication. Our lives would improve considerably if we practiced on a daily basis the skills and key lessons shared in these autobiographical narratives, including deep(er) listening, stronger intentions and abilities to collaborate, shared creativity, and the patience to learn and ask meaningful open-ended questions and wait for the responses that will be forthcoming.

We would do well, I believe, to learn and practice the difference between giving answers and offering responses. *Answers* can be off-putting and conversation-ending when they are declared as the "be all and end all" in open-ended conversations; *responses*, as I see them, are critical in keeping conversations alive and extracting the best ideas from the greatest number of individuals. I see this point as one of difficulty for several of our intercultural pioneers. At times greater discernment between the two might have yielded stronger and more effective results. There are very few *absolutely correct* answers when it comes to building something. There are always multiple pathways to birthing and growing ideas into programs and services. The best work of the pioneers occurred when they offered and were seeking responses rather than absolute answers.

The *Power of Story* should never be lost to the human family. Narrative story-telling is one of the most basic—and universal—ways we have to share and make meaning and sense of our individual and collective lives. Story-telling is also a thrilling opportunity to learn about one's self through others, and therefore become more self-aware. We all have our stories. The American mythologist, writer, and lecturer, Joseph Campbell (personal communication, March 16, 1979, Medford, MA) asked, "Where are you in your myth?" The writers of the narratives in this book have shared their responses to this basic yet profound enquiry. To all of this, I found myself continually asking my one favorite question—a mere three words: "Is there more?"

So much would not have happened without these twelve individuals. The ability that they have shown throughout their lives and work is that of understanding life as process, not merely as a product or a series of related products. Once they developed a product or service, they had the intuitive sensibility that their work would need continual review and tweaking. On a more pervasive and even universal level, we are not, and never will be, *finished* products. What is *revolutionary* about our lives is simply how profoundly we evolve over the course of our lifespan.

We offer a large gift of gratitude to these disparate individuals who we've come to know, respect, and admire for their commonalities and their differences—and for the ways in which they've offered their lives and their work for the benefit and betterment of humankind. In the end, that is what will remain.

Daniel C. Yalowitz has no conflict of interests to declare that are relevant to the content of this chapter.

REFERENCES

Goleman, D. (1995). *Emotional Intelligence*. Bantam Books.
Goleman, D. (2006). *Social Intelligence*. Bantam Books.
Goleman, D. (2009). *Ecological Intelligence*. Penguin Random House.
Kesey, K. (1981). *The Hundredth Monkey*. Vision Books.
Rumi, J. (1995). In C. Barks & J. Moyne (Eds.), Trans. *The Essential Rumi*. Harper Collins.
Saint Exupery, A. (1943). *The Little Prince*. Reynal & Hitchcock.
Yalowitz, D. (2021). *Reflections on the Nature of Friendship*. Booksmyth Press.

The manufacturer's authorised representative in the EU is Springer
Nature Customer Service Centre GmbH, Europaplatz 3, 69115 Heidelberg,
Germany. If you have any concerns regarding our products, please
contact ProductSafety@springernature.com

Printed and bound by CPI Group (UK) Ltd, Croydon, CR0 4YY
22/04/2026
02094859-0002